Best wishes,

Florence Stevenson

Harold Washington: A Political Biography

HAROLD WASHINGTON

A POLITICAL BIOGRAPHY

Florence Hamlish Levinsohn

CHICAGO REVIEW PRESS
Chicago

Library of Congress Cataloging in Publication Data

Levinsohn, Florence Hamlish, 1926-
Harold Washington: a political biography.

Includes index.
1. Washington, Harold, 1922- . 2. Chicago (Ill.)—Politics and government—1951- . 3. Chicago (Ill.)—Mayors—Biography. 4. Legislators—United States—Biography. 5. United States. Congress. House—Biography. I. Title.
F548.52W36L48 1983 328.773'11'0924 [B] 83-15418
ISBN 0-914091-40-9
ISBN 0-914091-41-7 (pbk.)

Printed in the United States of America.
First edition.
Published by Chicago Review Press, 213 W. Institute Place, Chicago, Illinois 60610
ISBN cl 0-914091-40-9
pa 0-914091-41-7

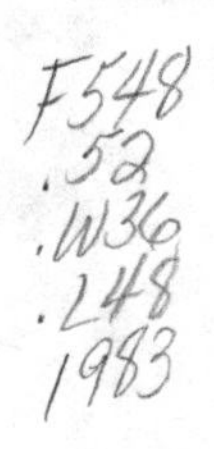

For Anni and Julie

What an unheard-of thing it is, in fine,
To love another and be equally loved!
What sadness and what joy! How cruel it is
That pride and wit distort the heart of man,
How vain, how sad, what cruelty, what need,
For this is true and sad, that I need them
And they need me. What can we do? We need
Each other's clumsiness, each other's wit,
Each other's company and our own pride. I need
My face unshamed, I need my wit, I cannot
Turn away. We know our clumsiness, we cannot
Forget our pride, our faces, our common love.

Delmore Schwartz

Contents

Preface

On Nov. 9, 1982, I was half-watching the evening newscast with a friend. Suddenly I sat up and paid closer attention. Harold Washington was announcing his candidacy for mayor. "Don't tell me he's going to try again," I said to my friend, "he is a glutton for punishment." Like so many in Chicago, I am an inveterate poll watcher and prognosticator. There had been talk that Washington would run again. I hoped he wouldn't. His try at the mayoral in 1977 had yielded only 11 percent of the vote. What a crushing disappointment. How could he expose himself to that again? Blacks just don't support their own candidates well enough and he is almost completely unknown among whites. He would probably do better this time, of course, since he won two Congressional elections since 1977, but still?

It was clear a few days before the primary election that Washington could win. The two white candidates would split the white vote and the black vote, if it went to Washington, could outnumber the two white candidates' votes because the black votes had been swelled by an incredibly successful voter registration drive. I could not believe it. My old college buddy the mayor of Chicago! A black mayor of Chicago! Winning the Democratic primary in Chicago was tantamount to winning the election. Most of us didn't even dream of such a possibility twenty years ago when we marched in the streets just to get the schools integrated, which we failed to do, and thirty years ago when we sat in at restaurants to get them to serve blacks, at which we did succeed. Other towns and cities, 233 of them, had elected black mayors. But Chicago? It didn't seem possible.

When friends learned that I had known Washington for over thirty years, they asked the inevitable question: "What's he like?" This book emerged from those questions. I hope I have answered them and, at the same time, answered the larger question that became such a heavy campaign issue: What does he mean when he says, "It's our turn?" I have tried to sketch the black experience in which Washington grew up and that inspired him to a career of public service that brought him to City Hall. I hope I have captured enough of that highly complex, difficult scene. I believe strongly that we all, in our own ways, are products of our environment. That each of us becomes a unique individual, with distinct drives and dreams, constitutes for me the great mystery of life. I have not tried to explain why Harold Washington became mayor while his brother Roy became a parole officer. I leave that to the psychobiographers. But I have explored his public life to find out what manner of man this new mayor of Chicago is.

I make no pretense of impartiality. I voted for him as student council president at Roosevelt College in 1948, for mayor of Chicago in 1977, again in Feb. 1983 and in April 1983. I viewed him as my candidate. I did not think he would win the two middle elections, though there was no doubt about the first and great fear about the last. I did not have faith that a black candidate could win in Feb. 1983 but I have voted for reform candidates all my life and Washington was surely another strong reform candidate. Having said that, I hasten to add that, though not impartial, I have tried to be objective, to explore and expose his warts along with his beauty marks.

I will be using the term racism throughout the text since that phenomenon looms darkly over Harold Washington's whole life, as it does for every black in the nation. By racism I do not mean race hatred, which also afflicts the victims of racism. A black can hate whites—many do. The treatment of blacks by whites has engendered race hatred among many. But racism is a different phenomenon: it is based on the power to exclude. Racism is the name given to the long-standing process by which whites have enslaved, lynched, burned, raped, exploited, and excluded blacks from the ordinary privileges of American citizenship. Even when they are guilty of no racist acts, most white Americans, unfortunately, have been raised with a racist psychology—"I don't want to live next door to them." They may not be able any longer to exclude nearly as much as they did before the enactment in the sixties and seventies of anti-discrimination laws, but there remains in most Americans the desire and power to keep blacks "invisible," a phenomenon made famous by Ralph Ellison in Invisible Man. *It is mostly that racism that I refer to in this book, the lingering vestige of the more brutal racist behavior that formerly characterized this nation. That there are degrees of racism is obvious. In this election, a wide continuum was displayed, from wondering whether a black could possibly be a good mayor to a full campaign of vilification and slander. It should be clear from these words that, for the most part, blacks cannot be called racist. When they attain the power to exclude and do, in fact, exclude whites, they, too, will deserve that appelation.*

I want to thank the dozens of people, most of whose names appear in the text, who have given me their time and assistance to put this book together. I also want to thank Linda Matthews for her thoughtful, concerned and careful overseeing of the book every step of the way. She asked the right questions. And Jane and Robert Hunziker, without whose kindness and generosity the writing of this book—and life—would have been more difficult and less pleasurable. Finally, and most of all, I want to thank Harold Washington for having created the opportunity for me to write this book that draws so many strands of my own life together and who put new life into the city I love.

Florence Hamlish Levinsohn
August 1, 1983
Chicago, Illinois

Introduction

Eighty years after that black titan, William Edward Burghardt Du Bois, wrote, "the problem of the twentieth century is the problem of the color line," voters in America's second largest city seemed determined to keep faith with his prophecy.

In a race dominated almost solely by race, Harold Washington, 61, gifted and black, was elected mayor of Chicago.

His spectacular victory lent credence to three propositions:

1.) White America suffers from historical amnesia.

2.) *Ceterus paribus* (all other things being equal), an intransigent white electorate still votes white and an equally stubborn black electorate is finally responding by voting black.

3.) Du Bois' prophetic color line is alive and well and living in the White House.

At the risk of appearing to scapegoat my colleagues, all three propositions have been diligently nurtured by the media. Not because the press is any more color-obsessed than its constituents, but because the press dutifully mirrors American society.

In reporting on Washington's campaign, an amnesiac white press acted as though the 1967 historic election of Carl Burton Stokes as the first black mayor of Cleveland, the nation's eighth largest city at the time, had never happened.

Scant credit was given to the dramatic progress orchestrated by blacks as mayors of 233 cities, including the major metropolises of

Atlanta, Birmingham, Detroit, Los Angeles, New Orleans, Newark, Oakland, Richmond and Washington, D.C.

The Cleveland 1967 election was characterized by the identical elements over which the press salivated in the Chicago 1983 election: a heavy voter turnout, a heavy black bloc vote and a balance of power white vote.

For Chicago, 1983, the results were percentage-point similar: 80 percent of the registered voters went to the polls; 97 percent of the black vote went to Washington; and his margin of victory over Bernard Epton was provided by an 18 percent white vote.

But this time, the reporting emphasized the black vote, which seemed to be shrugging off its shoe-shuffling somnolence by registering and voting in droves.

Blacks have always tended toward bloc voting—a pattern established by other more successful ethnic political blocs, the Irish, the Italians, the Jews and the Poles. But blacks have invariably vitiated their potential clout by neither registering nor voting in proportion to their numbers in the population.

Moreover, blacks have congenitally been guilty of rejecting superior black challengers for inferior white incumbents who breastfed blacks with economic security at the expense of political maturity.

Several years ago, I wrote, "An almost shocking example of the black voter's lack of ability to discern loyalty to the cause of advancing the interests of their ethnic group occurred in the April, 1964, Democratic primary in Chicago.

"Running for re-election in the 6th Congressional district was Rep. Thomas J. O'Brien, an elderly 14-term representative. Ill for several months prior to the primary, O'Brien had been unable to campaign in the predominantly black district on the west side.

"Running against him was a young black woman who had long been active in civic and civil rights programs. On primary day, Congressman O'Brien died. But that did not matter to black voters in his district. They went out anyway and voted for a dead white man over a live colored woman, re-electing O'Brien."

In the same year that Stokes pulled off his political breakthrough, black voters in 33 percent black Memphis overwhelmingly rejected the candidacy of black State Rep. A.W. Willis for mayor. In a field of seven, Willis ran a poor fourth with only 12 percent of the black vote.

Asked to explain this electoral anomaly, Willis lamented: "The Negro has been taught to be inferior. He thinks the white man's ice is colder, his sugar sweeter, his medicine better."

That lingering delusion has helped polarize black elected officials in a debate over the merits of a black presidential candidacy in 1983. Some who suggest "the time is not ripe" are also blinded by historical amnesia. They forget the sacrifices of civil rights pioneers who confronted a far more strident racism and they have learned little from the successes of other ethnic groups in politics.

Washington's election stunned America for two reasons. It happened in America's second largest city, generally regarded as one of the nation's most bitterly segregated cities. And it reversed a trend of declining black participation in the electoral process.

But black Chicagoans were galvanized by two major forces—a police force which had brutalized them for decades with impunity and Ronald Reagan, the most aggressively racist president since Woodrow Wilson.

As a rule blacks are middle-of-the-road, law-abiding, religion-loving, almost conservative people.

If they have docilely accepted oppression, it is because of a fervent belief in the American dream. "We shall overcome," . . . "By and by, when the morning comes, all the saints go down the river and home, we shall tell the story how we overcome and we'll understand it better by and by" . . . "Lift every voice and sing, till earth and heaven ring . . ."

No calls to action, no promise that "if we must die . . . we'll face the murderous, cowardly pack." Just keep praying and singing and believing in the American dream. In Chicago, the dream had begun to twist into a nightmare.

The first impetus for Washington's historic election may have been the year 1974, when his political mentor, the late Congressman Ralph Metcalfe, broke with the Richard Daley Machine after a prominent black professional and close friend of Metcalfe's was killed by a Chicago policeman. As usual, the policeman was not punished. The loyal black political lieutenant, raised in the fidelity of the William Dawson tradition of "to get along, go along and to go along, get along," denounced Daley's inaction, aroused the community, then two years later added independent insult to audacious injury by beating a Daley-backed candidate who challenged him for his Congressional seat.

Suddenly, blacks were doing more than hoping for a better tomorrow. Metcalfe's break was a turning point. The dream was being placed in escrow.

A second turning point was Ronald Reagan's election.

In deadly pursuit of neo-reconstructionist policies, the Reagan Administration methodically proceeded, with omnivorous malice aforethought, to assault the civil rights foundation of black progress.

In Chicago, the twin streams of lingering police brutality and galloping Reagan racism merged into a giant tributary that made "judgment run down as waters and righteousness as a mighty stream" to drown the Jane Byrne administration.

Here again, Washington benefitted from a third accident of history.

When Byrne was swept into office on a rising tide of black votes, she was hailed as a new sensitivity to black needs. Within two years, she had executed a 180-degree turn, replacing black appointees on the school board and housing authority with whites. Outside of a couple of "you Tarzan, me Jane" Madison Avenue gimmicks such as staying temporarily in a crime-infested public housing project, she managed to alienate the black community.

Ordinarily, black voters stay home in disgust or wring their powerless hands when they believe they have been betrayed by an erstwhile ally. This time, they thundered out of their homes to the voting booths.

Washington's election may signify a new trend of aroused black voter participation, even when blacks recognize they may not be able to guarantee success.

Black voters know the Rev. Jesse Jackson can't be elected

president in 1984. That's not the issue. At stake is the validity of the Wesley Carter thesis of black politics in raising electoral consciousness.

In 1956, Houston black newspaper publisher Wesley Carter insisted that a liberal coalition include a black as one of its candidates for the school board. When the coalition refused, Carter encouraged a black man to enter the race as an independent. Both the candidate and the entire coalition were defeated.

"We knew we couldn't win without liberal support," Monday morning quarterbacked Carter, "but we showed them they could not win without us, either."

Trying to convince a turn-back-the-clock administration that it cannot win without black support could well be, in John Foster Dulles' words, "an exercise in massive futility." No Reagan Republican wants or seeks black voter support. If Reagan can command the same majority of white voters as he did with the coalition he put together in 1980, the black vote will once again be consigned to the cellar of electoral impotence.

The second half of the 1980s may well typify more than ever the Dickensian ambivalence, "the best of times, the worst of times."

Blacks approach the second half of this decade in a spirit of the best of times—the largest number ever of black members of Congress, 22; black mayors running four of the nation's six largest cities (after November, when W. Wilson Goode is almost a sure bet to be elected mayor of Philadelphia); blacks now occupy key positions in some major corporations, serve on boards of directors, run major universities (the president of the nation's largest university, State University of New York, is black); black women head up the school systems of the nation's second and fourth largest cities as well as the nation's capital; despite the widening disparity between black and white, black family median income is the highest ever; black pupils have begun to make startling educational gains in major cities such as Pittsburgh, Washington, D.C. and New York City; and, as a final index of national acceptance, the percentage of Americans indicating approval of interracial marriage doubled from 20 percent in 1968 to 43 percent in 1983. In many respects, these are the best of times.

These are also the worst of times, a political dark ages for blacks.

Civil rights are out of fashion, Civil rights groups are feuding internally and externally. Their memberships are declining faster than an Olympic bobsled downhill. Former white allies have abandoned the struggle for racial equality because of spurious complaints about affirmative action being quotas.

America is bored with racial equality. The black press, once a mighty fortress of militant truths, has degenerated into a toothless tiger of genteel accommodation.

In this gloomy era of egalitarian retrenchment, blacks may be forced to turn inwardly in a revived exercise in self-determination and self-assessment.

One symbol of white superiority that irritates black America is the monopoly of white authorities—white experts, white scholars and white writers—collectively defining and authenticating the black experience. From newspapers and magazines to publishing houses and universities, whites dominate the analyses of black America's journey for justice. It is a galling fact of our lives.

Such an irritant in the interracial body politic, however, does not deny the existence and, if you will, the continuing need for empathetic white friends who are as knowledgeable as they are committed.

Florence Hamlish Levinsohn is such a friend. A devoted friend.

Not many whites are able to get inside the black experience with an involvement fueled by a rational head and a loving heart. As the reader will discover in this perceptive biography, Levinsohn does.

Back in the 40s and the 50s, when some of us were just beginning to enjoy the elysium of interracial togetherness while attacking the harshness of "separate but equal," Levinsohn immersed herself in these activities with a colorblindness that transcended all suspicion. I remember this energetic friend from our University of Chicago graduate student days, popping up at enough protest activities to keep an entire sorority busy.

In *Harold Washington*, she has chronicled a Horatio Alger

story, the rise of one man's black political power in white America. It is both a success story and a paean of praise to the country ambivalently described by Claude McKay, "I love this cultured hell that tests my youth."

But *Harold Washington* is also a testimonial to one white woman's faith in the black realization that singing "We shall overcome" is no substitute for voting to guarantee that we shall oversee.

Chuck Stone
Senior Editor
Philadelphia Daily News

Born to Politics

The bright-eyed, slender youngster, his hair clipped short, tiny sprouts of moustache on his upper lip, sits beside the tall, powerful looking father he adores, listening with awe to the speeches, the singing, the amens. It's not a church meeting, it's a political meeting, but the difference isn't always easy to discern. Politics, in the twenties and thirties in the black community, had all the fervor and much of the tone of a religious revival meeting. Listen to one observer of a meeting held in the mid-thirties on Chicago's South Side, quoted by St. Clair Drake and Horace Cayton in their *Black Metropolis* (published in 1945 by Harcourt, Brace and Company), a book to which I am indebted for much of the material in this chapter.

The meeting was in a very large room in an old, dilapidated building, probably at one time a dance hall. Between 250 and 300 persons were present, most of them workers and precinct captains in Alderman Dawson's organization. They seemed to be a rather poor, forlorn group for the most part, running from middle-aged to elderly, with a few young people scattered here and there. Apparently they were mostly southern migrants who still clung to the old traditional Republican ideology.

The first speaker was an elderly gentleman, a rock-ribbed Republican, a long-time member of the Second Ward organization. He said:

"We are worshipping a great cause. If I were a preacher I would take a text in the

Psalms: 'Oh, how well it is for men to dwell together in unity!' We need prayer more than anything else on earth. A lot of our folks seem hypocrites because of the misfortune that befell them here in Illinois, the home of Lincoln, who cut the shackles from the legs of your grandparents and made it possible for us to be here above the Mason-Dixon line. We should give some credit to the Republican party. Of course you have a right to be anything—Communist, Socialist, even Democrat; but first you should consult God. We are tired of white people using us as drawers of water and hewers of wood. In this cruel world no one loves anybody. They only crave for dollars. We are not as interested in this fight as we ought to be—there are too many empty chairs.

"I was in Mitchell's [Negro congressman] office and had a talk with him for two hours. He gave me some of his speeches and told me he gave 50 white boys jobs and 50 colored boys jobs. Now I am not prejudiced, but I asked Mr. Mitchell, 'Do you think you are doing us justice?' There are 434 white Congressmen to look out for the whites. We have fifteen million Negroes in America to help. Friends, get your heart in this thing!"

Another speaker took the floor:

"We are leaders of a family. Our family has become separated in the last four or five years. A lot of us cannot stand pressure. Yet it is painful to have a lot of children and they crying for food and bread. People have left their party affiliations—many have gone Socialist, Communist; some have turned their backs on the Republican ticket and turned Democrats because of poverty, hunger, and lack of work. It reminds me of the parable of Abraham just as he was about to sacrifice his son on an altar but a hand stayed him. I thought about that today downtown in the City Hall in the Council Chamber.

"There are many people now on WPA, some making $85 and some $105. All of that money comes from Washington. Send Dawson to Washington to get us more money."

This talk was followed by music. Miss Pitts of the Ninety-ninth Precinct sang "I'll Tell It Wherever I Go."

Dawson then addressed the meeting and introduced Stanton DePriest, son of Oscar DePriest, the first Negro Congressman from Chicago. DePriest said:

"History is repeating itself.

Lives of great men all remind us
We can make our lives sublime,
And departing leave behind us
Footprints on the sands of time

You know and I know the dire necessity of having a county commissioner. For thirty years we have been deprived of representation. You all know the slogan on which our government is founded, 'Taxation without representation is tyranny.' The same is true today, and I will be your county commissioner after November 8. The conditions are terrible at the county hospital. It is all the fault of the Democrats. The Democrats never played fair with the black man."

DePriest was followed by Representative Harewood of the state legislature (a Negro), who said:

"PWA, WPA, relief, etc., is here to stay. We need a man who can get the most for us. We need Dawson to protect us from American Fascists. We need more men like Dawson in the high councils of the Republican party."

Evangelist Essie Whitman was called on to sing two original songs she had composed about Dawson.

Dawson said: "We must have a record made of those songs. I like the part she sang about Mitchell having to grow up."

Mrs. Keller then addressed the meeting:

"It is up to us to make Mitchell moan and groan. We should give him the cramps because he has done nothing for us. Dawson is the man of the people and for the people. He is a friend of his race and the champion of his people. We need he-men of this black group to represent us. It is only seventy-five years this side of Emancipation—Lincoln would roll over in his grave. It is time we woke up our racial pride and sent Dawson to Congress. We want a fearless man to fight for the black race."

Two solos followed: "The World Is Mine Tonight," dedicated to the Republican party, and "Without a Song," dedicated to the Democratic party.

Alderman Robert R. Jackson closed the meeting with these stirring words:

"We must stick together to get somewhere as a race. Every Jew will hunt for and vote for a Jew. The same for the Irish and every other race. The Negro can't find a Negro's name to save his life. Look for his name until you find it! He's your own flesh and blood, and nobody is going to vote for him if you don't. We are going into the Second Ward to help William L. Dawson—by telephone, telegraph, and tell-a-woman, the great agencies of communication in the world."

Arthur Mitchell, who had taken over the Congressional seat when DePriest retired, was among the most venal politicians. Not only did he become a rich man through graft and corruption but he was known as a friend to few. In the Depression, a broke and desperate teenager went to Mitchell for help. His reply, reports Timuel Black, a long-time observer of and participant in black politics, was "I may be your color but I'm not your kind."

William A. Dawson, at that meeting running for Congress, was still a Republican, as blacks had been since the Civil War. Abraham Lincoln freed the slaves, blacks owed their loyalty to his party. But Franklin Delano Roosevelt could not be ignored; he was a champion of the poor people and slowly blacks shifted to his party. By his third term, they gave him a majority of their votes, but only a majority—52 percent; loyalty to the Republicans remained staunch despite WPA, CCC, and other New Deal programs that benefitted blacks in the Depression. That was no small issue: in 1935, at the height of the Depression, half the blacks in Chicago were on relief, 70 percent had annual incomes of less than $1000 and only five out of every hundred blacks had more than $2000. By comparison, thirty out of every hundred whites had more than $2000. As hard as life was and as much as the New Deal eased life a bit, a sizeable number of blacks retained their loyalty to the party of their savior. As hard as life was in 1935 in Chicago, it was a virtual paradise beside life for the parents and grandparents of those voters. They were poor, many of them hungry, many of them ill-housed in a ghetto, most of them doing the worst menial jobs in the city, even those who had graduated from college, but they were free citizens of this nation. They were no one else's property; they were not slaves. And while, in Chicago, Jim Crow kept them from good jobs, from entering many public places, from moving into most communities, they at least had a free community of their own, with their own newspapers, organizations, churches, and even some small businesses—in 1938, 2600 of them. They had schools, not the best schools, they were often short-changed by the city, but they were educational facilities denied their parents under slavery and in the South after Reconstruction. If whites denied them access to many things in life, they had patience. They had learned to do for themselves. They had their own hospital, undertakers, and their own banks and insurance companies. And they had the vote; they had their politics. There was reason to believe, to hope, that through education and the vote, with time, they would improve their conditions, perhaps even gain equality. It wasn't an easy life for most but it was a free life and they owed that freedom to Abe Lincoln.

Since 1876, Republican blacks in Chicago had been able to elect their own representatives, not every year but regularly enough to justify their continued enthusiastic activity, to justify those revival-type meetings that large numbers attended regularly. From 1903, when the last black Congressman of the Reconstruction was defeated, until 1928, there was no black in Congress. Then, from 1928, when Oscar DePriest was elected in the 1st District, Illinois's black representative was the lone black in Congress, the "watch-dog" for the rest of the nation's blacks, until 1944, when Adam Clayton Powell was elected in New York. Little wonder that sentiment ran high in those political meetings on the South Side of Chicago. They were the primary place where the aspirations for the future and the rage at injustice were codified and formalized.

There was a steady stream of clever, astute Republican politicians in the Black Belt, beginning in 1894 with Edward H. Wright, who became powerful enough to place a number of blacks in important city jobs.

Having been elected county commissioner in 1896, Wright gained the presidency of that body by a technique attempted years later by another powerful black in Chicago. Wright humbly approached each commissioner privately to ask for his vote. After all, he said, one vote could not elect him and it would be a vote of confidence for the only black on the board. They all gave him their "one" vote. When Wilson Frost, the Finance Chairman of the City Council, tried a similar trick almost ninety years later, it backfired badly. The white aldermen were not disposed kindly to this black man who now represented a real power base; a black had just been elected mayor. Wright had been one of the few blacks in government and represented less than 2 percent of the population of the city.

In 1900, there were 30,000 blacks in Chicago (1.9 percent). In 1922, when Harold Washington was born, there were 109,458 (4.1 percent). In 1940, the percentage doubled with 277,731, and in 1944, there were 337,000 (9.3 percent). In that year, the total population of the city was 3.7 million, more than in 1980. The black population in 1980 was estimated at 40 percent, though some people insist that it was even higher, that the census did not capture the entire population, leaving out many without permanent homes.

The big influx of blacks into Chicago in 1940 was the result of large efforts to entice them into the city to replace the European immigrants who had stopped coming to America with the entry of the country into World War II. There weren't enough people to man the plants and do the menial work. Good jobs, good homes, schools, racial tolerance were promised to southern blacks. Railroad fares were sometimes paid. They came in large numbers—to find only a few *good* jobs, many more menial ones, cramped, crowded housing in the ghetto, and dubious racial tolerance. But they kept coming. There was hope in urban Chicago for poor tenant farmers and sharecroppers in the South. The Old Settlers in the city, blacks who had been here in small numbers for many years, did not welcome those illiterate farmers and sharecroppers. They feared for their image as refined, educated, civilized people.

There had been hope in the Black Belt. The young men returning from World War I were filled with optimism and hope. They had fought a war for democracy. They assumed that the lessons of the war would be sustained at home, that life in the U.S. would be kinder to them. Then, one day, one hot summer day in 1919, three years before Washington was born, one year after the armistice was signed, a young boy swam over the imaginary boundary line in the lake. He was in the white swimming area. He was stoned. A fight broke out. He drowned. Blacks were enraged, especially those young veterans of the war. They fought the whites. And whites went to war against blacks. For six days, they roamed the streets of the black community, throwing stones, beating people up, shooting at random. Houses and businesses were bombed. People were snatched from streetcars and buses and beaten. Blacks took revenge, burning and looting. The police were either inept or uninterested in stopping the terror against blacks. The national guard was called in on the sixth day. The riot was over and so was much of the hope and optimism of the immediate postwar period.

Hope, however, was revived. In fact, the Black Belt, like the rest of the nation, had some prosperous years between 1925 and 1929. The terrible impact of the Depression that followed was made much worse by the contrast between those few good years and the succeeding years of despair. Of course, the black community was hit first. It was the most vulnerable. The few black banks closed before the white; black workers were fired first, black homes were lost first.

Still, most blacks clung to the Republican Party. It had seemed to serve them well for sixty-five years. "Big Bill" Thompson had wooed and won them with promises of jobs—with his friendship. He hired enough blacks that his opponents called City Hall "Uncle Tom's Cabin," though that was not an objective observation—the number was actually quite small. They were not lowly jobs, though. The last time, until Washington's administration, that a black served as corporation counsel was under Thompson.

But the new Democratic politicians were confounding the black loyalties to the Republicans. In Roosevelt's first election in 1932, most blacks stayed in the Republican column. Only 23 percent voted for Roosevelt, though the rest had no great love for Hoover. The presence of a white southerner as vice presidential candidate didn't help the Democrats, either. However, the New Deal was having its expected impact and in 1936, almost half the blacks voted for Roosevelt. In 1940, he had the majority but it was still only 52 percent. Only in 1944 did black Chicago finally swing heavily to Roosevelt, giving him a whopping 65 percent of its vote, after he came to the city with a message for blacks: end the poll tax, establish a permanent FEPC, extend equal opportunity to all.

Roosevelt had won over the blacks nationally. Locally, Democratic Anton Cermak had beaten Thompson in 1932 despite black support for the Republicans. Cermak had run on a reform but racist platform. He would clean up the corruption and graft. He would also clean out City Hall of the blacks. Blacks were dismissed from their jobs. But Cermak was assassinated shortly after his election. He may have been killed by the Mob, who wanted none of his reform, or he may have taken the bullet intended for FDR, next to whom he was standing at the time. No one has ever proven either theory. Edward J. Kelly followed Cermak into the mayor's office. He was, as Thompson had been, a friend to the blacks and restored to them their jobs and opened even more. He also opened more opportunities to the Mob and the Machine. Corruption and graft dominated City Hall. Black voter turnout, for many years second only to the Jews in the city, was crucial; Cermak had won without it but no savvy politician would turn his back on blacks for long. The combination of support for Roosevelt and the attractions offered by Kelly led many blacks to switch parties.

The first effort that had attracted black votes to the Democratic Party was the presidential campaign in 1924 when John W. Davis, who had an excellent civil rights record as an attorney, won about 20 percent of the black votes in the nation. Earl B. Dickerson, an early "race leader," was the regional director for the campaign. Roy Washington was a precinct captain.

Roy Washington had been an early Democrat, one of the first precinct captains—a lawyer, a Methodist minister, the son of a Methodist minister, though apparently lacking the oratorical skills so many black ministers have. Democratic precinct captains in the twenties, especially black ones, were not the same people to be found in the precincts of Chicago today, those with nothing else going for them. They were accomplished people with a mission. Washington helped elect Roosevelt; he had the wit to see that Abe Lincoln's party was no longer the party of democrats, that the wave of the future was with the Democrats. It can't be said he corralled a lot of votes in the twenties and thirties. Nor can it be said he corralled a lot of people to assist him as precinct captain. Instead, he corralled his family. His son, Harold, was passing out leaflets, canvassing voters, getting petitions signed, and poll watching in his early teens. All the children helped. They were paid a few cents to stuff and seal envelopes and do a variety of small chores.

Washington's brood was not all of his own making. Bertha, his first wife, was a restless woman in her youth, an amateur singer who had left a little farm in Southern Illinois as a teenager to seek a fortune in Chicago but who married Roy soon after and had four children in rapid succession.

Washington often refers to his birth in County Hospital as proof of his humble beginnings. He does not realize how much more about his family this birthplace reveals. In 1922, most births still occurred at home; hospitals were considered torture chambers and places of last resort, especially by the uneducated poor. However, a concerted effort was being made by doctors to convince women to have their babies in hospitals to reduce the disastrous infant mortality rate, especially among the poor, whose infant deaths were blamed on unclean homes. That filth may not have been universal among the poor and that maternal illness, malnutrition, and lack of prenatal care may have caused more infant deaths than the cleanliness or lack of it in the homes of the poor, the medical profession seems not to have considered.

For the rich, hospital birthings became a mark not only of advanced thinking but of the classiness that accompanied such thinking. Furthermore, the lovely accommodations private hospitals created for the rich woman in labor made having a baby almost like a trip to a first class hotel. This was enhanced by the fact that household help, following World War I, was difficult to find and the rich women could count on being well cared for—pampered—in hospitals.

For poor women, there were no such fancy accommodations; there were maternity wards, large rooms with lots of beds—no privacy and not a lot of personal care. But a hospital birth, even one in County Hospital, represented the best advice of a doctor. It was a mark of upward mobility, of advanced thinking, a departure from the ways of one's mother and most of one's neighbors, who still relied on midwives and home births.

Though she was poor, Bertha Washington did believe in the most advanced ideas. Harold was born in County Hospital, the hospital of the poor but one renowned for its medical care. She did not know that infant mortality rates in hospital wards were very high or that the unsterile conditions in many hospitals—prestigious hospitals—had resulted in several epidemics that killed hundreds of babies. Statistics were not very well kept in those days and it took doctors years to realize that hospital mortality rates were no lower than those for home births. Even when they discovered it, they were slow to release that information or act on it because, willy-nilly, they remained convinced that births they oversaw in the controlled conditions of the hospital were safer—and certainly more convenient for them.

In 1980, the infant mortality rate among poor blacks in Chicago was again the third highest in the nation. In 1983, County Hospital put up a plaque commemorating the birth there of the mayor of Chicago.

Bertha Washington's father had been the victim of a lynch mob. An outspoken man who took "no guff" from anyone, black or white, at a time when blacks defied whites at a risk of their lives, he was killed and his body placed on the railroad track to appear as an accident. There was some law and order in that little town near Centralia. His body was found but the killers weren't. Southern Illinois had seemed a refuge from the racist south where he had been born in slavery but it, too, was Southern.

Bertha left Roy and her children shortly after her fourth child, Edward, was born, when Harold was still a toddler. Not long after, she married a man with whom she had another six children before she separated from him. But Bertha, or Mother Dear, as she was called by all her children, was not a woman anyone could stay angry at. Sweet-faced—Harold has her face—good-natured, loving and lovable, imaginative, a bit of a ham actress, she kept her family close to her until her death in 1980. Though he remarried too, Roy Washington remained close friends with his first wife and, in fact, was thought of as a "second father" by her second husband's children. Mother Dear fed and entertained the whole brood regularly and her kitchen table was often the site of Roy's politicking for the Democratic Party.

Bertha Price was one of many such matriarchs in the black community. "The main stamping ground of the family for years was Mother's," Ramon Price says. Not a strict disciplinarian, she nevertheless set very high standards for her children, expecting them to get educated and cultured. Billie Holiday's records were impermissible because they were "too blue." Sunday School was required. Card playing wasn't permitted; it was a form of gambling. Daughters' dates were carefully supervised. And despite a small income, the girls had dance lessons and everyone had piano lessons. She ran regular family talent shows. She had seen Roy Washington through his toughest time, working to help him through Garrett Theological Seminary, Chicago Kent College of Law, and John Marshall Law School, and then to get a start in a law practice, not an easy task for any black lawyer but more difficult for a man without the connections of the Old Settlers, the men and women who were born and raised in Chicago and had ties in the community. Roy had come to Chicago from Lovelaceville, Kentucky in 1918 after attending Indiana University.

While her ex-husband shared some of Bertha's puritanical

ideas, his home was not quite the sanctuary that hers was. His children played cards. Billie Holiday was and is Harold's favorite singer.

In 1920, there were already ninety-five black lawyers in Chicago with only 110,000 blacks, one lawyer for every 1161 people, hardly a base from which to earn a living but the only base available, since lawyers were entirely segregated. Even for the Old Settlers who had broad connections in the community, it wasn't easy. For a newcomer, it was doubly difficult, made even more difficult by the fact that the majority of blacks were very poor, unable to pay even the small fees lawyers charged and certainly unable to provide the kinds of cases for which reasonable fees could be charged. There was no corporate law in the Black Belt in the twenties, very little civil law. Those who made money, "went downtown to white lawyers, and still do," Judge Eugene Pincham recalls. A few divorces, an occasional real estate closing, and the defense of those accused of crimes were the major cases—not precisely lucrative business in the twenties and thirties when not many were divorced, not many could afford to buy homes, and most of those accused of crimes were indigent. Many lawyers ended up working in the post office.

But there was legal work for the city. Those who labored for the party were rewarded. No precinct captain has, for over sixty years in Chicago, had to worry about earning a living if his party was in power. Certainly as president of the 3rd Ward Democratic Club after Edward J. Kelly came to power, Roy was in line to be rewarded. He became one of the few blacks in the Corporation Counsel's office, though he remained for many years in the police court at 48th and Wabash, in the heart of the ghetto, not one of the high prestige jobs in that office, jobs that normally went to whites. His last years were spent in Boy's Court. The whites he saw were the judges, bailiffs, and policemen in his courtroom. He also saw much discrimination in the treatment of accused black criminals by those whites. Because he was a prosecutor, the whites in the courtroom were courteous and respectful but that respect did not extend to the accused. A study by Marion Goldman of black lawyers contains ample testimony of what they describe as racism in the courts.

Washington was, therefore, in an awkward position. As prosecutor he was the natural ally of the police and the judiciary. As a black he was the kin of those accused, often unjustly, by policemen. He trod a delicate path. Eugene Woods, a veteran criminal lawyer, says that Washington was "one of the nicest men in the courts. He never took advantage of a defendant just because he was a defendant. He was so kind and fair that I could go to him and tell him when I had a guilty client, something a defense lawyer would never do ordinarily. It was very unusual for a defense attorney to take a prosecutor into his confidence. But I got to know him and talked to other defense lawyers who would say: 'You know, Roy Washington is really a different type of prosecutor. He realizes that, not only is the defendant indigent—lots of us took indigent clients—but that they were accused falsely! Now that's unusual. Every prosecutor just assumes the defendant is guilty. Not Roy. He is a different sort of fellow.' Maybe because he was a Methodist minister he had a kindness and a fairness. He took everything into consideration. And he never took graft. He was as clean as a whistle. Other prosecutors could be bought off. Not Roy. If he thought someone was guilty, he had them bound over to the grand jury right away. On the other hand, he would plea bargain for a fellow who was guilty but for whom there were some circumstances that made you sympathetic to him. He had to be punished all right but you had to be fair to him. But he always left it up to the judge. He would never make any deals. A thoroughly honest, decent man."

Roy Washington was a mentor to those beyond his own family, too. Judge Eugene Pincham recalls being a young lawyer and listening to Washington: "We were out there starving to death. He counselled us to work hard, to stick to it, to survive. He was very encouraging to us."

Honesty in a politician in Chicago was no small thing. The city was for many years controlled by gangsters in league with politicians who got rich on the gangster's thank you notes. Gambling and prostitution were as common as buttercups, protected as they were by the politicians. At one point, all the aldermen in the city were saloon keepers. Blacks introduced their own wrinkle—the policy racket, a notorious form of gambling, now earning for the state a healthy piece of revenue under the title, "Illinois State Lottery." When Senator Estes Kefauver came to Chicago in 1950 to investigate organized crime, Congressman Bill Dawson told him, "It's good for my people. It provides lots of jobs." Illegal policy, or the numbers racket, flourished for nearly seventy-five years but most particularly under the protection of Bill Dawson. But, in fact, the racket employed fewer people than was generally believed—in the mid-forties, it was estimated at 6,000, with a weekly payroll of $26,000. The payoff to the Democratic Machine at that time was estimated to be half a million dollars a year. The total take was alleged to be $18 million. Everyone got paid off. It was the most lucrative business in the ghetto. In 1945, St. Clair Drake and Horace Cayton, in *Black Metropolis*, estimated that the policy bankroll tripled in World War II. The take has risen, of course, as personal income has risen and as population has grown.

In 1974, Illinois followed the lead of New York and other states and attempted to take over the rackets. The gross revenues from the Illinois State Lottery in 1981-82 were $334.7 million. Operating expenses were $10.3 million. The commissions paid to Control Data Corporation, which runs the lottery for the state, and to the agents who are ordinary shopkeepers and who sell the lottery tickets along with their other merchandise, were $23 million. Prizes totalled $160 million. The net revenue to the state was $140.6 million. In 1982-83, it was $214.1 million.

The state lottery has cut seriously into the policy, but there are still those who prefer it. There is a legal lottery "station" as they were called in the heyday of policy, on every corner of the city. But for every legal station, there is probably another station that is not legal, receiving the same protection from the police and politicians as did the early stations and using the same numbers as the legal lottery. A legal lottery ticket costs a dollar or more; a policy ticket costs no more than a quarter.

Drake and Cayton discuss the cult of policy. "It has a hold on its devotees which is stronger than the concrete gains from an occasional winning warrants. It has an element of mystery and anticipation. It has developed an esoteric language. It organizes, to some extent, the daily lives of the participant."

A policeman I know starts his 3 o'clock afternoon shift by driving to his station to buy $20 worth of lottery tickets, legal ones—he is, after all, a policeman. Every day, following roll call, he and his partner drive the mile to his favorite station before they begin their tour of duty. For his $100 a week for the past five years or so, this man has won $500. He is waiting for the big win. He doesn't play the horses, nor does he play cards. Numbers is his game.

In a time when blacks were completely excluded from business and industry, from the mainstream of American commercial life, policy became a community institution. The men and women who profited from the racket invested in the community, creating scores of legitimate businesses and supporting local philanthropy. Drake and Cayton estimated that about 20 percent of the businesses in the black community in the early forties were owned by policy people. That policy was a criminal activity was not important to most. What was important was that at least one multimillion dollar business succeeded in the ghetto. It was the only kind of business that could succeed—self-contained in the ghetto, except for the payoffs downtown. It did not need huge capital investments, not available to blacks, nor did it need technological skills, also not much available. That it succeeded only with the aid and comfort of the political machine was again not important to most. The Machine was opening to blacks more and more opportunities within the structure. There was promise that things would improve, that blacks would finally move into the mainstream. In the meantime, one got what one could. Life in the black community for the large majority has not changed. Policy still thrives.

According to all reports, Roy Washington was never involved in the ghetto's biggest business. "He was an absolutely honest man."

Washington's children and Bertha Price's children also regarded him as an honest, decent man, a kind, generous, decent man, they say. Life in the Price household, two blocks away from the Washington household, was not easy after Bertha separated from her second husband. They lived among the hoi polloi at 47th and Michigan—the elite of the community lived along Michigan Avenue near 47th Street—but not *of* them.

Across Michigan at 47th, on the north side of the street, was the most famous concentration of black hoi polloi in the city, the Rosenwald Garden Apartments, built in the mid-thirties by Julius Rosenwald, owner of Sears, Roebuck & Co. It was to house the poor, but it was the best housing available at the time and so was immediately grabbed up by the middle class. Built on a square block, around an interior garden, the five-story buildings were not luxurious—did not have elevators—but they were clean, comfortable and safe, with entrances off the garden and a 24-hour security guard on the premises. A roof promenade, a small playground for young children, and benches in the garden provided an "oasis in the desert." "Rosenwald was the first opportunity blacks had to live in a respectable apartment on a first-rate street," says Earl B. Dickerson, in his nineties now, a famous white-haired attorney, businessman, and politicial figure on the South Side, who now lives in another of the enclaves that the black wealthy have carved out for themselves, this one on South Lake Shore Drive. Dickerson, however, is no longer a struggling young attorney; he is one of the wealthiest blacks in the city.

Bertha's family lived in a basement flat, as they are called in Chicago. Like most black women in the thirties in Chicago—in the forties and fifties, too—who had to support their families, Bertha worked as a domestic, cleaning the houses of white housewives who could still afford the few dollars in severely straitened Depression budgets to pay others to clean, cook, and wash for them. There were no other jobs open to black women with a high school education. The thousands of clerks and clerical workers who serviced the overwhelmingly white stores and offices in Chicago did not include a black woman among them. Ramon Price recalls the many afternoons he went, with a note, to Roy Washington's office at South Park and 47th Street, and returned with a few dollars to buy groceries, pay for a ballet lesson, pay the rent. Domestics earned only a few dollars a week. "Roy was generous," Price says. These were not his children, but Bertha had been his wife, the mother of his children, and he was her friend, such a close friend that her children saw him as a second father. When he died he left a legacy to the Cook County Bar Association, the legal association founded in 1914 by black lawyers because they were excluded from the white association, designated to assist young blacks to get a legal education.

The elder Washington was a family man, attached to his children, to his ex-wife's children, but mainly to his third son, Harold, for whom he was a model. Eugene Woods recalls the visits young Harold made to the courtroom where his father worked and Judge Richard Harewood recalls seeing the youngster at political meetings with his father through the years.

Eugene Woods says he thinks Roy Washington was using his job in the corporation counsel's office as a stepping stone to a political career. It was a way to make friends, meet important people in the Party. Perhaps Woods is right. More likely, Washington had no choice. All too many lawyers were working in the post office, one of the few decent jobs a black professional could get in the city. The job was, indeed, helpful in building a political career but it was also a way to earn a living in those lean years. There is no question, however, about his political ambitions. Unfortunately, he was an honest, fair man who did not always see the handwriting on the wall, who did not always anticipate the chicanery of those whom he had labored so long to elect. When he finally tossed his own hat into the ring, in 1947, to run for 3rd Ward alderman, he did not anticipate that Mike Sneed, the committeeman, would double-cross him to work for the election of Archibald Carey, a Republican. (No, Virginia, the election in 1983 was not the first one in which party stalwarts have double-crossed their candidates to work for their opponents.) It was said that policy men backing Carey had bought off Sneed. It was also remarked that Sneed had never enthusiastically backed Washington. And it was rumored that Bill Dawson, well on his way to being the black Democratic boss, had been the culprit.

Following the election of Carey, Dawson was able to remove Sneed from the committeeman's job in the 3rd Ward and replace him with his own man, C.C. Wimbush.

Carey was a well-born, highly connected man in the black community. His father was a minister of a large influential Methodist church and a very visible Republican. When the election results were in, it was clear what had been going on: the strongest Democratic precincts went for Carey.

"Dawson used Carey to keep other Democrats in line," Judge Harewood says. " 'If you guys don't toe the line, I will put a Republican in there,' he was saying. He didn't want a Democratic alderman out there. It was easier to control a Republican, who couldn't get elected without the help of the Democrats." Later on, Harewood said, Dawson rewarded Carey for his cooperation by running him as judge on the Democratic ticket and getting him elected.

It was clear that no effort was being made to elect Washington. Dawson was so bold in his betrayal that a full-page ad in the *Chicago Defender*, the major black newspaper, on April 8, four days after the election, that listed all the Democratic candidates did not even include Washington's name. Why didn't he see that highly visible handwriting? Dawson had systematically dumped all those who were not his loyal associates. Why should he treat Washington any better?

Why didn't Roy Washington see the handwriting on the wall? Only eight years before, in 1939, Earl Dickerson had been double-crossed in the first of the many knifings that Dawson inflicted. The popular Dickerson was the choice of the Democrats to run against the still Republican Dawson for the 2nd Ward aldermanic seat. But, though a Republican, Dawson had ingratiated himself with Mayor/Machine Boss Edward J. Kelly who asked the 2nd Ward Democrats to support him. They objected. Dickerson was their man. Kelly compromised. He hoped they would support Dawson but he would not take away their jobs if they didn't. In a three-way primary, Dickerson won. Every morning as he emerged from his house, he found Dawson waiting for him to make a deal. Dawson would bring his Republican organization into the Democratic Party and thus strengthen it. He would see to it that Dickerson won this election if, in turn, Dickerson would go downtown to Kelly to recommend that the party boss turn over the 2nd Ward patronage to him. Kelly was already inclined in this direction. But a word from Dickerson would be the clincher. In the following year, Dawson promised, he would support Dickerson for Congress if he supported Dawson for the aldermanic seat. He didn't want the Congressional seat, he said, he didn't want to leave Chicago. Dickerson agreed. He won the election. Dawson got the patronage. The next year, Dawson double-crossed Dickerson and supported the incumbent Arthur Mitchell for Congress in exchange for Mitchell's support for him the following term. Dawson wanted that Congressional seat after all and kept it until he died in 1970. Furious, Dickerson challenged Dawson for the Congressional seat.

"Trying to pay back the loans I made to try to beat him kept me in debt for five or six years, but of course, he had control of the Machine by then, aided and abetted by Kelly," Dickerson says. "Dawson was a man who would do anything for power. But he would never have had the power if he had not been catering, obsequiously, to the whites who controlled everything," Dickerson adds.

Did Harold Washington pursue so diligently, so single-mindedly a political career to avenge the betrayal of his father? He refers to him often but rarely mentions that betrayal. Did he say, in 1948, the year after his father was betrayed by the Democratic Party, that he would be the first black mayor of Chicago because he was so enraged at the treatment of his father? Or did he just catch the bug from his father? Politics! But he would not be naive about the motives and actions of the party bosses.

In 1950, Mayor Martin Kennelly testified before the Kefauver Committee on Organized Crime that Dawson was the primary cause of the outrageously wide open gambling in Chicago. "It only exists because of Dawson's sponsorship," Kennelly said. Later, when it was time to prepare the slate of candidates for the mayoral election, Dawson cast the deciding vote against Kennelly and slated Richard Daley. And thus, most people agree, began Dawson's decline and "the demise of substantial political power in the black community," in the words of Timuel Black, long-time observer of black politics. Daley was no friend of blacks.

Washington remained in the party, but he was never the enthusiastic activist he had been. Instead, he concentrated on his law practice and on making money. There is a rumor on the South Side that he died one of the wealthiest blacks in Chicago. Judge Harewood says he left his wife and children an inheritance of half a million dollars, made in what Harewood calls "kitchenettes," namely buying up buildings with large apartments and converting them into smaller units, a widespread activity in the late forties and fifties when the need for housing for blacks was so pressing. His estate consisted almost entirely of that real estate. His son, uninterested in real estate or in money, made no effort to maintain or even collect the rents on the properties his father bequeathed him, the effects of which came back to haunt him in the mayoral campaign when he was exposed as a "slum landlord."

Roy Washington was not a socially prominent man, as so many black professionals were. Harewood says, "He was not our kind."

Though he belonged to one of the prominent black fraternities, Phi Beta Sigma, he did not move in the inner sanctum of black professionals—the Kappas, the Alphas, the Frogs, the Snakes, the fraternities and clubs that dominated the social life of the black upper class. He was a "diamond in the rough, a big, jovial sort," says Judge Sidney Jones. Though his second wife, Arlene, who was a social worker, did participate in some of the many social clubs of the middle class, Washington was not a social climber, not a man of great mobility. He was a private man, a family man, not given to small talk or to sharing confidences. His life was a busy one—a law practice, prosecuting attorney, his family, politics, and visiting minister to several Methodist churches in the community. He also prized his relationship with his brother, Booker (yes, Booker Washington).

Like so many other blacks, but not those of means, Roy Washington lived most of his life in the confines of a few square blocks—49th to 47th (two blocks), Wabash to South Park (now King Drive, five blocks). He did not travel, did not seek those other connections with life. His home was at 49th and Michigan, the courtroom where he worked so many years was at 48th and Wabash, one block north and one east. His ex-wife's home, where he spent so much time, was at 47th and Michigan. Four blocks west, on 47th Street at South Park, was his office and the Democratic Party headquarters. There is, in those words, an implication that Washington lived a highly circumscribed life. This big, jovial man did not know much more than existed in those few blocks.

But what a few blocks they were! Those few blocks were the hub of the Midwestern black world. It was where you went when you came to Chicago if you were black and if you were a curious white. And it was where you went on Saturday afternoon if you wanted a taste of the high life—or the low life—in the black community.

This was Harold Washington's stamping ground, too, until he went off to the army upon graduation from high school. DuSable High School, the new school built for blacks, in which Washington was a member of the first graduating class, was one block north of his home and one block east. The Hall Branch library, fondly recalled by all the kids in the neighborhood for its librarians who were eager to put books in the hands of black children, was at 48th and Michigan. And two blocks south was Washington Park that offered a mile across 51st Street of playing fields, paths to run for the aspiring track star—Washington made his first mark as an athlete in high school, a star hurdler—and to bicycle, bushes to make love behind, and trees to sit under and contemplate and talk under on a hot summer day. On Michigan Avenue, open double-decker buses offered a cooling excursion on a hot summer night, the wind blowing, the sounds and sights of the city exciting to youngsters who did not normally dare go much beyond the confines of their own neighborhood because they would be chased and beaten. From the top of the bus, when it reached 12th Street, one could see, on the east, in the distance, the lake, the museums that were replicas of Greek temples, and close by, Grant Park, with its decorative gardens, statues, Buckingham Fountain, and the Art Institute with its famous lions. Beyond was the boat harbor with the hundreds of sailboats tilting in the breeze. On the west side of Michigan were the massive fancy hotels and tall buildings.

But the real activity, the day-to-day life, was on 47th Street, a metropolis in itself. Stores of every variety, taverns, and restaurants lined both sides of the street. In the el station at 47th and Calumet was a big newsstand with magazines of all kinds, including Buck Rogers and The Shadow. In the Palm Tavern, any evening, but especially on weekends, the elite of the black world met to eat. Though not among the elite, Washington's family joined that set for dinner at the Palm. A block away, the fancy hustlers, policy kings, and other sophisticated night people crowded Nelson Sykes' Brass Rail. In the Southcenter Building, above the Southcenter Department Store, doctors, lawyers, dentists, and accountants had their offices. Roy Washington's office was in that building. It would be Harold's, too, when he finished law school. Down the block a bit was the Regal Theater, one of the stately palaces built in the twenties to offer movies and extravagant "stage shows." Every great black musician, comedian, dancer played the Regal on weekends. They were "glamorous creatures out of the sky"—Duke Ellington, Count Basie, Earl "Fatha" Hines, Louis Armstrong, Ella Fitzgerald, Sarah Vaughn, Billie Holiday, with a camellia over her ear. Earl Hines and Louis Armstrong lived not far away in those days when Chicago was the preeminent home of jazz. The late thirties was Duke Ellington's most fertile period. Beside the Regal was the Savoy Ballroom, with its boxing and wrestling matches, basketball games, parties and dances, where the big bands played to wildly enthusiastic dancers. The Metropolitan Theater was also on that corner, an ordinary movie house where kids went for a dime on Saturday afternoon to see the serials and eat popcorn and talk, to sit through two shows, laughing and whistling through the movies yet able to repeat all the dialogue when they got home to their mothers.

Saturday afternoon was carnival time at 47th and South Park. Everyone came to shop in Henry C. Taylor's Haberdashery next door to the Palm Tavern, one of the few black-owned businesses, and in all the other shops that lined the street: groceries, jewelry, records, clothing, linens, anything and everything, including pawn shops for those who were temporarily broke. The Big Red clanged to a stop on 47th Street, bringing shoppers from the east and west. On South Park, the jitney cabs, those big black ancient cabs that were the true buses on the Parkway brought their passengers for a dime from north and south. In the shops, the Jewish grandfather sat at the cash register and the rest of the family and an occasional black clerk served the customers. It is not completely amazing that a large number of young blacks became fluent Yiddish speakers after working in the shops on 47th Street. Even the kids who shopped there learned a few words.

Edgar G. Brown worked the sidewalk at the corner with his bullhorn exhorting the people to be proud of their race, to stand up straight and tall and demand recognition as the true great race of man. Down a few feet, a sword swallower entertained the crowd, and farther down, magicians vied with blues singers and guitar players for the audience and the pennies. Ministers preached the gospel denouncing sin and heresy. And they all competed with the sounds of jazz blasting from the speakers outside the shops. Through the crowd strolled the omnipresent Irish detectives in their dark fedoras, their black Fords parked nearby. And the Irish cops in uniform were always on hand.

Chili Mac is still there and those who grew up in that little square return regularly for the "best chili in town." The Chinese restaurant is gone but the people who as kids stood in front and made the sign of the slashed throat to the Chinese inside still laugh at their antics, remembering how they raced away after threatening the lives of those Chinese restauranteurs with their dangerous signals.

There was another black business on that corner, the Ben Franklin store, one of the businesses the policy people opened to create good will in the community. It couldn't compete with the Woolworth's across the street but it offered jobs to local people and decent merchandise.

Over west a block, on Calumet, was the notorious Red Light district, where whores sold themselves on the street and the police looked the other way except for the few minutes when the pimps and madams made their payoffs. Over east, across the street from the 48th St. Police Station where Roy Washington was a prosecutor, Joe Louis was one of the many fighters who boxed at Bacon's Casino, where sporting events were held almost nightly. Down south aways, at 63rd Street, White City Amusement Park had a roller coaster and a tilt-a-whirl and dozens of other wonderful entertainments. It was open to blacks. The roller rink next door was not. It was, in 1947, the site of one of the first picket lines in the city and blacks did finally skate there.

It was raucous, exciting, liberating. Politics, religion, sex, music, film, books, sports, commerce, the practice of law and medicine were all there in that little metropolis where friends met every weekend to talk, argue, shop, listen, watch, to absorb and participate in the life of the black community.

A circumscribed life for an adult? Perhaps. For a youngster? Hardly! But it was, except for the Irish cops and the Jewish shopkeepers, all black. It was the black community's response to white Chicago that would not permit it to eat in its downtown restaurants, attend its downtown movies, shop in its downtown stores. Oh, they weren't barred from the movies and stores as they were from the restaurants. Whites were willing to sit in a movie house or shop in a store with blacks but breaking bread was another story. But even in the movies and stores, they were made to feel unwelcome. A gesture, a word was enough. It would be twenty-five years before blacks would decide that they would no longer tolerate that exclusion and simply ignore the not welcome signs in the eyes of the whites downtown. It would be only a few years, however, until Harold Washington would travel every day on the el from 47th and Prairie to Chicago's downtown to join the first integrated community in the city and begin the journey that would take him to the fifth floor of City Hall.

It would be several years before he would begin that leg of his journey, though. First, he had to serve his country in World War II. He was drafted in 1942 and was soon sent overseas to the South Pacific, where he built runways for the air force in the Philippines as a member of the Air Force Engineers. Building runways in the heat of an invasion and after, when snipers continually fired on the crews, was not the safest task in the war but it was a lot safer than actual combat. Washington would have preferred combat. Not because he yearned to put himself in danger. He and all other blacks in World War II except two units were not placed in safe positions for protection, as were the sons and relatives of so many government officials and their friends. Blacks were considered incapable of combat duty.

For over three years, Washington burned with the stigma of not being courageous or smart enough for combat.

It was no less stigmatizing to be placed, as all blacks were, in segregated units—all black with white officers, many of whom trained for their jobs by reading a manual entitled, "How to Treat Negro Soldiers," as if they were separate from the human race. Nevertheless, he rose to the rank of First Sergeant, second to the highest rank among noncommissioned officers.

His high school buddy, Dempsey Travis, was almost killed in a revolt he started to protest mistreatment of black soldiers on his base in the U.S. Tim Black rose to the highest rank of noncommissioned officer but was broken to private again after he voiced his several protests. Such events were common among blacks in the armed services in World War II. All the black units had black noncom's, but there was a quota that permitted only a handful of black commissioned officers. Washington was in one of the higher status units; the engineering corps required more skill than the service units. But the opportunity to excel was limited by his color. He went almost as far as he could go, restraining his anger and resentment, as he has done most of his life.

Early White, who served through his whole overseas tour of duty and who was to re-emerge later in his life as an adversary, is chronologically the first in a long list of Washington admirers interviewed for this book. "He was one of the most likeable fellows in the unit," White says, "a brilliant fellow with a sharp wit, a good friend."

A need to excel has, somehow, in Washington's life, always overcome outward displays of anger and resentment, has taken precedence over other motives, though those emotions have, at times, had a powerful impact on him in ways not always perceived, perhaps not even conscious. There can be little doubt, however, that his dedication to racial justice was strongly fueled by the three years spent in the South Pacific helping to fight a war for democracy as a victim of racial prejudice and discrimination. A man of great wit, that terrible irony was never lost on him.

A Dream Realized

"There's a new college downtown, man, that's gonna be together. They don't discriminate."

"Yeh, and I'm a purple ostrich."

"It's the truth. A coupla fellas were in here just last night raving about it. Roosevelt College. I guess they named it after FDR."

Lou Roundtree stared at the bartender in disbelief. And cynicism. There had to be a hitch. Sure, the University of Illinois down at Champaign accepted blacks in the college but they had to live and eat separately. Life on the University of Illinois campus in 1946 could hardly be described as nondiscriminatory. The city junior colleges also did not discriminate but they were two-year colleges that represented no challenge to the intellectually gifted, especially to men who had served three or four years in the Army. Any high school graduate could enter.

A real college in Chicago that did not discriminate? Could it be true? Roundtree had applied for admission to the University of Chicago and been rejected. So had several of his friends, veterans like himself who, because of the GI Bill, were encouraged to try for the best. But there were at the University of Chicago in 1946 only a handful of black students. Chuck Stone, one of those few blacks at Chicago, had done his undergraduate work at Wesleyan College, the only black there at the time. "All the blacks in New England colleges knew each other," he recalls. "There were so few of us, we always kept in touch." In 1946, one year after the close of World War II, most blacks were limited to black colleges or state universities where everything but classes were segregated.

Roundtree slipped off the barstool, went to the phone, and asked for the address of Roosevelt College. Thanking the bartender, he paid for his beer, and went out to catch the Big Red to go down to 231 S. Wells, where the operator had said Roosevelt was located.

It was true! The dingy corridors of the dilapidated old office building at 231 S. Wells were filled with people of all races. "The atmosphere was like nothing I'd ever seen before. All those faces—like a little U.N.—you didn't see that in Chicago or anyplace in the U.S. in 1946." Roundtree stopped someone to ask if there was a lunchroom. People in the corridors were one thing—people eating together was something else. "Sure," the student said, "if you can stand the food. Right through that door, B&Gs." (B&Gs was an early fast food chain in the city. Ernie Simon, a well-known radio announcer, was fired from his job after referring to B&Gs as Bugs and Germs). Roundtree went through the door and stopped, to stare at the people sitting in groups in that grungy restaurant. He sat down and ordered a cup of coffee. Beside him were sitting two white men, a white woman, and a black man arguing fiercely about Gandhi. On the other side of him was a similar grouping—they were reading from a book and laughing. All over the restaurant, interracial groups were drinking coffee and talking together.

He returned to the corridor and took the rickety elevator to the seventh floor where he'd been told the admissions office was located. What were the requirements, he wanted to know. An acceptable score on the entrance exam, he was told. Could he take the test? Of course. Fill out these forms. Have your transcripts from high school sent to us.

A man standing next to him struck up a conversation. "What unit were you in? Were you overseas? What have you been doing since you were discharged?" The kind of questions being asked of returning veterans all over the country. When the man left, the registrar told Roundtree that he had been talking to the president of the college. "I'm going to like this place," he said.

He went home to tell his mother of the discovery. A graduate of Spelman College, a small black southern college, his mother was overjoyed. Her son had been restless, uneasy, since his return from the Army. A southern black college was not for him, he insisted. Thank God he had this opportunity. As he was leaving home to register for classes, she eyed him with alarm. "You can't go downtown dressed like that"—a pair of army pants and a cotton T-shirt.

"Don't worry, mama, it's a very casual atmosphere," he reassured her. Casual it was. Army pants were almost regulation—the majority of the students were veterans.

Roundtree entered Roosevelt in September, 1946, along with 3,948 others. In the year since the college had opened with 1,300 students, enrollment had swelled to more than twice that number. Word of the highly unorthodox college had spread quickly. Blacks were not the only ones barred from the local colleges. Asians, too, were not accepted. And while the news of the annihilation of six million Jews had worked on the consciences of many American college administrators and, while the University of Chicago had never discriminated against Jews, there were still quotas under which only so many Jews were admitted to many colleges. Students poured into Roosevelt, from as far away as California and New York, but largely from the Chicago area, from the black ghettos, from Lawndale, Albany Park, and Rogers Park, where most Jews then lived, from the South and Northwest sides and from the suburbs. Though no records of race and religion were kept—on principle—it is estimated that the student body was one-eighth black, one-half Jewish, and the rest others.

Word had reached Harold Washington the previous spring and he was already enrolled when that bartender told Lou Roundtree about Roosevelt. He had entered the summer before, shortly after he was discharged from the Army. It was a spectacular world, this Roosevelt College, for a young man who had spent most of his years in a segregated world and in a world where the Democratic Party was the ruling political force. There was a challenge in the air and he was ready for a challenge. There were new ideas in the air and he was ready for them. In his classes and in B&Gs, he met Communists, socialists, anarchists, Trotskyists burning with revolutionary zeal, and liberals burning with idealism. It was the time of the founding of the U.N., the emergence of the Third World, the start of the Cold War with the consequent fear of American Communists—a time of great hope and great despair. Hope, however, was uppermost in the Roosevelt community. The very existence of the college itself engendered hope. A poll taken by the college newspaper in February 1947 showed that 75 percent of the students had enrolled because of the "nondiscriminatory progressive principles."

"We thought everything was very simple. All you had to do was propose some solutions and publicize the wrong policies and everyone would see the wisdom of our words. That's what we felt. We lived in a dream," recalls Mark Jones, later a judge of the Circuit Court.

The other 25 percent of the students came to Roosevelt merely because it was an open enrollment college to which they had easy access. Except for the junior colleges, there were no public colleges in the city. Tuition at Roosevelt was low. Some of those 25 percent were serious scholars. Some were careerists. They had no interest in or knowledge of politics. But Roosevelt's spirit was inescapable. Even those who came only because they had no other choice were swept up in that spirit. Some emerged as conservatives on many issues—on the Cold War, on domestic "subversives," but even they shared the commitment to racial and religious equality.

> Roosevelt College has husbanded the formula of working and living together with all races and creeds. Here the Negro studies Shakespeare while seated next to the white-skinned youth. Here the ex-GI, who helped take the Normandy beach and prays by the yellow light of the Menorah, plays bridge during his leisure moments with his Japanese-American friend (*Roosevelt Torch,* Jan. 16, 1947).

The revolt at Central YMCA College that led to the founding of Roosevelt began prior to World War II. A group of professors protested, among other things, the handling of money by the administration and the trustees. The revolt failed; several people were fired. In 1945, Edward J. Sparling, president, resigned after refusing to turn over demographic data requested by the trustees that he suspected would be used to establish a quota system to deal with the tide of returning veterans. Though no crusading liberal, Sparling's action provided "the great altruistic cause around which the already discontented faculty could rally," according to Rolf Weil, president of Roosevelt since 1965. Looking back, Weil says that the trustees of the Y College were probably no worse than any others of their time but Sparling had a strong commitment to integration, a vision of a college that did not discriminate against minorities at any level. He rounded up financial support, including that of Marshall Field III and the Rosenwald Fund, and led a group of 68 faculty and many students out of the Y to form the first integrated private college in Chicago and one of a tiny handful in the nation. Only at City College of New York was there the same atmosphere.

A report from the dean of faculties, Wayne A. R. Leys, to the board of trustees on Dec. 17, 1945, says:

> If it is foolhardy for 68 men to resign their jobs without assurance of future security, the faculty of Roosevelt College was foolhardy.
>
> If it is impossible to remodel an 11-story building in 33 days, equipping it with classrooms, library, laboratories, and offices, Roosevelt College was an impossibility.
>
> If it is absurd for a new college to offer such subjects as advanced calculus, to apply for accreditation six days after the opening of school, and to graduate a class at the end of the first 17 weeks, then Roosevelt College is absurd.
>
> If it is radical to teach future labor leaders, as well as future businessmen, the mysteries of accounting; if it is radical to supply Jews, Poles, Japanese and Negroes as well as Anglo-Saxons with the tools of language, then Roosevelt College is radical.
>
> If it is impractical to give employed men and women during the evening hours courses of standard quality in history, chemistry, and music, Roosevelt College is impractical.
>
> I am proud to say that Roosevelt College is in these ways foolhardy, impossible, absurd, radical and impractical.

Washington immediately threw himself into the activities of the college. In December, 1946, he was named to chair the first fund-raising drive by the students, with a goal of $3 million. At the same time, he was named to a committee that would assist in the citywide efforts to outlaw restrictive covenants, the legal means then used to prevent minorities from moving out of their ghettos. From the beginning, he was regarded as an astute, honest, intelligent leader, reports G. Nicholas Paster, then director of student activities.

Roosevelt also had its "thieves and gangsters" among the students, as Ben Harrison fondly calls the cronies with whom he regularly stole off to an unoccupied classroom to play poker with scraps of notebook paper, a version of liar's poker, to avoid detection by then dean Leys, who kept his ear to the ground for those bets that may have been the only acts at Roosevelt considered sinful. "You wouldn't find Harold sinning with us," Harrison recalls. "He was a straight arrow. You could tell that he knew already what he would do with his life and he wasn't wasting time. But he wasn't offensive about it. He didn't sneer at the bums who were just fumbling along. Serious but not stony-faced. He was always good for a laugh. We admired him."

For its first two years, Roosevelt raced toward becoming a full-fledged college. Bringing a faculty together, organizing classes, creating a library came first. President Sparling's vision of a nondiscriminatory college was not limited to the students. Discrimination against minorities was even greater in the selection of college faculties. Rolf Weil, a Jew, recalls his first job search prior to his graduation from the University of Chicago in 1950. Armed with that very prestigious and still uncommon Ph.D., he went to the university officer who handled job opportunities for graduates. "With almost no exceptions," he says, "the institutions that were looking for faculty made clear that only white Anglo-Saxon Protestants need apply." He was hired by Sparling. So was St. Clair Drake, a black anthropologist who had recently published, with Horace Cayton, the monumental work, *Black Metropolis,* and who would awe generations of students with his quirky brilliance and extraordinary knowledge. The world expert on the Creole language, Lorenzo Turner, was hired, too, to teach Shakespeare. (Turner chuckled at the move in 1947 from Wells Street to Louis Sullivan's Auditorium Building on Michigan Avenue. He had been a waiter in his youth in the elegant restaurant that was later converted into a library reading room.) Walter Weisskopf, Helmut Hirsch, Otto Wirth, Hans Tischler, Sigmund Freund, and other refugees from Hitler's Europe who lacked American credentials but whose brilliance was unquestionable were also hired. So was Rose Hum Lee, not only Chinese but female, a combination rarely found in the professorial ranks.

Of course, the students, most of whom had not been in any other college, didn't know that the presence of these people was as unique to the setting as their own was. Nor did they realize that the endless conversations in the cafeteria and in the professor's homes in which they were fondly and enthusiastically treated as equals was unique to college life.

> April 15, 1949, Dear Miss Hamlish, If Mohammed will not come to the mountain, then the mountain must go to Mohammed. I have missed our conversations. Have you been ill? Or only otherwise occupied? Yours, Helmut Hirsch.
> Sometime in 1955, on the flyleaf of *The Psychology of Economics,* "To Flo, who provided some of the friction for some of the sparks, if any, in this book. Walter Weisskopf."

So much for ordinary faculty-student relations. An audacious editor of the college paper even dared to use his columns to spell out the qualifications of a professor:

> A College professor is learned—not from the standpoint of a singular phase of his subject or even from his subject alone. Somewhere along the

> line he must have become completely identified with the general search for knowledge through the medium of his specialization (*Roosevelt Torch,* Dec. 12, 1946.).

How could Roosevelt's students know that most colleges frown deeply at—some expressly forbid—love affairs between faculty and students, marriages, yes, even friendships. If anyone at Roosevelt was frowning, and no doubt some were, they only told each other.

Which is not to say there wasn't a lot of frowning at Roosevelt. If there was less concern in the college about who was sleeping with whom, there was more concern—frowning concern—about politics, both school politics and world politics, about race relations and economic development, about the emerging nations and about the rise of the Cold War. Eminent men and women were invited from all over the world to inform the Roosevelt community about the latest theories and developments. And when they were introduced to the students and faculty, it was often Harold Washington who sat on the platform with the speaker and the faculty host, who, indeed, was often the person who introduced the speaker.

At the reception for Harold Laski, world-renowned English economist and Nobel prize winner, President Sparling introduced his guest first to Wilberforce Jones, a popular student leader. "Wilberforce!" Laski said. "That is a wonderfully famous name in England. He helped to end the slave trade." Jones smiled broadly. Sparling then turned to the next person in the receiving line and said, "And now, Mr. Laski, I'd like to introduce you to Mr. Washington."

Once the faculty and course offerings were in place—subject to additions every year—it was time to create some of the other organs that make a college live: clubs, a newspaper, a student council. Clubs proliferated weekly; some had only four members but it didn't matter. The *Torch*, independent of faculty control, was founded and Lou Roundtree spent fourteen hours a day in the *Torch* office; it became his obsession. Though not quite an obsession to the others who put out the *Torch* in its earliest years, it was an ardent passion. Not only did they report all the news, but they regularly admonished the students and faculty. Roosevelt must be clean, orderly, respectful, tolerant, intellectually demanding, and realistic.

> Roosevelt College progressives must face reality. People are primarily interested in their immediate welfare. Therefore, we must appeal to the self-interest motive, not to a patriotic or high sounding political or social ideal.
>
> Our object should be to make each student at Roosevelt College an ambassador of good will. To do this each individual must be convinced that his personal aims and those of Roosevelt College are in accord. (*Roosevelt Torch*, Jan. 12, 1947).

The *Torch* won several national awards as best college newspaper.

The staff of the *Torch* was generally considered to be a group of fair-minded centrists—middle-of-the-roaders. None of the radicals—the Communists, Trotskyists, anarchists—could take time out of their politicking for such mundane tasks. But a centrist at Roosevelt in the late forties was a staunch liberal in the outside world, particularly on the subject of race relations. Not even a suggestion of racism in the college was tolerated. Neither racism nor any other kind of bigotry.

Winston Kennedy, editor in 48-49, was widely known and respected as a centrist. But in the tradition of Roosevelt centrists, when he saw racism, he exposed it. He detected what he considered racism in the college theater. (Yes, a theater had been organized, too.) "I felt that the theater was a rather rigid organization and racist, in its casting and development of leadership." He said so in the newspaper. The theater fought back, denying the charges. Kennedy held his ground. One night, late, near deadline, the cartoonist brought in his contribution to the fight—a theater decorated with swastikas. Kennedy ran the cartoon. The theater director was enraged. He demanded Kennedy's expulsion. "I was hanging there on a limb," he recalls. Washington saved his skin. They were both friends, both centrists, both careful, thoughtful people.

Kennedy's father had visited the president. He was unmoved; he was ready to expel Kennedy. Washington then went to Sparling. The swastika was certainly an overreaction, he said, but political cartoons are often overreactions. The important thing, though, was that the *Torch* had a charter as an independent organ. Yes, Kennedy had been indiscreet. But he was the editor and he should not be censored. The issue was freedom of the press.

Sparling listened. He and Washington were friends. They respected each other, understood each other. Sparling called Kennedy in to tell him that he thought the problem could be solved by a public apology to the theater.

"I published the apology, for the swastika. I did not back down on my charges," Kennedy says. He graduated with Washington at the end of that year.

In 1948, Roosevelt moved into the historic "white elephant" at Congress and Michigan that it had been able to buy cheaply. The Auditorium, built in 1890 by Louis Sullivan and Dankmar Adler, and acclaimed as their most outstanding achievement, had been a cultural center of the city for many years but, with the Depression, had been all but abandoned. Used as a servicemen's center during the war, completely abused and disfigured, it would require massive renovation before it could be habitable. Stained glass windows and Sullivan's elaborate wall and ceiling decorations had been painted over. Neither of the two electric systems worked adequately. The elegant marble staircase that led up to the second floor, the castiron stair rails, the solid mahogany panels, great arches, and every other inch of the building was solidly encrusted with layers of paint and dirt. Within a year, enough of the 400 hotel rooms and 136 offices and stores had been converted to labs, classrooms, offices,and lounges to move in, though the great artistic renovation of the Auditorium Theater would have to wait for twenty years and the complete renovation would be done gradually over the next few years.

Perhaps the most important conversions for the students were the store fronts on the first floor and the offices on the second. They didn't mind attending classes in grungy rooms but a place to meet and eat had been desperately missing on Wells Street. At last, the Roosevelt community had a comfortable, attractive cafeteria and lounge. Those who return to visit today bemoan the loss of that first cafeteria to a sidewalk required by the widening of Congress Street for the expressway.

The new cafeteria in Crown Hall on Wabash Avenue seems smaller because it is not graced on two sides by walls of windows looking out onto Michigan and Congress; it looks out on the L tracks. The great high ceilings and massive windows in that original room created an openness that surpassed almost any eating place in Chicago. The food wasn't much better than B&Gs, but there were no waitresses hovering about to insist the students buy something. It was not a commercial establishment, though it was operated on a lease to a restauranteur. It was the gathering place. Win Kennedy, the *Torch* editor, wrote an irate editorial complaining that some students sat there for hours over coffee, making it impossible for others to find a table at which to eat, "disturbing the traffic patterns." Some tables were informally reserved, held for certain cliques all day by a system of rotation beginning with breakfast and only ending when the cafeteria closed in the early evening.

On the second floor, above the cafeteria, was the lounge that was also used as a meeting hall, where there appeared a continuous stream of speakers from all over the world, exhorting the students and faculty to understand the modern postwar world. The lounge was also the site of Joe Siegal's Friday afternoon jazz concerts, a singular contribution to the life of the college. Admission was a quarter. The music was unfailingly exciting. Some students danced—others just listened. The room that was named for Governor Altgeld was always crowded on those Friday afternoons. Siegal was another of the campus heroes.

Every college has a student council. It is *pro forma*. It governs student activities. Historically, it has been a vehicle for young people who aspire to public office, the first run for election, the first elected position. Mark Jones, the first Council president, later became a Circuit Court judge, having paid his dues to the Democratic Party. Ray Clevenger, the second president of the Council, went on to serve in Congress as a representative from Northern Michigan. Washington was the third president. He served first as a member, then as vice-president, and finally as president.

But student councils traditionally are not weighted down with authority; their scope of responsibility is minuscule by comparison to the administration. And most students know this. At Roosevelt, which was and is a commuter school and a school in which many students work, often at full-time evening jobs, the role of the student council was even more questionable. And large numbers of students were deeply, cataclysmically, involved in world politics and had no interest in or time for student government.

Under Washington's leadership, the student council struggled to acquire a larger role in the college. Whether it was to enlarge his own role or because he believed in his mission is not clear. What was clear was that he did succeed in raising the awareness of the student body. Everyone was aware that the council was a serious body acting on behalf of the students. Everyone was conscious of the table in the cafeteria that was filled throughout the day with council members engaged in "strategic discussion."

> "Student government must be functional," said Harold Washington, chairman of the Council Executive Board. "More service to the student

> body will be the aim of the council this year," he continued . . . "The Student Council must be an efficient service organization which not only serves the immediate needs of the student community but has the vision to see into the future and plan a constructive long-range program."
> (*Roosevelt Torch*, Nov. 8, 1948).

In the sixties, as part of the student revolt against arbitrary authority on college campuses across the country, one of the strongest demands made was for student representation on faculty senates and boards of trustees. In the forties, at Roosevelt, this was one of the most hotly debated issues in the College. In its third year, 1948, characteristic of the college and unlike most other colleges, it was finally decided that the students would, indeed, have representation on faculty committees. It was decided that for those committees named by the president, students would also be named by the president, from a list of thirty nominated by the students. For the committees elected by the faculty, student representatives would also be elected. Also characteristic of Roosevelt at that time, the nominations for student representatives were conducted as if they were nominations to the Congress of the United States. "There were deals going down all over the place," recalls Lou Roundtree. "All of us had our favorites. By the time we got to the meeting, we had a pretty good idea of what was going to happen except for one person. What would Harold do? Well, it went around and around and then Harold got up to make his speech. Don't you know? The great compromiser! It was all worked out to everybody's satisfaction."

When Washington and the other nine delegates went to the first regional meeting of the newly founded National Student Association in the spring of 1948, they took with them a proposal for student representation on faculties. They were supported by their political kinsmen at the University of Chicago who proposed a "Bill of Rights" for students. Both measures were roundly defeated by the delegates from other Illinois colleges. In 1948, it seems, college students weren't, as a famous Chicago politician once said, "ready for reform." (The NSA was accused in the late sixties of being funded by the CIA.)

Washington and Frank Brown were the only black students at the NSA confab, which was held at the University of Illinois at Champaign. The group slept in student housing. Finding a place to eat together, however, was not so easy. Restaurants in Champaign didn't serve "coloreds." Bernard Jaffee finally hit on a scheme to get the delegation served after they had been rejected from several restaurants. He explained to the manager of the restaurant that he was the coach for this team of athletes. "Oh," the manager exclaimed, "that's different." He ushered them in, and served them. Black athletes had gained some access in 1948. The manager didn't ask if this was the first coed athletic team in history.

Washington was the only black in the group that went to Springfield in 1949 to try to talk to the legislators about the coming probe of "subversives" at Roosevelt and the University of Chicago. Sen. Paul V. Broyles (R. Mt. Vernon), the author of several bills outlawing the Communist Party and requiring loyalty oaths for teachers, and chairman of the seditious activities investigating commission, had set dates to conduct hearings at the two institutions. President Sparling promised cooperation. "We will welcome and cooperate fully with a fairly conducted investigation." Washington had another view of the matter. Louis Roundtree wrote in the *Torch,* March 14, 1949, "Unhampered by what Harold Washington, Student Council president, termed 'dilatory parliamentary tactics,' the Council passed resolutions condemning the Broyles bills and the proposed investigations pending in the Illinois legislature. . . . The Council passed an eight point program of resolutions and tactics to fight the Broyles bills, and register protest to the 'spirit and purposes of the proposed investigation.'" Washington won the support of the majority of the council despite accusations by those who opposed him of using his own parliamentary tricks.

Washington and several others went to Springfield to carry out the Council's resolutions. The group arrived in the early evening of the day before they were to visit the legislature. The question was: where were they to sleep that night? Washington excused himself, saying he would spend the night with friends. Win Kennedy, Dale Pontius, and the other members said goodnight and went on their way to find lodgings in a tourist home. They met Washington, as planned, the next day at the Capitol. "We assumed that Harold really did have friends and wanted to save a few bucks. We only realized later that, in his characteristic way, he was being sensitive and considerate. Springfield was a completely segregated town. Had he stayed with us, we might not have found lodgings. We never knew where he stayed. He never said a word about it. Had we been more sensitive, smarter about such things, I don't know what would have happened. We might have slept in the car."

Washington helped lead the opposition to the investigation and to the Broyles bills, which were passed later that year. With Gus Savage, who later was elected to Congress with Washington, he also led the plan to reorganize the Student Council to make it more effective. He also organized and ran a political science study group. He was an acknowledged leader on what is euphemistically called the campus. When it was time to represent the college in the community, he was often the representative who described its ideals and its guiding spirit. His integrity and his leadership ability were never doubted. His word was good. Nor was his intellectual ability ever questioned. "Everybody sat and listened when Harold talked," Roundtree recalls. In a course on Shakespeare, another on the Civil War, another on economic planning, in a wide range of courses that reflected an inquiring mind, in a fiercely competitive atmosphere, Washington was consistently an excellent student. He had charisma, oratorical skills, and the ability to mediate disputes. "If there was a conflict, large or small, Harold could see both sides and mediate it," recalls Esther Grunsfeld Klatz. Another classmate, Marcie Brower, recalls that "he was very careful about what he said, very respectful. He gave the impression of great stability."

In the atmosphere of Roosevelt College in those postwar years, great stability was not a garden-variety trait. Though the majority of students were veterans and older than the ordinary college student, the atmosphere was charged with a youthful excitement that belied stability. Perhaps it was precisely because it was the postwar era and because so many of the students were veterans—not just ordinary veterans but highly idealistic ones. They had fought a terrible war for democracy overseas and they now wanted to continue that war at home. Perhaps the excitement was not so youthful, after all. Certainly there were those who would have resented that appellation. And, indeed, asked if Washington had seemed more mature than others, several people insisted that the college was filled with mature young men—and women. What Washington had, they say, was a remarkable ability to keep cool, to reason carefully, to walk a cautious middle line, to avoid getting entangled with anything that was extremist.

That middle path that Washington walked irked some of his friends. They were his friends and they respected him but they would have felt a lot better about him if he had not been, as Earl Durham says, "reluctant about street action." Durham recalls his amazement at seeing Washington join the picket line in front of the office of the Real Estate Board of Chicago that was protesting discrimination in housing and supporting Alderman Archibald Carey's ordinance calling for open housing. It was the only time he joined a street action. Washington's participation in that sole street action, however, was not as inconsistent as it first appears. The other actions of Durham and the other more radical types at Roosevelt were organized around issues raised not by a city alderman but by the radical groups themselves: an effort to gain jobs for blacks at Goldblatt's, an effort to open the White City Roller Rink to blacks, sit-ins in restaurants that refused to serve blacks.

Some of those street actions were highly informal, spontaneous, like the one conducted by Mark Jones and Al Grossman.

"We decided to have a beer and went into the Elm." The bartender stared at Jones a moment, then barked at him, "I ain't gonna serve you. You're a trouble maker."

"Well, ok," said Jones, who had never been in the Elm before. He turned to Grossman who continued the conversation they had been engrossed in on the way over.

"We sat there, smoking and talking for an hour and a half, just ignoring the bartender. He glowered. We just sat there."

An early sit-in, one of the many that occurred all over the city when black and white students attempted to eat and drink together in restaurants when they tired of Woolworth's, Walgreen's, Wimpy's, Pixley's, Power's, and Thompson's, cafeterias where there was no service involved, where coffee was a nickel and the food was terrible. Only Ric Riccardo and Toffenetti's welcomed mixed groups. The others were polite: the men didn't have ties, an obviously near empty place at midnight didn't have a table, there would be a half-hour wait. "We'll wait." "Well, it might just be an hour." This was Chicago; the law was clear; it had been written before the turn of the century: discrimination in public places was illegal.

Some restaurant sit-ins were planned. At the eating place closest to the college, Anne's Rendezvous, where the owner had consistently turned blacks away, a group of a dozen or so CORE members planned an action. They entered en masse, sat down at the table nearest the entrance, and refused to move. They sat for two hours without even a glass of water on the table. They then left. The next night they returned and repeated the action. And the next night. Owner George Annes called the police. The police, to the amazement of all, refused to arrest them. The law was on their side, the police told Annes. He was bewildered. He had no choice but to negotiate. Several days later, he told a reporter from the *Torch,* "I would like to commend CORE and the students of Roosevelt College for their alertness in protesting instances of discrimination." Years later, he told Mary Lou Edelstein Kaplan, who had been a frequent customer at Anne's, that he "had learned a lot from the students." Understandable. Students sat in his restaurant every night, after the cafeteria closed, until Anne's closed at two. Arguing, loudly, all those weighty questions of race, sex, politics, religion, history, physics, education. And then they went home to Rogers Park, Logan Square, 43rd Street, 61st Street, having bid George Annes goodnight.

Restaurants weren't the only places that didn't want to serve blacks. The families of some white students weren't always so happy to receive them either. Charlotte Grossman Wallk remembers the shock of having Washington and Gus Savage arrive first at a party at her house after she had argued long and volubly to convince her parents they should risk their neighbor's censure, that she could not have a party without inviting her black friends. "Oh, my God," she said to herself as she ushered Washington and Savage into the living room to meet her parents, "they could have done me a favor and arrived second or third."

Of course, there were other kinds of parents. Roundtree recalls arriving at midnight many evenings to drop the two Sachs' daughters at home after a night at the printer when their mother insisted on feeding them, "Jewish-mother style. We would protest that we weren't hungry, that it was too late, but we didn't move her. We had to eat."

The picket line at the Real Estate Board was not organized by CORE. Though it was the work of students, it was of a different order. It was an effort to support an ordinance introduced into the City Council by Archibald Carey. In 1949, he was at the peak of his prestige in the black community. A "street action" in support of him on such a crucial issue as open housing was not in the same class as other radical actions. Washington might safely participate. Or at least a little more safely, since *any* street action in those days was considered hare-brained, irresponsible, crazy. In staying away from them, Washington may have been protecting his father's reputation.

More likely, he was protecting his own chances of being admitted to law school. Any street action could lead to jail (in fact, arrests were rarely made in those years; that development had to wait for the sixties) and an arrest record was an almost automatic barrier to acceptance to law school. Any serious contender for such a berth would be foolish to take such a risk. Furthermore, anyone in 1949 even considering a career in politics had better keep his nose clean. There was a growing "red scare" in the country and it was a long tradition in America that any radical activity was viewed as Communist subversion. In 1947, President Truman wrote executive orders founding the CIA and the National Security Council. In the Congress, J. Parnell Thomas was leading his House Committee on Un-American Activities (HUAC), which included Karl Mundt and Richard Nixon, on a crusade to expose and condemn "Communists." In his 1967 book, *The Committee,* Walter Goodman spends 35 pages on the year 1947 alone, in a 500-page book that spans the years 1938-1967.

Shortly before graduation, I approached my department chairman, well-known for her conservatism, for a fellowship at the University of Illinois where I would go to work on an M.A. She replied, "I'm sorry, Miss Hamlish, I cannot give you any recommendations."

"But my record in this department has been among the best," I was breathless.

"Your academic record is unimpeachable, Miss Hamlish, but your morals are not."

"Morals?"

"You are an intemperate young woman."

"Intemperate?"

"Did you think I didn't know what you've been doing?"

"Doing?"

"All of that extracurricular activity is what I am referring to, Miss Hamlish."

"Do you mean my political activity?"

"I don't know what *you* call it." One didn't come right out and call someone a Communist at Roosevelt, but we all understood the symbols.

She looked down at my feet. Politics was bad enough but Roman sandals too? I was given an assistantship instead of the more prestigious fellowship. Perhaps because I didn't score high enough on the Miller Analogues. Or perhaps because I lacked that crucial recommendation. Indeed, she may have given me a bum rap. Washington was smarter.

Washington may have believed that the picket line at the Real Estate Board was safer because its purpose was to support the Carey legislation. Or he may have believed so strongly in the open housing ordinance that he was willing to take the risk. Hindsight on such questions is rarely accurate. Looking at his record, though, it is hard to avoid the conclusion that he believed it was safe enough, that his father would not be flayed for having a crazy son and that the police would not arrest the participants of this action.

It was a glorious fantasy that Washington shared with Jerome Robbins, with whom he went on to Northwestern Law School: he would be the first black mayor of Chicago. The spirit at Roosevelt engendered such fantasies. The open atmosphere, the warm encouragement and support of faculty and students stimulated fantasies of fame, fortune, and political power in many students. Many prepared for those futures by reading, writing, arguing, practicing. But for many more, the high spirits in the college, the sense of an extraordinarily privileged experience, a sense of other-worldliness overwhelmed such wordly preparation. It was as if they were taking time out of life for a great adventure. Later, they would settle down to the tasks of life. For Washington, on the other hand, his life at Roosevelt was, very consciously, the first step in his career. He was heading for the top ranks of political life. He was a staunch liberal and would remain so but, though he shared many of their values, he could not identify himself with the radicals.

What is most interesting about his role on that volatile campus is that, as much as they resented his absence from their ranks—he was a strong charismatic leader who could have helped their causes greatly—the radicals of the left were respectful and warm in their relations with him. His "reluctance about street action" and other radical activities was a friendly, respectful reluctance. He did not, as many middle-of-the-road types did, ridicule and shun the radicals. He was kind to the legendary anarchist, Joffre Stewart, who chained himself to a barber chair next door to the college when the barbers refused to cut his nappy hair and was jailed over and over again for demanding that haircut. Stewart did not receive the same kindness in all quarters of even that most unconventional atmosphere. Walking shorts on Michigan Avenue in the late forties! Sandals were mad enough but shorts?

Several years after they graduated, Stewart ran into Washington, as he often did, standing on the corner of 47th and South Park outside the Democratic headquarters chatting with a friend. Stewart gave them one of the leaflets for which he was already famous, and exchanged a few words. When he was on his way, Washington explained to his friend, Albert Pritchett, that Stewart was an old friend from Roosevelt, a single-minded, dedicated crusader for justice, one of a kind, a good friend. No one was too outrageous to elicit Washington's graciousness. He earned the respect of the radicals as they earned his. Not that they didn't argue, often long into the night, but there was a mutual respect, his respect for their radical activities, theirs for his pragmatism. It was understood that they shared the same ideals and that there was more than one way to pursue them, though it was often forgotten in the heat of an argument. It was understood that the path one chose was determined as well by temperament as by political expediency. In his arguments as well as in his activities—there were more of the first, of course—he was more temperate, more cautious than the radicals. But he was not less idealistic.

Frank Untermeyer, a young assistant professor of political science, dropped in to visit Shirley Waller (who had changed her name from Wallowitz to avoid the stigma of a Jewish-sounding name), one of his favorite students, in her West Side apartment. He hoped to have a cup of coffee and some conversation. Shirley was a brilliant student and a stimulating talker who went on to write a significant book in economic theory before she died a few years later. To Untermeyer's dismay, Waller's apartment was in complete disarray. Washington, in a pair of white overalls and a painter's cap, was on a ladder, painting the walls. He earned extra cash as a house painter but volunteered to paint gratis the apartments and rooms of friends who could scarcely afford the price of the paint. Many of Roosevelt's students were on scholarships, supporting themselves with part-time jobs, having come from poor families. They were often the first generation to go to college. Washington had a special fondness for those highly intelligent, hard-working students. Especially of the women but even of some men students, he was a few years older and seen that way by most. A paint job for their shabby rooms and apartments was a small gift he could give them. They gave him in return the respect and admiration that fueled his dream of one day becoming the first black mayor of Chicago.

Kindness, a sharp wit, honesty, hard intelligence, charisma, the life of the party—over and over again these words echo in the words of Washington's former associates at Roosevelt College—faculty, students, administrators. "But he was always an enigma," recalls Charlotte Grossman Wallk. "He was an entirely public person. Through all the beer bashes, endless meetings, endless conversations over coffee, Harold revealed nothing of his private life. It was as if he didn't have one, as if he was entirely engrossed in his work, his intellectual work and political work." Well, Mark Jones recalls that they were both, at one point, "interested in the same lady." Jones doesn't reveal who won. But it remains true that Washington didn't engage with others in the story-swapping about family, friends, lovers that went on regularly even in the overheated political climate at Roosevelt. He probably confided in Wilberforce Jones, with whom he was more intimate, whom he took home to family dinners, who called his mother, as the family did, Mother Dear. Jones died after a long illness in 1980. Perhaps Washington confided in few others, trusted few people well enough to share his private life with them. A stronger impression is that he had little interest in those intimate details of life, that he was consumed with his work, with enlarging his knowledge, with building a political career, and with expanding the liberties and opportunities of blacks. And his own liberties and opportunities. Pragmatism is no sin.

New York State Prosecutor Thomas Dewey was the odds-on favorite for president in 1948. President Harry Truman was fighting for his political life. Henry Wallace was the candidate of the Progressive Party, begun by idealistic liberals but slowly being captured by the Communist Party. Wallace had lots of followers at Roosevelt, both liberals and radicals. Dewey, too, had followers, especially those in the Commerce Club, who represented the conservatives in the college. The forthcoming election was argued dizzyingly through the days and nights by students and faculty. Washington and others organized a mock convention in May, 1948. It may have been the only open convention in the country that year. Nominations flew almost as fast as the rhetoric. Caucuses met and met again. The stakes were high. Like every political event at Roosevelt in those years, this one would have momentous importance—to the Roosevelt community. Anne's Rendezvous was their smoke-filled back room. The wheeling and dealing was intense. When the election was finally held, William O. Douglas was nominated for president and Wayne Morse was the vice-presidential nominee. As so often happened at Roosevelt, often to Washington's dismay, idealism won over the hard political realities. The actual candidates had been set aside, forgotten. But the results of that election revealed an idealism strongly tinged with pragmatism, the pragmatism so characteristic of Washington. The college community could not support Wallace, the candidate of the left, nor Dewey, the candidate of the right, nor Truman, the incumbent, whose record included dropping the bomb on Hiroshima, creating an internal security agency, and opening the Cold War. William O. Douglas and Wayne Morse were among the purest souls in the country, leading liberals in the nation, utterly clean of any leftwing associations, beloved for their support of democratic institutions and the expansion of democracy. Those who did not love them respected them.

The nominations were viewed as copouts by some, those who wanted to be a realistic political force, as foolish idealism by others, but for most, including Washington, they were viewed as a clear expression of the will of the majority at Roosevelt, who, given the chance, would elect those whom they could trust to promote the general welfare of the people. As he always did when events didn't go exactly as he hoped, Washington grinned broadly and quipped, "Right or wrong, I have but one life to give to my country. The people have spoken." And with that, he dashed off to another meeting.

The college experience is often the pivotal one in a person's life—a sudden awakening of intellectual concerns, the acquisition of skills previously undreamed of, the first sexual experience, knowledge of the world beyond home. Few colleges, at few times in history, in few places, have offered an experience to equal the one at Roosevelt in those immediate postwar years. While there was ferment on many campuses, the unique blend of political ferment with the lowering of racial and religious barriers that occurred at Roosevelt was unique. It had a profound impact on Chicago, creating the first truly interracial, interreligious community from which the student returned to every neighborhood of the city, never to forget the lessons learned there. "It made me appreciate the feelings of blacks—an experience most ordinary people couldn't get," says Marshall Dickstein, who served on the student council with Washington and who was one of those "athletes" at the NSA meeting in Champaign. Dickstein grew up in Albany Park and has spent most of his adult years in the northern suburbs. He still cherishes the memories of his college years.

For a young man looking forward to a life in politics, a black man who has grown up within the confines of the Democratic Machine on the South Side of Chicago, the experience of Roosevelt College in those years, the opportunities open to him there as they could have been nowhere else at the time, cannot be underestimated. Pivotal? Indeed!

Keeping A Low Profile

The last honor having been bestowed upon him—election to class president—Washington graduated from Roosevelt in August 1949. In September, he entered Northwestern Law School, the university where his father had briefly been an undergraduate. In three short years, he had gone from the dingy halls at 231 S. Wells to the hastily painted narrow corridors at 430 S. Michigan to the oak-panelled walls of Northwestern Law School; from the small, crowded classrooms on Wells Street to the more spacious but spare classrooms on Michigan Avenue to the first-year lectures in the hallowed Lincoln Hall, a replica of the ancient British House of Lords at Northwestern; from Wells Street under the L tracks to Michigan Avenue across from Grant Park to Lake Shore Drive; from a brand-new racially integrated, low-cost experiment in higher education to the 100-year-old law school steeped in educational and racial tradition—Washington was the only black in his class.

As he had done at Roosevelt, he entered school politics and was, in his last year, elected treasurer of the Junior Bar Association (now called the Student Bar Association). His election in 1951 was not a little ironic, considering that it had been only five years before that the Chicago Bar Association had admitted blacks to membership and then only at the insistence of the University of Chicago Law School, which had finally added a black lawyer to its faculty and wanted to avoid the embarrassment of having one of its own barred from membership in the local legal association. Washington's father had been permitted to membership only in the Cook County Bar Association, founded in 1914 as the black counterpart of the CBA. No small coup it was, then, that his son was elected treasurer of the Northwestern student branch of the American Bar Association.

That election was possible because, while the school maintained its nearly lily-white tradition, accepting one—perhaps two—black students a year, the climate was hospitable enough to those who were accepted.

Interestingly, the law school at Northwestern has not discriminated against women for many years. Women were not encouraged to be attorneys just as they were not encouraged to be doctors or stock brokers, but of those few who did apply for admission to Northwestern, a higher proportion of women were admitted than men. In 1949, while Washington was the only black in his class, there were six women. Three dropped out, two finished early by attending summer sessions, leaving Dawn Clark Netsch as the only woman to graduate with Washington. Netsch soon rose to the top of her class. She speculates, though she insists it is only speculation because she has not done the research to discover whether it is true, that until the seventies proportionately more women than men applicants were accepted to the law school because the women tended to be among the best candidates. Only the very best women even considered the idea.

So for both women and blacks, Northwestern was a relatively comfortable place to be. Judge Eugene Pincham, who preceded Washington as the only black in the class of 1950, and who had come from a southern town where Jim Crow still dominated the landscape, was pleased to discover the warmth and cordiality that he received from his fellow students and the faculty at Northwestern. And if there was an occasional slip, it was overlooked if not unnoticed, he says. Certainly, had there been any large-scale bigotry in the school Washington would have failed in his bid for election to the JBA.

That he assumed he could win is both a testimony to the faith and self-confidence in the integrated world that he had acquired at Roosevelt and to that bold streak in his personality that led him thirty-four years later to the fifth floor of City Hall in Chicago. To say that elections represent a challenge that Washington cannot ignore is to understate the case.

Unlike most young blacks of his day, but like those young people with whom he had made the great leap forward that Roosevelt College represented, he had a vision—a dream—of what he could attain. Pincham reflects on those years to say, "The true evil of segregation and discrimination is not that it denies opportunities, though of course it does that, but that it denies us vision. I couldn't dream of a black mayor of Chicago. I couldn't even dream of a black judge—there was only one in Chicago. How could I hope to attain that goal? Had we been able to dream such dreams, just think of what we might have done, considering that when the time actually came it took only six months to win the mayoralty." That Washington did dream of being the first black mayor of Chicago, while his fellow blacks were merely dreaming of "surviving," as Pincham puts it, is an indication of his bold imagination as much as it is a tribute to the unique experience at Roosevelt that enabled people to have big dreams. That it took him thirty-four years to accomplish his dream is testimony to the racism that has afflicted Chicago. He dreamed, but that evil that Pincham views as the lesser one succeeded in keeping the dream merely that for thirty-four years. Most mayors are elected when they are in their forties. Even the black mayors of other cities—most of them—were elected in their forties. In Chicago, where politics has always been tightly controlled and where racism has abated less than in most other cities, the black who dreamed of being mayor in his twenties and who began preparing himself for a political career when he was fifteen, had to wait for that dream to come true until he was sixty-one.

Elections to the JBA at the law school were, in the words of A. Arthur Davis, the vice-president when Washington was treasurer, a "popularity contest in which the students simply elected the people they liked best but for whom there was nothing much to do. The president met with the dean occasionally but we hardly met at all." The election merited a story and a picture in the school newspaper, but the JBA did not play the highly-charged role at Northwestern that the Student Council had at Roosevelt. Most alumni do not even recall its existence. The significance of the win for Washington was instead symbolic: it was another election victory, highly symbolic at that law school because he was the only black in the class. However, in his characteristic way, he attempted to enlarge the scope of the JBA by proposing a series of committees whose tasks would be to promote more "fellowship" among students, faculty, and alumni. Fellowship—what a wonderfully polite word. At Roosevelt, it has been "service to the student body." One didn't speak of service in 1949 in law school; one spoke of fellowship. It isn't difficult to discern utilitarian motives in the proposal, however. Closer contacts with faculty and alumni could not but help enhance the opportunities for students. Getting a good job in the legal business, as in most other businesses, depends on who you know and how well you know them. In addition, closer contacts with faculty could not but help enhance the knowledge of the students. Much practical advice and theoretical discussion that never take place in class do take place in personal exchanges between faculty and students. There are some who say that the most important things they learned in school were learned in conversations with professors outside of class. The proposal, however, seems to have died on the vine. Davis can't even recall it.

Washington knew that his own chances for a job in one of the big white law firms in downtown Chicago were probably nonexistent. Even in 1983, thirty years later, there was only one black member of a prestigious white law firm. Furthermore, he wasn't sure yet whether he would want such a position; one doesn't easily build a political base on which to win elections in the black community as the only black working in a white law firm. And a black couldn't hope to win an election in any but a black community. On the other hand, there was that challenge: he might just want to try to be the first black man hired by a big LaSalle Street firm.

Though it admitted almost no blacks, Northwestern Law School had for many years admitted enough Jewish students to constitute a *minyan* (A Jewish quorum, the ten males required for a religious service). In fact, Jerome Robbins, who moved from Roosevelt to Northwestern with Washington, recalls exactly ten Jews in their class of 162. Ten was just enough to constitute a chapter of a Jewish legal fraternity, a response by some Jews to being excluded from the traditional fraternities. Bigotry, it seems, did occur outside those oak-panelled corridors. Robbins was approached by a fellow Jew at DePaul Law School with the idea of reviving at Northwestern Nu Beta Epsilon, a Jewish fraternity founded there years before by Barnett Hodes, who later became a prime mover in the Democratic Machine and who was a member of one of the few large Jewish law firms in Chicago. Robbins agreed to the idea on the condition that the organization accept an interracial, interreligious chapter at NU. Robbins had helped found the first such fraternity in the country at Roosevelt and had enjoyed the experience. Besides, he says, "It was our way of snubbing our noses at those who snubbed us. They had baseball games, beer busts, and parties and didn't invite any of us minority people—not the Japanese, the blacks, the Jews. Those Christian fraternities formed a nice little ingroup from which we were excluded. So we formed our own."

There are those who deny that there was bigotry. They insist that the problem lay in the strong distinction that existed between those who lived in the dormitory, Abbott Hall, and those who commuted. The commuters left at the end of the school day, the defenders insist, and were therefore automatically excluded from the social life of the school. Well, maybe. Maybe not. Are baseball games normally played in the evening? Well, perhaps the commuters didn't choose to come back to the campus on the weekends. It was certainly true that Robbins, Schwartz, Secaras, Washington, and the other members of Nu Beta Epsilon were commuters and, in addition, worked at jobs after classes and often on weekends. But the fraternities? Weren't they professional fraternities? All their members weren't Abbott Hall residents. Were they merely, as all fraternities but the one that Robbins organized at Roosevelt, restricted to white Christians? Or Jews or blacks, for those who "snubbed their noses at those who snubbed" them?

Nu Beta Epsilon wasn't a highly prestigious fraternity, nor did it provide any of the tangible benefits that fraternities normally do. Its members met only irregularly for what Robbins calls "some silly meetings and an occasional lecture." The members disavowed all the secret symbols and rituals usually associated with the fraternity and conducted themselves for the most part as a small intellectual society. When Hodes visited a meeting, "his eyes popped out of his head at the sight of a black, a Japanese, a Greek, and a few Jews,"—ten in all. Washington was the black. Robbins "managed to schlep" Washington into Nu Beta Epsilon, though he had not even made an effort to enlist him in his similarly interreligious, interracial fraternity at Roosevelt. Such a group at Roosevelt held no interest for Washington. He had little interest in mere social activities and he certainly did not need to join that fraternity to make a statement about integration. But at Northwestern Law School, the only black in the class, as one of a dozen minority students blatantly excluded from the recognized fraternities, it was a worthy organization to join, a worthwhile statement to make.

John H. Secaras was the Greek who joined the newly constituted fraternity. There is a little bitterness in his voice when he recalls the exclusion of ethnics at Northwestern. The warmth that Pincham recalls seems not to have touched him. "I had only a few friends," he says, "Harold was one of them. He was a very interesting, well-balanced man. I didn't even try to join those other fraternities. They didn't feel right to me. I stayed with my own kind." Secaras adds that he, like most of his friends, had to work his way through college, leaving little time for socializing. "I did write for the *Law Review* [one of the honors accorded second and third-year law students] but even then I was not accepted. It didn't bother me. I knew I was a good fellow. If they didn't want my company, that was their loss." Membership in Nu Beta Epsilon was obviously a statement that Secaras was eager to make, too.

Were women, once accepted, also discriminated against by that all-male student body? Well, as the top student in the class and as associate editor of the *Law Review* in her third year, Dawn Clark Netsch "could hardly have been looked down upon," she says with a smile. She worked hard, often leaving the school only at ten or eleven in the evening to walk the mile to her rooming-house because she did not have the carfare for the big red. She didn't have much time for socializing and, in fact, there wasn't very much social activity in the school. "There was more discipline in the school then than there is now," Netsch adds. She began teaching there in 1965 and a few years later introduced the first course in race relations law.

Though Washington is described by Elaine Tigler, the law school's veteran librarian, who retired only in 1983, as having been "political," he seems rather to have been quite an average student. Like the rest, he worked hard to make a respectable record and maintained, by comparison with his college years, a low profile. He obviously kept a high enough profile to be elected, in his third year, an officer of the JBA, but he is recalled by no one else as having been politically active. Smart enough to hold his own in a highly competitive atmosphere, witty and charming enough to be recalled fondly, but an activist, a star? No, there seem to be no such recollections by any of his classmates. He learned soon enough that those who raised their profiles very high were seen not as heroes as they had been at Roosevelt, but as "loud-mouths."

"A lot of students in law school think that it's good strategy to keep a low profile because there is so much flak flying," reports Francis Allen, a professor at NU at the time, now at the University of Michigan. Whether the difference between Roosevelt and

Northwestern Law School was the difference between a college and a professional school, as Allen implies, or whether it was the difference between a school largely populated with ethnics and one almost entirely populated with WASPs is a question sociologists and psychologists love to play with. It's an intriguing question, particularly in view of the present situation. "There is so much more activity now," Netsch reports. "There is a student representative at faculty meetings and students are much more involved." There are also a lot more blacks and ethnics in that student body now.

Washington quickly underwent the personality change required to fit his new situation. He learns fast. His wit and good humor were appreciated at the lunch table in the basement cafeteria at 357 E. Chicago Avenue, Marshall Winokur and Harold Shapiro recall, but he was no longer the "big man on campus," the stellar personality admired by all. He was just another law student struggling to get through school, which took most of the day, five days a week, and to earn some money in the evenings and weekends to supplement the $75 GI Bill stipend—one very capable, highly intelligent student in a class that is described as a "very distinguished large class from which many members went on to be famous"—A. Arthur Davis now heads the largest law firm in Iowa. Netsch, the only woman to graduate from Northwestern with Washington, has served four distinguished terms in the Illinois Senate and teaches at Northwestern. Don Rubin became one of the best known attorneys in Chicago. Robbins and his partner, Allen Schwartz, are well-known in the field of school law, Martin I. Steinberg, James Richards, and James S. Quinlan are judges, Secaras the acting regional solicitor for the U.S. Department of Labor for Region 5, Harold Shapiro a partner in one of Chicago's largest firms. Frank Nicholas, the "character" in the class, became a great entrepreneur, the big daddy of the baby food business, having bought and made a multi-million dollar business of the nearly bankrupt Beechnut Corporation. Numbers more are in prestigious firms, on the bench, and in government. That the only woman and the only black in that graduating class are the ones to have made distinguished careers in elective office is a fact to contemplate.

Were they, because they were so much in the minority, driven to seek greater public acclaim than the others? There were those, in the fifties and sixties, and earlier, and even today—most victims of discrimination—who shrank into the role assigned to them. Others, a handful, sought—seek—to rise far beyond that role as a signal that they would not accept it, that they demanded recognition as talented individuals, that the role is a falsely, cruelly conceived one. Were Netsch and Washington among that handful? Or were they attracted to public service because their uniqueness dramatized for them the needs of the community, especially of the deprived, the minorities, the disenfranchised? Until very recently, it was not easy to find a professional woman or black outside the ranks of the serving professions: teaching, medicine, law, social work. There were almost no women or black engineers, architects, physicists, though of course there were precious few doctors and lawyers, either.

To some extent, politics is an extension of that serving role. The phenomenal rise of women and blacks in politics reflects the continuation of that long tradition of service to the community (though that tradition was often not so much chosen as enforced—women and blacks did not have access to the other professions). Most likely, as the evidence of their careers indicates, both factors were operating for Netsch and Washington. As the star performer in her class, Netsch early on displayed a powerful drive for recognition and achievement, a woman who would overcome the barriers normally placed against those acquisitions by women. And, as the only black in the class of a first-rate law school, Washington, too, displayed that drive for recognition and achievement. At the same time, both their careers have been notable for dedication to service in the community.

So it was the combination of the drive for recognition and the drive for public service that propelled these two unique individuals in that class of '52 at Northwestern Law School to attain stature in the world of politics. Netsch had to wait longer than

Washington; she taught for twenty years, entering politics only when it was clear that a woman could be elected. For Washington, having grown up in the politics of the South Side, he could enter the arena immediately but, as a black, he, too, would have to wait—twelve years—before finally being slated for public office.

Building A Political Base

The phone rings for Harold Washington in the 3rd Ward office. It is Bishop Ford, leader of the Church of God and Christ Church, one of the most prestigious on the South Side. "Harold, I'm sending my son over to you. Will you take him under your wing? He needs a steadying influence."

"Send him along, Bishop. No promises, but I'll do my best."

Washington didn't make promises he couldn't keep. But his best seems to have been quite enough. For the next fifteen years, Charles Ford spent most of his spare time, not in the streets but in the 3rd Ward Democratic headquarters or in activities in the community for the ward. His nights were spent—long, late nights—talking, arguing, planning about organizing, about issues, about the rules of politics, about how to get support for issues and for candidates, about how to pressure for what you want.

Ford was not a complete roustabout. He was in college and was already involved in politics, serving as assistant precinct captain in his precinct. His father just had very high standards for him and hoped to tame the restlessness he saw in his son. Washington was hardly the man to tame anyone but he was a good man to help others channel their energies. Channeled Ford was. He served as president of the Young Democrats under Washington's tutelage for several years and then took over Washington's role as political consultant to the group. After spending fifteen years deeply involved in 3rd Ward politics, he slowed down, though he never stopped completely. In 1983, as district manager in the Department of Human Services, he campaigned for his boss, Jane Byrne. He had no choice. Had he campaigned for his old mentor and friend and Byrne won, he would have been out of a job he loves. When the primary was over and Byrne lost, Ford happily turned his long-honed political talents to the campaign he had hardly imagined possible when Washington taught him the rules of politics in the late fifties and early sixties.

Washington taught hundreds of men and women the rules of politics but, Ford says, he would never have had that role in any other regular political organization, only in the 3rd Ward where Ralph Metcalfe was boss. Metcalfe may not have been Washington's mentor but he was his maker.

In 1952, following Richard J. Daley's election as party chairman, great changes occurred in the political structure of Chicago. Daley set immediately about dumping all the people who might have some ideas of their own, who might not play ball, who might not acquiesce in his control. C.C. Wimbush, Dawson's man in the 3rd Ward, committeeman and state senator, was a man whose concerns for the welfare of black people were well-known, not a man Daley wanted around. More importantly, he didn't want Dawson's man around because he was in the process of removing Dawson's power. Wimbush was first stripped of his committeemanship and replaced by Ralph Metcalfe and then dumped from the state slate.

But Daley was never a stupid politician, selecting people merely because they would say yes to him. His people had to be that unusual blend of loyal and smart. Metcalfe was a shining star in the black community, an Olympic track star, a graduate of

Marquette University, a handsome, elegant gentleman, a highly intelligent man with obvious leadership qualities. He was also a Catholic, a large factor in Daley's selection of people to run the organization. It wasn't easy for Daley to deal with blacks; being Catholic made them a little more acceptable.

In 1952, only half the voters in the 3rd Ward were Democratic. According to William Grimshaw, of the Illinois Institute of Technology, in 1951, the 3rd Ward ranked 33 among 50 city wards in the size of its Democratic plurality. In 1955, after only three years of Metcalfe's rule, that rank had risen to 8 and helped sweep Daley into the mayoralty. By 1961, the ward ranked first.

Getting ahead of my story a bit, in 1977, after Metcalfe broke with the Democratic Party, that ranking fell to 27; in 1979, after Washington broke with the party, the rank fell to 45—out of fifty. Voters were either casting their ballots for independents or they were staying home on Election Day. They were no longer giving the Democrats those large pluralities Daley had received from 1955 to 1967. Blacks were marching, finally, to a different drummer by 1967. The civil rights movement had finally had its impact.

Metcalfe, then, was no mere yes man. The most powerful evidence for that was to be found in his alliance with Washington that began shortly after he took over the 3rd Ward. In the same year that Metcalfe moved into 366 E. 47th Street, Washington moved into his father's law office kitty-corner from the ward office. He was struggling to earn a living but he was spending more time in the ward office. Most observers agree that he sacrificed his law practice for his politics but that tradeoff is not so remarkable when we realize that the young black lawyer's opportunities for an interesting practice were almost nil. It would have been more remarkable if Washington had been able to put in the long, tedious hours of grinding out simple divorce decrees, real estate transactions, and minor civil suits that it took to build a practice. It was not in his nature. Nor did he have any great interest in making money. In fact, most of his friends laugh at the suggestion that Washington might have plugged away more seriously at his law practice to earn money as most of his peers were doing. "Harold never gave one damn about money," they agree.

Washington never gave one damn about *any* material possessions except books. In the sixties, his good friend, Charles Freeman, now a judge on the Circuit Court, with whom he later shared an office at 63rd and Peoria, received a phone call from his wife, enthusiastically telling him about a remarkable sale on leather coats she had found. Should she buy him one, she wanted to know. And shouldn't he ask Harold if he wanted one, he desperately needed a new coat.

"Go ahead and buy two," Freeman told her. He gave the coat to Washington. He was thrilled.

Several months later, he and Freeman arrived at the office at the same time. Bennett Johnson, an old friend, was with Washington.

"My God, your coat looks like new!" Washington exclaimed.

"Why shouldn't it?" Johnson asked, "he doesn't sleep in *his*."

Washington did, indeed, sleep in his sleek new leather coat, Freeman says. He worked late into the night in their offices, long after the heat was turned off, wearing his coat to keep warm. When he finally got tired, he put his head down on the desk to sleep.

"He's gotten better about that in the last few years," Freeman adds. "He's paying more attention to his clothes." Perhaps the experience of Capitol Hill and then the mayoral election campaign made him conscious of his appearance. On the other hand, one of his first acts as mayor was to retire the huge mayoral Cadillac limousine and request from the city pool an Oldsmobile for his own use.

He did move out of the small apartment in which he had lived into a larger one, which he had redecorated, in the same building, a modest one by the standards of the previous mayor but by most standards a lovely old building. It is a bachelor apartment, overflowing with books and papers. Not all of his books. Many of them have been lent away over the years, never to be returned. County Commissioner William Harris recalls his laughter when Washington first tried to avoid lending him books and, after relenting, insisting that they be returned. "We both knew I'd never return them," he says. "He has thousands. He would never remember and neither would I."

Freeman became as close to a best friend as Washington has. They shared an office for eight years and throughout that time often talked into the late hours. Washington loves to talk. And play chess. But he does not love to socialize, to party, attend dinners, and mix in that way that most people do. Like his father before him, he is active in none of the social clubs and fraternities that are so popular in the black community. In those earlier years of the fifties and sixties, he did enjoy an occasional evening at a saloon but Cecil Troy, owner of one of the bars he visited regularly, says he obviously got restless and left earlier than some. "He dropped in for a couple of drinks and some conversation and then left," Troy says.

Talk, a game of chess, a book, a woman, and work, mostly work—that is Washington's life, the life of a serious man, but one with an endlessly buoyant sense of humor, not humor that is easily recorded, consisting as it does of a wink at the right moment, a phrase that relieves tension or makes light of something he wants to avoid, or a playful quip about an absurd situation. There is no Miller's jokebook in Washington. He sees the absurdity of so much in life and cannot resist remarking on it, wryly, even slyly at times. Only rarely is his humor at someone else's expense though he has, Freeman says, been known to deliver a sharp barb to someone "who deserves it."

Though he confides his private thoughts to almost no one, Washington talks freely and expansively about politics and intellectual and social issues, and because he has been mentor to so many and loyal to those he taught, most people find it comfortable to accept him as a man dedicated to work and uninterested in the sociability ordinary people enjoy, a private man who demands respect for that privacy. His life is politics. He has said over and over again, "Politics is a jealous mistress," William Harris says, "and that's what it has taken. He doesn't have the needs that other people have. He needs politics the way other people need families and ordinary social things. He needs politics the way other people need sleep and food."

Washington also seems to be different from ordinary people in his need for sleep. Harris recalls many times when Washington was on his feet steadily for many hours after only a five-minute catnap sitting up. "His energy seems endless."

When it was time to be sworn in as mayor of Chicago, Washington asked his old friend, Freeman, to perform that duty. They could exult together. It was a sign of the love and respect he felt for the friend who had, among many other things, bought him a sleek leather coat that he would never have bought for himself and who had loyally travelled to Washington, D.C. when he was inaugurated to his Congressional seat.

It didn't take Ralph Metcalfe very long to recognize the skill and intelligence of the handsome wiry young man who seemed to sprint around the Democratic Party headquarters. This young man was clearly destined to go far—Metcalfe needed that kind of talent. He was determined to move the 3rd Ward, to build a strong organization, a service organization that would genuinely help the people and would, at the same time, inspire their vote, for him, for Daley, for the solid Democratic ticket. His ambition was not only for himself but for his community.

"Any thinking politician knows he needs the youth of the community to build an organization and Metcalfe was smart enough to know that," Charles Ford says. He also knew that young people do not necessarily a silent organization make, that there is bound to be a certain amount of intellectual tumult if youth are encouraged to build their own organizations. Ford adds, "Metcalfe took large significant risks with Washington and the Young Democrats but it paid off." In Metcalfe's first several elections, the 3rd Ward vote was second only to Daley's own ward. He built a powerful machine of his own, based largely on the youth in the ward, that eventually sent him to Congress in opposition to Daley, with a thundering plurality.

Without Washington, Metcalfe probably could not have accomplished what he did, most observers agree. Clever as he was, Washington was cleverer. Skilled as he was, Washington was more skilled. More important, Washington had foresight that Metcalfe, along with most others, lacked. "Harold could think ahead, on behalf of the folk," Albert Pritchett, a Young Democrat in the fifties, who headed up Metcalfe's sports programs for kids, and is now assistant to the County Assessor, says. "Metcalfe was a good politician, a smart man who knew exactly what he was doing, but Harold was his chief advisor. Ralph depended on Harold for his intelligence, his ability to think, especially to think ahead."

Through the years in which he built his own organization, Metcalfe met regularly with a group of people whose ideas he had come to respect. "But the meeting didn't start," Freeman says, "until Harold arrived." If he didn't show up, Metcalfe sent people out in search of him, to his apartment, his office, the local saloon, the street corner where Washington often stood for hours and talked with anyone he happened to meet.

Years later, when he was in the State House, Washington decided it was time to create his own think tank. He and Metcalfe had fought for many years over many issues. He was not the thinker Washington and his friends were. It was time to cut loose, to stop being Metcalfe's advisor, to begin having his own advisors.

They met in Freeman's office, including several who had been in Metcalfe's group. One night, Metcalfe arrived, uninvited, early. He had been tipped off. If Mohammed would no longer go to the mountain, the mountain must go to Mohammed. He sent his wife, Fay, up to Freeman to grease the way. He left his driver out in front to see who came in. It was intolerable that Washington had gone off like this on his own. Washington and the others were polite but Metcalfe's continued uninvited appearances at these sessions led, Freeman says, to their dissolution.

The Young Democrats in Chicago were organized in the thirties. What is there about political parties that must grade people by age? The Republicans, too, have a youth organization. Youth is defined as somewhere under thirty-five. Few other organizations engage in age-grading. Even churches, those other paternalistic, often monolithic organizations, restrict their age-grading, for the most part, to their Sunday schools for the truly young. Even then, for the main purpose of the church—the worship—there is no age-grading. Another of the few organizations to indulge in this practice—and it seems to be a function of earnings rather than learnings—is the Junior Chamber of Commerce.

The purpose of the Young Democrats and the Young Republicans is ostensibly to train young blood to take leadership in the senior party. The implication is that a man or woman under thirty-five is not ready for membership in those stellar ranks of politicians. More likely, it is the fear of competition from the dynamism of the young that creates this artificial structure. In fact, in Chicago, under Machine rule, there was little room for real leadership in the ranks of the regular organization. Leaders were largely hand-picked by the bosses, less for leadership ability than for loyalty, though it would be a mistake to assume that all those who rose to prominence in the Machine were incapable of leadership and did not exert their ability from time to time. Certainly Ralph Metcalfe, while he was entirely loyal to Mayor Daley for more than twenty-five years, was a leader in the black community.

It was said by many that Daley needed him more than he needed Daley.

A clear indication of his leadership was his effort to put new life into what had been a largely defunct Young Democrats group. Why he decided it would be more effective for his organization to rejuvenate this so-called youth group than to recruit these young men and women into his regular ward organization is not clear. Perhaps he was simply afflicted with the prejudices of the regular organization. Or perhaps he had no real choice; they would not be eligible for membership in the regular organization. The former seems to be the more acceptable explanation. He wanted their support but not their competition. That he wanted a strong YDs, however, is very clear.

His first move was to install aggressive, intelligent Winston McGill as president in 1954. McGill, now program director for the Department of Housing and Urban Development (HUD), was a student at the University of Illinois at Navy Pier, majoring in political science, wanting to learn something about real life politics. "I was a true volunteer. No job, no political aspirations, just a free spirit wanting to know how the whole thing worked." He made an immediate impression on Metcalfe. The job was to assess the situation, figure out how to recruit new members, to revitalize the organization, how to interest young voters in the political process. McGill went to work and the organization began to grow. But he was busy in school and could no longer handle the enormous load of work the job with the YDs involved. After a year, he asked to be relieved.

Meanwhile, Washington was making his mark. he was already well-known among the young people in the 3rd Ward. He was the logical person for Metcalfe to turn to. Washington happily took on the responsibility. Though he served only one year as president, he was the leader, the organizer, the political advisor for nearly ten years. "When he finally left us on our own, we knew we had made it," Ford says.

Within a couple years, the YDs had completely turned around—an active membership of 200, a mailing list of 2,000, twenty-five working committees. "If you didn't want to work, you weren't made to feel too comfortable," Ford says. "We were there every night, often late into the night, organizing, talking, arguing." Washington taught classes in the parliamentary procedures he had learned at his father's knee in the Democratic Party and later at Roosevelt: the tactics of running a meeting, of caucusing, maneuvering for position, of snowballing, of stalling—the skills needed for winning on issues, for getting candidates nominated and elected. "He seemed to know it all, maybe just instinctively." There were also classes in precinct work and there was precinct work itself. Washington organized First Voters—Age 21, an effort that took YDs into the homes of as many first-time voters as they could locate—about 300 prior to each election. A team of YDs went to the homes of youngsters reaching or just having reached voting age whose names were supplied by precinct captains. They explained the electoral process, the importance of registering and voting and of joining the YDs. By 1961, they had swelled the ranks of the registered voters so impressively that they were able to bring in a huge plurality, second to no ward in the city.

By 1961, about 75 percent of the precinct captains in the 3rd Ward were also YDs. The organization was also self-sustaining. It raised all its own funds with dances, rallies, queen contests—huge affairs, according to Harris. It was also distributing food to the poor and performing a wide variety of services to the community, a mirror image of the parent organization.

Well, not exactly a mirror image. "We wanted to be a spearhead for the senior party, to take positions that would make it easier—would provide support—for the black committeeman to take positions in the parent organization in opposition to the mayor, in favor of blacks," Harris explains.

By 1960, the 3rd Ward YDs was the most popular and powerful organization on the South Side. People came from other wards where the regulars did not encourage independence in the YDs. Freeman lived in the 8th Ward and, on graduation from the University of Chicago Law School, went looking for a political organization to join. Young lawyers needed political organizations, most especially black lawyers needed them. Freeman was actively discouraged by his alderman. he joined the 3rd Ward YDs. Its reputation had spread throughout the South Side.

Earning a living was problematic. Building a law practice, as his father said, took long hours and hard work. Washington preferred to put his long hours and hard work into politics. In 1954, with no will to build a private practice and with a will to build a political career, and with the death of his father, he went into the Corporation Counsel's office to take his father's slot.

A former associate in the Corporation Counsel's office, former Judge Harry Iseberg, offers a view widely held among whites in City Hall in 1954. "There weren't too many black lawyers out there, you know, and the few there were were doing very well in private practice. They didn't want to go into public service."

But Washington was not his father. He stayed in the Corporation Counsel's office three years, first handling menial traffic tickets in Traffic Court and then moving up to the new division concerned with housing code violations and demolition orders. That job was no more his kettle of fish than a private practice. He was not a mirror image of his father who had persevered for twenty years as a city prosecutor of small crimes. The next step was a job as aldermanic secretary to Metcalfe.

A secretary is, after all, a secretary. A boss is, after all, a boss. Some bosses are more tyrannical than others. Some secretarial positions are more degrading than others. Some secretaries have a higher estimate of their own worth than others. Some are more restless than others. All that being so, a secretary, restless or not, working for more or less of a tyrant, the bottom line is that a secretary is hired to do the boss's bidding. Harold Washington, a graduate of Roosevelt College and Northwestern University Law

School, an army veteran, already a well-known political figure, was not a happy secretary. With the political clout he had by now acquired, he secured an assignment as arbitrator with the State of Illinois Industrial Commission, an agency that arbitrates worker-management disputes over worker injuries.

Washington was the only black arbitrator. He was also, by some accounts, one of the most intelligent and fair-minded. Harold Katz, an attorney, a colleague of Washington's in the state legislature, says he always liked to have Washington hear his client's cases. He knew "they would get a fair and wise decision." It was not a bad job for Washington, a more bookish, meaty job than the previous ones. By 1964, it was paying him about $8,000, hardly a living wage but he didn't need or want much. It was good experience. Judge Claude Whitaker, who was at the time the only black commissioner, says that the arbitrators for the commission did more personal injury trials than any judge in a regular courtroom. But personal injury is, after all, personal injury. It is not politics. What Washington wanted was not a job behind a desk adjudicating personal injury cases, as much compassion as he might have felt for the injured—the injured who came before the Commission were largely black, management was white. He wanted a political career. He wanted an opportunity to run for public office. But there were precious few slots open to blacks in the Democratic Party. They could represent their own constituencies as aldermen or state representatives or senators but even in the largely black wards and districts, whites often continued to hold those seats. In 1954, for instance, only about half the seats in the legislature that represented blacks had black representatives. There was one Congressional seat open, first captured by Oscar DePriest in the late twenties and held by blacks ever since, held by Dawson from 1942 to 1970 when he died, and Metcalfe took it over to hold it until his death 1978. In 1972, a second seat was given to party hack George Collins in the 7th District, the West Side. Collins was killed in a plane crash in 1974 and his seat was given to his wife who has retained it. Those elected who stay loyal to the Machine were reelected over and over again. Needless to say, most stayed loyal. In the late fifties and early sixties, there were, in other words, no city or statewide slots and only a few representative slots open to blacks. Washington would have to wait until 1964 when a fluke would occur in the electoral process before he would be slated for public office by the party.

Elective office inside the Democratic Party in the early fifties and sixties—and of course earlier—was also closed to blacks. "You're not ready," they were told. "When you elect a black mayor you can have a black chairman," they were told. The regulars repeated over and over again what Washington called "the picture on the wall speech!" "See that man in that picture [Daley]. He wouldn't like your talking like that at all."

Daley didn't like it. He didn't like being charged with racism. He didn't like being reminded that Bill Dawson had cast the vote that got him slated for the mayoral. He didn't like being reminded of the large pluralities blacks were turning in or of the fact that those pluralities were the ones that were keeping him in office. Daley didn't like being reminded that, under the system, the blacks were fairly and logically entitled to a bigger piece of the pie—more jobs, more money spent in the community, more elective offices, more control of their own destinies. He didn't hear these reminders—these charges—from the regulars, from Metcalfe or his fellow committeemen and aldermen. Those charges were coming from the Young Democrats, most especially from the 3rd Ward YDs, from Harris, Ford, Freeman, McGill, and from Washington, most loudly and clearly from Washington. They weren't said to Daley's face. They didn't meet with Daley. They had their own organization. They weren't even addressed to Daley. Washington wasn't crazy. They were general charges levelled against the senior party by the YDs, on the floor of meetings of the Central Area Committee of the YDs, comprised of the black wards, and on the floor of the Cook County YD meetings. They were said in caucuses and in committee meetings. But there were always those loyalists—toadies—who took the word forward to curry favor with the bosses.

The 3rd Ward YDs under Washington's tutelage were talking about change. "Washington was always ahead of his time," Ford says. "Not many addressed themselves to those issues." But "we weren't flaming revolutionaries," Ford continues. "We felt the best way to bring about change was through the party apparatus. It was the slow way. It required discipline. We learned the discipline that the people who got up on soapboxes never learned. Oh sure, you could get some people to listen to you but then what?"—that famous party discipline, practiced in all monolithic organizations from the Communist Party to the Birch Society. The YDs questioned the fairness of the organization in its treatment of blacks but it never questioned its basic tenets. That there may never be fairness where there is also uniform acceptance of ironclad discipline from the top, that party discipline and fairness just may be completely contradictory concepts, opposed to each other in their very nature, did not occur to the YDs then, nor did it occur to Washington, it seems. One may disagree and criticize inside the organization but when one meets the public, one closes ranks behind the party dictum, even if one violently disagrees with it. It is understood and accepted that when one takes one's disagreements to the public, as Metcalfe was to do in 1974, punishment is swift. Washington, too, was to receive that punishment in the years ahead. He was always aware of that possibility but he had no choice. There was no other avenue to a political career. It was not so crass as that, though. He did believe in the basic tenets of the Democratic Party. He thought they needed reform to create that fairness he sought but it would be years before he would finally reject the party as a viable organization to achieve social change. That true social change only comes about as a consequence of deep social upheaval he did not countenance. That he would lead what was in fact a social upheaval in 1983, he didn't dream.

That party discipline was basically undemocratic and unfair seems not to have been an issue. It is said by the party loyalists that the party is no different than any other organization: you don't bite the hand that feeds you. A representative of IBM does not appear on television and state views contrary to the company's. Likewise, the president's cabinet members do not publicly state personal views in opposition to the president's. Dan Rather does not make public pronouncements that disagree with CBS. If they do, they are either fools or want to be fired in order to collect severance pay. But a political party is ostensibly a voluntary organization whose major purpose is the election of public officials. Its major figures are elected officials. The trough is the public one, funded by the citizenry. If a political party functions democratically, if its members gain nominations for office on the basis of merit and popular acclaim, if the elected officials are responsive to their constituents, there would be no need, no justification, no rationale for a solid front that reflects the chairman's ideas. In fact, the National Democratic and Republican parties function more or less on this model. There has hardly ever been a united party position in the Congress or the Senate. Senator Allan Cranston, on the one hand, and Senator Strom Thurmond, on the other, are both members of the Democratic Party, take positions far to the left and right of the party on many issues and are not punished by the National Democratic Party or by their local organizations. Their punishment comes from their constituents.

In Chicago, under the Machine, to take a position on an issue in opposition to the party is to bite the hand that feeds you or, alternately, to run independent of the Machine, as several aldermen and women do. The so-called independents in Chicago are actually Democrats who attend the national conventions and who work for Democratic candidates in national races. Only in the city and state legislative bodies and other elective offices must a person who holds a position contrary to the party on some issues run as an independent candidate and be tagged as an "independent." The Chicago Democratic Party has, for about sixty years, functioned just like IBM or CBS, but unlike those companies, that functioning is illegal, unethical, and destructive. None of the principles of a democratic organization have operated in the Democratic Party of Chicago. It is a voluntary organization only for those who volunteer to abide by "party discipline." Its members gain the prized nominations to elective office not on the basis of merit and public support but because of loyal service to the party and clout with the party chairman. And the elected officials it produces are responsive not to those who elected them but to the party that named them to that position.

Washington decided, about 1960, that the YDs would elect a black county chairman. They were ready and they would not wait until they had a black mayor. It would take time. A lot of wheeling and dealing would have to be done. But, unlike the senior organization, the YDs were more fluid, more open to change, more susceptible to suggestion and persuasion, to verbal arm-twisting and elbow-bending. He began talking and aroused enthusiasm. Yes, indeed! To those remarks that "You are not ready," the 3rd Ward YDs had retorted with angry laughter. To the remark that they would get the chairmanship when they got a black mayor, they howled, "Are you out of your mind?" Now they were ready, with Washington, to plan their moves. Bill Harris was selected as their man. Washington, Freeman says, was too outspoken to be the candidate. Then, at conventions, meetings, social gatherings, they made their moves. In 1964, four years later, Bill Harris was elected county chairman of the YDs, an election that Ford compares to the mayoral election in 1983.

Mayor Daley said the YD wasn't worth the trouble it caused. "Control those people," he told his committeemen. But the committeemen were in no position to control their young people. They were the ones who were bringing in the votes on Election Day.

Daley didn't much care for the goings-on at YD conventions, either. Those resolutions demanding action on behalf of blacks—open housing, open public accommodations, more jobs, better health care, more humane police, an end to discrimination. Most didn't pass, of course. Most of the YDs were junior versions of the white Democratic regulars. But they got a hearing and some did get through. Washington seemed instinctively to know how to operate on a convention floor—like the legislative floor where he was later to operate in the same way on the same issues. He had plenty of help from those he was teaching—quick learners they were, eager as they were to learn those ropes, some of them with their own shrewd political instincts.

Washington and his folk became national heroes to black Young Democrats across the country. For blacks in the Democratic Party, Chicago was only worse than other places. It was a matter of degree. Regularly the YDs came to Chicago for advice. The 3rd Ward headquarters buzzed regularly with the accents of people from all over who would later gain prominence in their own state and local organizations.

The lounge of the 3rd Ward headquarters was never big enough to hold comfortably all those who wanted to drink and talk late into the evening there. It was one of the more congenial, pleasanter places to drink on 47th Street and was always crowded, not only with the Young Democrats, with Washington and his friends, but also with the endless stream of hangers-on for whom the party headquarters was a place to meet and drink though they did not always attend the meetings in the large hall adjoining the lounge and rarely had business to transact in the little offices off the hall. But the drinks were cheap, the company was stimulating, and they knew they were always welcome. It was part of the strategy of Ralph Metcalfe to keep an open door to the community. He was a good host. They repaid him in votes and loyalty.

Most of those who were active in the Young Democrats in the fifties and sixties—mostly men in their twenties and thirties, a wide range of people including uneducated manual laborers and highly skilled professionals, heavily weighted with the latter—were infused with a sense of social purpose. It was the postwar era. Most had been in the war, in segregated units, and came back to go to school on the GI Bill, filled with the feeling that the end of the war, the founding of the UN, the desegregation of the armed services, and a feeling of optimism in the air would lead to great changes. In 1954, the greatest victory for blacks since Reconstruction occurred with the Supreme Court's overturning of school segregation. In 1955, Martin Luther King led the Montgomery bus boycott. And CORE led a group of Freedom Riders through the South. The ferment among blacks and their white supporters was growing almost daily. True, the Southern whites were committing heinous crimes against blacks who were demanding such simple things as the right to use the same public washrooms and eat at the same Woolworth's lunch counters. But there was an optimism abroad in the land.

As with all social movements, the work of bringing equality to blacks was done by a few, by those young men and women in college and already graduated, young professionals, World War II veterans who had been influenced by that postwar mood in the nation. There were, behind them, alongside of them, hundreds—thousands—of ordinary blacks, marching, meeting, rallying—social upheaval. The 3rd Ward YDs saw themselves as the northern urban complement to Martin Luther King's activities in the rural south. They saw themselves as the electoral arm of the movement. They would work through the party apparatus. Washington was the leading exponent of that theory. But he was wise enough to know that this was the slow route. It was the surest, he believed, the one that would endure after the soapboxes had broken down and the marchers had been exhausted.

There were many in those days who disagreed. Washington counted some of them among his friends and talked and argued into the small hours of the night with them. He went so far as to attend some of their many meetings and offer his advice when it seemed appropriate. But, as he had at Roosevelt, he steered clear of any public association or endorsement of the radicals and even those not so radical who were merely attempting to bring pressure on the major political parties.

It was considered pretty radical in 1960 to organize opposition to the Democratic Party. People still remembered the Progressive Party and its fate when it was taken over by the Communist Party. Besides, Mayor Daley was riding a crest of popularity rarely enjoyed by a political figure. Nevertheless, when Lemuel Bentley, Bennett Johnson, Luster Jackson, and other friends founded the Chicago League of Negro Voters, Washington spent long hours, often late into the night, helping them put together "A Plan to Increase the Power of Negro Citizens." It was the first effort by blacks to create an independent political action committee and while he could not openly endorse or work in the organization, he could not ignore it, either. He couldn't. But he *was* a regular party man and had to protect himself. It was one thing to criticize on the inside, quite another to attack from the outside.

Washington didn't have a lot of faith in this new vehicle. His friends were well-intentioned and needed encouragement but the city wasn't ready for independent politics. Daley was getting stronger by the day. Still, it had to be done. There had to be a voice in opposition to the racism of the Machine.

In fact, the League of Negro Voters pulled as many votes for its candidate for city clerk, Lemuel Bentley, as the Republican candidate for mayor—60,000. And its six aldermanic candidates did reasonably well under the circumstances.

"We knew we couldn't win," Luster Jackson says, "but we had to make a start to begin to arouse the people to get them thinking another way. And we had to put pressure on the Machine."

The next year, in the judicial election, the League convinced both Democrats and Republicans to slate one black judge for a higher court, lifting him from the municipal court to which black judges were normally relegated.

But the League could not sustain itself between elections. It was a one-issue organization with nothing to keep it together after the votes were counted.

In 1963, the same group organized again, in the same way, calling itself Protest at the Polls. The announcement for its two-day conference at the University of Chicago said that its goal was to "Contribute to the civil rights movement in Chicago by adding to its new thrust the decisive element of electoral action." Its stated goals were not so different from those of the 3rd Ward YDs: "Develop means of increasing the quality and quantity of Negro representation on local, state, and national levels." But this was independent politics, not party politics. "The need is for grass-roots activity of dedicated people, *regardless of their past political affiliations* [my italics]. . . .This is a call to a conference to help fuse the new militancy of direct action with [the] might of the ballot in the Negro community of Chicago in this one hundreth year of freedom." Washington once again, quietly, took part in the planning. Tim Black describes him as a consultant, a private, unpaid consultant.

By the mid-sixties, serious out-to-win independent candidates were emerging. Johnson, Black, Jackson, Bentley, and the rest of their group worked hard in those campaigns. A.A. "Sammy" Rayner and William Cousins won aldermanic seats in 1967. Others followed. Only a handful, to be sure, and they lasted only one term, either by choice or because the Machine brought in their big guns to defeat them, but those activities continued, steadily, laying the groundwork for the eventual defeat of the Machine, for Washington's eventual emergence as an independent himself. Thoughout those twenty-three years, Washington retained his friendships with the men and women who started the League of Negro Voters and it was to them that he went to assess his chances for a victory in 1983.

As for the other, more radical, elements, most particularly the Committee on Racial Equality (CORE) that had been organized in the mid-forties and had engaged in such direct actions as that famous restaurant sit-in at Anne's and other confrontations with white authorities, Washington kept a long arm's distance. He had made that fateful decision that his work for social change would be within the party structure and, because the Democratic Party was the monolith it was, such a decision does not permit even a glancing acquaintance with confrontational politics. To do so would be to voluntarily drop the knife on one's neck. There is, however, something to be said for the fact that this soapbox is broken and the marchers of CORE were long ago exhausted. There are those who insist that it served its purpose and died naturally. Others disagree. A serious conclusion awaits a thorough analysis of the civil rights movement.

A district manager in the Department of Human Services, two County Commissioners, a couple of aldermen, the assistant to the County Assessor, a program director for HUD, several judges, lawyers, social workers, and the mayor of Chicago—not a bad lineup of talent and achievement from a membership of about 200 YDs. It is not unlike the list described at the end of the last chapter—the 1952 class of Northwestern Law School. That list cannot be in any way attributed to Washington. He was fortunate to be a member of such an illustrious class. But the YD roster can in large measure be attributed to Washington's skill in organizing and training his fellow YDs and to his charismatic ability to attract to that organization so much native talent. Most of those people now say that they don't believe they would have made as much progress had it not been for that pivotal experience in their lives, the intellectual stimulation and the political savvy they gained under Washington's tutelage.

"He has few peers who can explain issues and chart a course of action," Ford says. "He would have made a great teacher," Freeman adds. "He is truly concerned about issues and can convey that concern like few others," Pritchett adds to the litany. What is significant about that group of men is that most of them spent all their lives in government jobs. Many began with a letter from Metcalfe. But those letters long ago ceased to have any importance, ceased to be necessary. Those men rose in the ranks because they were talented, not something that can always be said of those who work in government jobs. Some have served the party loyally. Certainly the alderman have had to be loyalists. But Eugene Sawyer and Clifford Kelly are no mere loyalists—they regularly take independent stands, they are regularly irritants to the regulars. In the context of the Chicago City Council, which has for years been a mere rubber stamp for the mayor, even a little independence is noteworthy and theirs has been more than a little; as Washington's was in the State House.

As County chairman, Bill Harris made the county YD financially independent of the regular organization. The 3rd Ward group had long since become independent, a crucial factor in their efforts to serve as an irritant to the senior party. "If you have to go to them for money, they can call the tune," Harris says. The aspiration to gain that chairmanship would have been vain, indeed, had the 3rd Ward YDs been dependent on Daley for funds to run the organization.

But raising funds is no small job. It takes lots of effort and time and the men and women who came to the YDs in the late sixties, after Washington's crew had graduated, were not so energetic. Organizations that are not monoliths tend to go through a variety of stages, depending on related factors. The YDs had been largely dormant when Metcalfe took over the 3rd Ward, but in an earlier period it had been a vital organ, a large contributor to the growth of the party. The graduation of Ford, Harris, Freeman, and others left the organization in a weakened position. Washington had already withdrawn, saying, "Stop looking at me. Start making your own decisions," Ford says. He wanted to work in the regular organization. Ford took over as political consultant after having served as president but the organization began to decline.

Three explanations are offered: Freeman says that, over the years, the 3rd Ward became second only to the West Side as a deprived, decaying area. Housing declined as it decayed, was burned down, and not replaced. No new building was done. The population was sharply reduced. The fabulous 47th Street became a ghost town. The famous corner was one of the worst crime—

drug scenes in the city. The Ward headquarters left, as did most of the businesses. Some of the wonderful old houses along Michigan and South Park (now King Drive) remain. McGill still lives in his beautiful old family residence at 49th and King Drive. The Rosenwald Apartments still stand but the hoi polloi no longer lives there. The devastation in the community is great enough so that the YDs can no longer rely on it for those bright, energetic, well-educated young people who made the organization such a vital force.

Harris offers an entirely different, political, explanation. He says that the senior party assumed a more dominant role in the activities of the YDs. Most crucially, the group was no longer permitted to elect its own officers. They were named by the senior party. Presumably, Metcalfe no longer trusted the Young Democrats to govern themselves. Or perhaps Daley put the screws to him. In addition, Harris says, the group was no longer financially independent of the senior party. Sounds as if the quality of leadership had seriously declined, as if perhaps Freeman's explanation adds weight to Harris's.

Ford says that, indeed, the quality of leadership did decline, that the Young Democrats could no longer attract the intelligent, energetic people it had in the previous fifteen years because the Democratic Party could no longer appeal to their interests. The civil rights movement had radicalized them, made them impatient with the slow process the party insisted upon. He does not add that, through the sixties, the party remained largely intransigent in its relationship with the black community and that effect was finally being recognized, that blacks were no longer filled with hope for a future under the Daley Machine. Unfortunately, the civil rights movement had been effectively killed by the assassination of Martin Luther King in 1968. There was no longer a viable civil rights movement in 1969, at the end of Ford's relationship with the Young Democrats. There was not much for young, energetic people to do in politics.

Furthermore, there was a pall over the land. Richard Nixon had been elected president on the promise to end all the programs that the Democrats had created to upgrade blacks. Nixon said they didn't work. He lied. They worked well. Many, many blacks—not enough—had profited educationally, socially, and economically from the passage of the Civil Rights Acts and the anti-poverty programs. The effect of Nixon's election was strongly apparent in many ways. What was not quickly apparent, however, was the pall it placed on blacks and white liberals—almost a paralysis. If this country could elect a president of Nixon's calibre in 1968, it was clear that it rejected and resented the progress made by blacks in the preceding ten years. It is often argued that Nixon won the election because he promised to end the Vietnam War. That argument is specious. Those who most opposed the war opposed Nixon. Those who voted for Nixon were voting against the social upheavals of the sixties, the upheavals that took place in opposition to the war and those that occurred to achieve racial equality. Nixon won by only a small margin but it was clear from his election that the majority in this country were opposed to social change. Such a revelation, for a few, would be a stimulant to work even harder toward one's goals. For most, it had a paralyzing effect.

Meanwhile, on the local level, Mayor Daley was getting older and consolidating his power. Earlier he had listened with one ear to blacks and had, indeed, given them some "rewards"—no more, Harris says, than he absolutely had to, but enough to encourage them that things could be even better. Between 1955 and 1968, Daley operated in a national mood of optimism and hope. He benefitted from that. He didn't need to give much to be acceptable because there was always the promise and the belief that there would be more. And some of the things he did were not very well understood. Most people, Harris said, were, for instance, optimistic about the future of the massive public housing projects Daley built in the ghetto. There weren't many who saw them as disasters waiting to happen, as horrible solutions to decaying housing, as a means to prevent blacks from moving beyond the ghetto boundaries. They were seen by most, Harris says, as a good solution. But in the seventies, the disaster began to happen. The enormous villages of blacks, erected to look like prison fortresses, were not maintained properly, not policed properly, not serviced adequately by the community, had no amenities to make life anything more than mere survival. They were not the commodious, congenial urban villages envisioned by planners in the fifties and sixties, planners who still insist on their good intentions. They were, instead, prisons in which poor blacks were confined for the duration. Just what does urban planning mean?

The presence of those prisons in the black community depresses those who don't live there as well as those who do. The acres of huge, bleak buildings are a constant reminder of the true condition of the black community—unemployed, undereducated, restless, deprived—there but for the grace of God go I.

To all of this, Daley responded in his later years by giving more to his own native constituency and less to what he viewed as essentially a foreign constituency, Harris says. And no amount of entreaties were effective. The community reacted. In 1963, the 3rd Ward gave Daley the second largest plurality in the city, second only to his own ward. In 1967, they gave him only slightly less. In 1975, the plurality had shrunk drastically from a rank of 3 in '67 to 23 in '71 to 31 in '75. The 3rd Ward was not alone. The entire black community gradually withdrew its support for the Machine. It voted independent when it could. When it couldn't, it stayed home. And continued to stay home until 1982 when it registered 100,000 new voters in preparation for getting rid of the latest and crassest version of Machine politics and 1983 when it accomplished that.

The decline of the Young Democrats was both a cause and an effect of that denial of support. Young blacks refused to work any longer for the Machine because they were infected by the community's resentment of it. They would offer no more leadership that denied them full citizenship. So the combination of despair at Nixon's election, the takeover of the YDs by the regulars, the devastation of the 3rd Ward, Daley's denials all had their effects on the Young Democrats. It is also possible, if one is inclined to the great man theory of history, that Washington's withdrawal from the 3rd Ward YD had a part to play in its demise.

"He was our candidate. We would have gotten pretty nasty if Metcalfe had named anyone else. He was the most popular person in the ward, the person who best exemplified the kind of elected representative we wanted," Commissioner Harris says. Washington had finally been named to run for elective office—the state rep's seat. It was a new seat, not an inherited one. It was not party procedure, not a normal election, it was an opportunity for more blacks to gain those seats. Metcalfe had to fight hard for him in the slating committee. Washington was not exactly Daley's favorite son. But he was Metcalfe's and he was the 3rd Ward's favorite and for this unusual election, he was the best candidate. Daley finally agreed, in part because he needed to put a liberal on the slate to offset the independents who were making a stink out there. He needed a few liberals on the ballot.

The ballot was an at-large one—long enough to reach the floor, and some—with 236 candidates, Republican and Democratic, listed in no particular order except party designation, for an election out of the control of the party because the candidates were not running in a given district but at large. The election was the consequence of the failure of a recalcitrant legislature—in reality, the party leaders—to agree on the reapportionment of districts required by the Constitution every ten years based on the census. The struggle was finally resolved in the court when the state was ordered to hold the at-large election. The two parties slated only 118 candidates each for 177 seats.

It was a wonderful opportunity for blacks and white liberals. If candidates were to run at large, they could run their own slate. After a brief period of hesitancy among some groups, the sturdy independents, who had begun fourteen years earlier with the League of Negro Voters, put together what they called a Third Slate, with 59 candidates, the difference between 118 and 177. On June 27, 1964, they announced their slate. Daley reacted swiftly. He got his own blue-ribbon candidates, among them Adlai Stevenson and Harold Washington, Abner Mikva, Harold Katz, and Robert Mann. Then, on August 17, the Illinois Election Board refused to permit the placing of the Third Slate candidates on the ballot because of "insufficient signatures" on the nominating petitions. Well, perhaps the Board actually did find enough real errors in the signatures to eliminate them.

The Third Slate people were dismayed, of course, but they

responded by putting together the "orange ballot," that urged people to vote for eighteen of the slated candidates, three Republican, the rest Democratic. Washington was number 106 out of 118 Democrats on the regular ballot, not exactly a dominant position. He was a number 8 out of 18 on the orange ballot.

It was a statewide election. Hardly any voters knew any candidate except their own incumbent. It was a wild and wooly lottery. The voters were expected to choose 177 candidates from the total of 236. Some people closed their eyes and picked. Some voted only for those they knew, one or two, perhaps three or four, giving a decided edge to the incumbents. Some voted all the Democrats, some all the Republicans. But those liberals and blacks who received one of the thousands of orange ballots passed out across the state had an edge of their own. They could, with a fair amount of faith, vote for the candidates on that ballot, knowing that they had met the standards of an organization especially created to take advantage of the absurd situation to liberalize the legislature. Washington had another advantage few others had: the 3rd Ward Young Democrats.

Adlai Stevenson, with his illustrious family name, was the top vote getter. Only slightly lower on the list, Washington went to Springfield in January, 1965, with one of the largest vote totals in that election. He got the votes of the liberals who had voted the independents' recommendations and he had a political organization he had built over fifteen years. No candidate on that ballot could have asked for anything more.

It is May 25, 1983, almost a month since the Inauguration, and I am at Washington's campaign headquarters at 53 W. Jackson where a skeleton staff is finishing up campaign business. Washington and the white majority in the City Council are locked in a bitter struggle for control. The city is waiting anxiously to see how the new mayor will resolve the problem. The white ethnic supporters of County Democratic Chairman and Alderman "Fast

Eddie" Vrdolyak are rooting for their side. Blacks and white liberals are rooting for their side. Many whites—including many in the press and many among the liberals—are certain Washington cannot win. Many blacks are certain he has the skill to pull it off. Some of the blacks are betting big money on him.

A volunteer stops me to ask, "How's the book coming?"

"Fine," I tell her.

"How far along are you?"

"Almost finished. I have still to write the chapters on the period right after law school and then the one on the Congress."

"Well, the second will be easy, but that first one, wow!"

"It won't be as easy as the rest."

"He sure keeps those years a secret. It's as if he's got a veil spread over those twelve years until he was elected to the legislature. No one knows anything about them."

"Not quite no one."

"He never talks about those years. If you read his biographical sketch, all you can see is that he worked at a couple of nondescript jobs."

"The Industrial Commission was not exactly a nondescript job."

"Well, maybe not. But it's hard to imagine Harold just working at a job, even if it's a decent one."

"You're right about that."

"Well, what did you find out?"

"Only that those were the years in which he was building his political base and refining his skills."

"Oh."

In the State House

Every morning when the idiot card arrived, Adlai Stevenson III, blue ribbon representative from the Near North Side, looked at it and laughed and tossed it in the waste basket. His seat-mate, Harold Washington, regular organization man, studied it hard. Though he was more independent than most, and though he had already moved his office out of the regular Democratic head-quarters, he could not afford to completely ignore that piece of paper. He had to vote with the party some of the time, especially on those issues the liberals and Republicans were bringing in to loosen the grip of the Machine. On the other hand, he had to vote his conscience. He resented this piece of paper arriving at his desk telling him how to vote as much as he had ever resented anything in his life. It was an assault to the dignity of these men and women who had been elected to represent their constituents. It was an insult to him, who had been elected to represent a black con-stituency. It was surely one of the greatest indignities visited on party members, among a long list of indignities. It made a sham of the General Assembly, of the election process which was already a shameful sham perpetuated on the electorate, with its fraud and vote-buying.

"It's easy for you to be independent," he said to Stevenson one day after he had taken another chance at ignoring the idiot card. Each time he voted with the liberals against the Machine, he could feel a nail being set in his coffin, but he could not vote against his own conscience on many matters, especially on civil rights and civil liberties. At the end of the second session, in 1967, the Independent Voters of Illinois ranked him number 4 in the House; his voting record was only three points from the top score a liberal could make. He had voted his conscience with the liberals. He was named Best Legislator of the Year by the IVI.

Stevenson was very moved by Washington's comment. "I repeated it to my wife," he says, "and I realized how fortunate I was. I had a chance to be independent without being punished and survive, even move ahead, because of it. I have always felt differently toward the regulars since then, much more sympathetic and understanding and even a little guilty" (shades of his father).

How does it happen that so many politicians in Chicago (and elsewhere at various times) have been forced to be slaves to a political machine? Why was Stevenson able to make a political career as an independent while the majority of his colleagues were not? The contrast between Stevenson and Washington is as good an illumination of that question as any to be found. They represent the extremes of the story.

Stevenson began with an illustrious background. His father had never been an independent in the strictest sense of that word because he never served as an elected representative but only in an executive office, the governorship, which is automatically a more independent role. He was known, however, in political circles as an extraordinarily intelligent and talented man, a liberal for his time, having served in the Roosevelt administration and championed the cause of the United Nations as its first alternate delegate. Though he won a huge vote, he lost two presidential elections to General Dwight D. Eisenhower, in both cases carrying and extending the Democratic image of liberalism as opposed to the strict conservatism of Eisenhower and the Republicans. Though his image as a liberal was blemished by his apparent collusion with John F. Kennedy in the Bay of Pigs invasion of Cuba, he nevertheless remained, in the minds of most liberals, one of the stellar figures of the postwar era.

His son inherited that mantle. His own career has not been as liberal as his father's but he has generally been regarded as free-thinking, independent of the Machine that dictated the lives of most other elected representatives.

But Stevenson's political heritage was not all that he had going for him. He was also a member of Chicago's moneyed class, though not as rich as some. Money is a crucial key to political independence. Campaigns cost money. A poor man with connections with other poor people cannot operate independently.

Even money and political heritage, however, are not enough if there is no natural constituency for independence. Rober Mann and Abner Mikva, two well-known Chicago independents who served with Washington in the legislature, had neither the first nor the second prerequisites but they had those constituencies. For many years, Hyde Park—the community that surrounds the University of Chicago—has had a national reputation as one of the few powerful liberal political bases in the nation but more importantly as a bastion of anti-Machine politics in Chicago. How well I recall Hyde Park on Election Day in 1952 when Stevenson first ran against Eisenhower. I had worked my precinct from 6 A.M. until the closing at 10. We had gone 98 percent for Stevenson. I reasoned that if we went almost 100 percent, the rest of the nation went 51 percent. That was how we reasoned in Hyde Park in those days. I went home for a short nap and then hopped on my bike to go to the local victory party at the IVI headquarters. It was empty save one glum person. The television set was on. Eisenhower had won. I was shocked. Could I really be so far removed from political realities?

In 1983, after Washington's election, David Canter, one of those who labored in the independent vineyards of Hyde Park politics for most of his life, said to Washington, as they discussed Canter's job in City Hall, "Get me an enemy! For more than thirty years, City Hall has been my enemy. Now the enemy is me!"

Stevenson also had a liberal constituency—it was called the Lakefront, though not, in those days, as big as it has become in recent years with the construction of hundreds of high rises where

Chicago's wealthy live, including a heavy concentration of Jews, traditionally the most liberal voters in the nation.

Compare Washington. His father had been an early Democrat, not an official in the Roosevelt Administration but a precinct captain, struggling for a place of his own, defeated in the end by venal bosses. He was poor, his friends were poor. And his constituency consisted of people struggling for a little political power in the face of white dominance, discrimination, exclusion—not independent, unable to make any real political choices because they were constantly forced to make deals to get even a small slice of the pie, at the mercy of those who had learned the tricks of political exploitation. It wasn't only true in the black community; it was true in every poor community and many that weren't dirt poor but were just beyond it. But it was worst in the black community because it was the poorest.

So there was Washington: no grand political inheritance, no money, no independent constituency. Ony a fierce desire to build a political career, a fierce desire to use politics to improve the lot of his people. Only his natural endowments: no help from the outside except the Machine. Little wonder Washington made Stevenson feel guilty.

How did the Machine exploit people like Washington and all those lesser people who did not have such high ideals and were therefore more easily compromised? "Stick with me and you'll be rewarded—a better job, Congress, a judgeship, a city job. Vote against me and you will be punished. There'll be no money, no workers, no help from the organization," Daley regularly reminded those whom he picked for elective office. Kelly did it before him. Punishment was swift. When Washington finally broke with the Machine, he faced a $200,000 barrage against him for his seat in the legislature.

The story related in this chapter is the astonishing one of how Washington managed to keep the support of the organization for fourteen years despite continued excursions into independence and continuous battles with Daley. "He was the only black legislator to ever take such independent positions and survive," one of his colleagues says. This is also the story of a man who was recognized by many of his colleagues in the House as one of its most brilliant members but who never attained any official position of leadership and who had to wrest from the Machine a position beyond the House, a position for which most of his colleagues agree he was eminently qualified—a seat in Congress, won as an independent sixteen years after he was first slated for office. It is the story of the collusion of one of his colleagues, Corneal Davis, who wanted to retire from the House but remained at the request of Daley only to prevent Washington from moving up in the hierarchy. It is the story of a decade of conflict and pain as a reluctant Machine man.

It would be ten years before Washington would again be named Best Legislator of the Year. Over those ten years, he would buckle under party discipline regularly. He learned quickly that the party exacts its pound of flesh. When it was time to be reslated for his second term, Daley scratched his name from the slate. People who ignore the idiot list do so at the risk of their political careers. Cecil Partee, a colleague who had long since proven his loyalty, intervened. All this stuff that Washington was doing was really harmless. None of those civil rights bills would ever pass. Corneal Davis had been trying to get open housing for years. The majority would never break ranks to vote for open housing or a stronger FEPC or for most of the legislation Washington was proposing. It was nothing new. Washington actually made the party look good. He was a maverick, sure, but a harmless one, and if the party tolerated him, it would show the world that the Machine was not quite so monolithic as it seemed, that the boss was not so dictatorial as he seemed. Washington was clearly star material. He could be used—and controlled. He was a rare orator among a crowd of accomplished orators. He clearly had the respect of his colleagues. He was smart and well-educated. Even if they didn't vote with him too often, they admired him. But could he be controlled? Well enough. He was a maverick and he would occasionally hold out his vote until he got what he wanted but it looked like he wouldn't turn on the party on its crucial issues: election reform and governmental reorganization, the pet legislation of the liberals and Republicans to reduce the power of the Machine.

The Fair Housing Act he was fighting for was still a crucial piece of legislation since Corneal Davis introduced it years before, but some things had improved for blacks. Open housing was still far in the future but open public accommodations were not. In 1964, when he got to Springfield, Washington found Cecil Partee living at the St. Nicholas Hotel and was himself able to get a room in another respectable hotel. Since 1955, Springfield had dropped those barriers he faced in 1949.

Washington was slated again, but he won largely with Partee's help and his own ward's support. In Jim Taylor's ward, the Machine had quietly dumped him. The precinct captains were instructing people to vote three for Taylor, leaving out Washington, what is called a bullet vote instead of the traditional split of one-and-a-half for each candidate.

"Can I see your palm card?" Bennett Johnson asks a precinct captain in Taylor's ward as he travels with Washington to visit the precincts on Election Day. The precinct captain figures that if this guy is talking, friendly-like, to Taylor, he must be okay. He turns his hand over and reveals the card he uses to instruct voters. "Taylor—three votes," it says. One and a half of those votes was supposed to go to Washington.

Taylor was the fair-haired boy. He had been a professional boxer and a Streets and Sanitation worker. "Daley picked him up with both hands and breathed the breath of new life into him. He made him a political figure. He doesn't know anything else," Johnson explained. Taylor is barely literate, cannot speak. He hates Washington, the silver-tongued orator, the well-educated maverick.

Washington went back to the legislature and began work again on his Fair Housing Act and the rest of the bills he had sponsored or co-sponsored the session before. In the first session, he had put together a huge list of sponsors to bring in the fair housing bill—most of the liberals and blacks in the House. The bill had been tabled as it had for years before. So had his bill to put more teeth into the weak FEPC. His bill to define real estate offices, banks and savings and loan associations as public accommodations forbidden to discriminate against people because of race, creed, or color was also tabled. In fact, all of the civil rights legislation in that first session had either been sent back to committee or tabled. An effort to raise revenue by imposing a tax on employment which, unlike the sales tax, places the burden of taxation only on those employed, failed to pass. Obviously, the honorific title, Best Legislator of the Year, is not the same as the most successful legislator of the year. The honor is bestowed for good intentions, not accomplishments, unless simply making the effort, raising consciousness, as it were, is viewed as an accomplishment. Voting "right" on the liberal agenda in 1965 was as much as one could ask—actually passing such legislation in Illinois would have to wait nearly fifteen years, fifteen years after the U.S. Congress passed its omnibus Civil Rights Act of 1964. Some of those who voted against civil rights legislation said that the federal law was sufficient. Washington and his co-sponsors said that this excuse was an evasion of the state's responsibility, that the federal act was not specific enough in such areas as housing and did not have enough teeth in it in matters of employment.

His colleagues came to view Washington soon enough as the major advocate of black rights in the House. Harold Katz, another of the blue ribbon candidates in that at-large election, says that Washington often saw black issues where he and other colleagues did not. "Sometimes it seemed far-fetched to me," he says. "Like all social pioneers—martyrs—he would sometimes take positions that go beyond what seemed logical." But Katz, like most of his colleagues, "admired his willingness to stand up on issues and his eloquence in presenting them."

Stand up on those race issues he did. He used every parliamentary trick he could find to win and, when he lost, he "licked his wounds graciously," says William Redmond. He would come back the next year to fight again. Partee, always the favorite of

Daley, disagrees. He was a sore loser, Partee says. Perhaps Partee had a private view of Washington that others did not share. But considering Washington's extraordinary penchant for maintaining his privacy—he seems to have spent almost no time in socializing with his colleagues—it seems more likely that Partee simply imagined a display of anger or pique by Washington because it seemed so unlikely that he could maintain his dignity under the barrage of fire he received. The rest of his colleagues agree with Redmond. He was a gracious loser, despite many losses. Katz says, "In all the years I've known him, we've never had an argument. I have never even gotten angry at him. He is a thoroughly likeable person." That feeling seems to be shared by all those close to Washington's political career. But he had, as Katz says, "that independent streak that Partee never had." Perhaps Partee was a little resentful.

Parliamentary tactics were Washington's forte. On issues he opposed he would, for instance, Katz says, write endless "tiresome" amendments to stall the process, not because he thought they would pass but to enable him to bargain. "It didn't bother him that it upset people or the Democratic Party. He was the only black legislator who was willing to do that."

Chicago was, and still is, described as the most segregated city in the nation. Open housing had been a major priority of Washington's for many years. It had been the one issue on which he joined a public street demonstration while still at Roosevelt. It remained a goal throughout all his years in the legislature; he brought up a version of the Fair Housing Act every year, finally getting it in 1979, after he had been elected to the Senate, getting it only with the help of Governor James Thompson, the first governor to support it, but more importantly after Daley's death when the Machine had begun to lose some of its control over the members of the legislature.

In 1965, acknowledging his debt to the Democratic Party and Ralph Metcalfe, Washington stewed over the idiot list. He paid his dues by voting with the Machine against election reforms and other bills that threatened the hold of the party on the electorate. But he carefully selected those votes, just enough to stay on the inside but taking chances all the time. In the process by which the legislators pay their tributes to benefactors—the resolution—Washington offered a resolution to commend his main benefactor, Ralph Metcalfe. But he also offered a resolution in memory of Reverend James J. Reeb, the Catholic priest killed on the main street of Selma, Alabama, where he was working with Martin Luther King to prepare for the eventful second march to Montgomery from Selma to demand the right to vote. Reeb was a rebel priest, not beloved by Cardinal Cody nor by Richard Daley. By memorializing him in the annals of the legislature, Washington showed his solidarity with the march.

Washington did not march himself, throughout the sixties when marching was endemic to activist blacks, except for the mainly ceremonial march through Chicago led by Martin Luther King in 1965. Everyone who had the smallest commitment to civil rights marched that day, even Bill Berry, who was generally not favorably disposed to street demonstrations, committed as he was to building bridges to the white business community for the Urban League. Any public figure who claimed to be involved in the civil rights struggle could not stay away from that parade of 30,000 down LaSalle Street. But Washington stayed away from all the rest of the marches and demonstrations. His work was in the legislature, others would work in the movement. It wasn't always easy for him. A natural leader, a charismatic figure whose presence, he knew, could make a big difference in those daily struggles with the city for more opportunity for blacks. There was a leadership void that he could have filled. And there was a void in him as well. He had a dream of being a leader, a significant leader in the struggle for equal rights. Instead of being in that struggle, providing that leadership, he was surrounded by political automatons who would not be led by anyone but a Machine mouthpiece. But he had chosen the legislative path, which had tied him to the Machine. Being a maverick in Springfield was one thing, being a civil rights leader in Chicago was another. He would have been dropped from the ranks of the party within minutes had he made one speech for the movement in defense of black rights, in opposition to Daley. He made a few quiet visits to meetings, saying little, staying, uncharacteristically, in the background. And he fought, behind the scenes, with Metcalfe over his support for the school superintendent, Benjamin Willis, whom the movement was trying to unseat. But that fight never went public. Washington was not, as Katz suggests, a martyr.

To the civil rights movement, however, Washington made one very signal contribution when it was, in effect, over. He celebrated the movement by bringing into law a state holiday memorializing the birthday, January 15, of Martin Luther King. It took four years. The year after King died, in 1969, he introduced the measure. It was passed but vetoed by the governor. He tried another tactic, this time simply asking for a legal holiday. It was tabled. Still another tactic was tried. This one succeeded. It became a school holiday. The next year, he introduced the bill again. Again it was tabled. Finally, in 1973, with the help of Partee in the Senate, the bill was finally enacted and signed by the governor.

Despite failures, plenty of them, Washington was over the years successful at bringing in a variety of legislation that provided some protection and assistance to blacks:

- In 1965, he led the successful fight to reform consumer credit.
- In '71, he won a bill to provide protection to witnesses in criminal prosecutions.
- In '72, he successfully rewrote the archaic Illinois Code

of Corrections and succeeded in getting the legislature to provide special treatment to small businesses in the letting of state contracts.

- In '70 and again in '74, he managed to put more teeth into the FEPC.
- In '76, he succeeded in convincing the legislature to save Provident Hospital, the major black hospital, with a $15 million grant.
- In '77, he led the fight to reform the Currency Exchange Act.
- His leadership in the passage of the Human Rights Act in 1979 is detailed later in this chapter.

He fought regularly with Metcalfe over issues such as Chicago's school superintendent, but when the arguments were over, he closed ranks and observed party discipline. And, as the years passed, he hewed more closely to the idiot card in Springfield. He loved politics. He loved the legislative process. He lived the legislative process. He could not bear to think of a life without it. And without the support of the Machine, in all those years until the mid-seventies, a political career for him would have been impossible. There was neither organization nor money available to him to run as an independent and beat the Machine. And it would have been political suicide to run as a Republican in the 3rd Ward of Chicago. In those years, a few blacks had run as independents and won one term but none had ever won a second term after the Machine brought in its big guns, nor did many independents even win a first term. Those were the days of the heaviest vote buying. "In all neighborhoods, the Democrats could buy votes because a dollar or ten dollars or even a dozen eggs were more important than an independent vote. 'Course, some people took the money and voted the way they wanted but the election returns showed pretty well that the money was well spent, that people were easily intimidated into voting the way they were told," Tim Black says.

Theodore Johnson, a precinct captain in the 2nd Ward for twenty years, recalls going downtown to pick up his payoff money for Election Day, only to be informed there was none. "There'll be no votes then," he told the party representative. Obviously, that candidate was not getting the party's support.

Most of the blue-ribbon candidates who had been elected in that at-large election were defeated when the redistricting took place, when the Machine was once again able to control the election. Some managed to stay, though, and, with an occasional injection of new blood, the liberal bloc continued to try to enact reforms. Washington cooperated on the floor. He cosponsored some of their bills—they cosponsored some of his. He spoke for their bills often because he was an unusually effective orator, able to phrase, clarify, explain, to put together a coherent statement of the position, to persuade better than most, according to James Houlihan. But he kept a distance, for political reasons and for personal reasons. He preferred his privacy and he preferred not to be associated with the liberals beyond the House floor or committee. He did not join them in the Democratic Study Group, nor did he join them for dinner or for evening chats that make up the social life in Springfield. He went back to his hotel to read, his favorite pastime. He made appearances at some of the events sponsored by lobbyists and others but, for the most part, he stayed to himself with his books.

Washington has always insisted he would prefer to stay at home and read. Like so many of us, another life looks more attractive—the peace and quiet, the life of the mind, as opposed to the hurly-burly, the active life, of the politician. But he could have gone on to graduate school in political science and become an academic. He would have been a fine teacher and would have been able to spend his life surrounded by books. He could, that is, had he not been black or been willing to accept a job in a Southern black college. There were precious few other opportunities in the academic world of the fifties for blacks. But knowing the drive and ambition of Washington, had he truly preferred this life, he probably would have tried it. In fact, politics is clearly his first love. It was clear at Roosevelt, though he was viewed as an excellent student and scholar. It was clear in his decision to go to law school, not exactly the haven of scholars. It was clear in his activities in the 3rd Ward. He could have settled for a civil service career. Yes, he loves his books—he reads two or three a week—but he loves politics more, whether because he is living out a career denied his father or because, as a youngster, the excitement of the political life infused him with an energy and a will to make it his own, or for other, more diffuse reasons, we cannot say. But it is certain that long before his father was so cravenly cast off by Dawson, Washington was already deeply into the political experiences of his father, into following in his footsteps.

In Springfield, he worked hard and kept to himself. "He is a workaholic," says another of his seat-mates, Louis Caldwell. "He's not a social gadfly," says Adlai Stevenson, "very good-humored, easy to like but not a high liver as some of them in Springfield are."

In the first years, Washington brought in a large number of bills, on a great variety of subjects, many on civil liberties and civil rights but in many other areas as well. As the years passed, he recognized that new bills were not necessarily the best tactic to get what he wanted. Eager new legislators learn that lesson soon enough. "You work with agencies, with all kinds of people," Houlihan says. "You work as ombudsman. You learn what the body will accept, what you should introduce to prepare them for bigger stuff. You learn to bend, you've seen the results of your work and move ahead accordingly. You become a lot more selective." Wahington's famous patience became more apparent over the years, not only in his bringing up year after year the same legislation but in his parliamentary maneuvering. He stalled the

Machine for several years in its effort to get a stop and frisk law to legitimatize the actions of the Chicago police. For years, Washington brought the House procedures to a complete halt, Katz says, in his efforts to prevent the enactment of that law. He lost, in the end, as he lost many other battles on issues of civil liberties and civil rights. David Goldberger, a lobbyist for the American Civil Liberties Union, says that he was "the hardest-working, most effective ally in beating back assaults on civil rights and civil liberties, one of only two or three in the House."

"I watched the frustration he experienced watching all that yahoo legislation get passed, without ever losing his dignity. Lesser men would have hurled books. I couldn't understand how a black man could take some of the guff he had to swallow and keep his dignity on that floor, no matter what. There was always an undertone of racism in those debates on those issues. But he kept his dignity," Goldberger says.

He couldn't afford to lose his dignity. He was there to win a war, not a few battles. A crucial part of that war was the solid stream of amendments he managed to tack onto every appropriate bill and the amendments to guarantee that blacks would get a certain quota of the jobs involved. It was a matter of tradeoffs. He cooperated to win the votes on many issues when he was guaranteed that those issues would include equal opportunity provisions for minority job seekers, children in school, contractors seeking business and so on. This often involved coalition politics that Houlihan says he was so expert at.

"It was clear from the beginning," Katz says, "that Washington was another breed of cat. He always had that independent quality that was particularly marked because of the subservience of everybody else in the organization. He was the only one who ever opposed the organization and survived in the early years." He was not only a maverick, Black adds, "he was also a good politician." Black speculates that Metcalfe maintained his ties with Washington and protected him from Daley's ire "because he was such a good organizer and because he was smart and tough. He admired him and, after all, Metcalfe had no particular love for Daley."

Independent though he was, Washington paid more obeisance to the party as the years went by, trading his reputation as Best

Legislator of the Year for a modicum of safety in his seat. Below are his rankings by the IVI for the years 1967-75:

Year	Rank	Net Score	(Highest possible score)
1967	3	11	(16)
1969	9	13	(28)
1971	14	12	(33)
1973	33	20	(61)
1975	42	9	(39)

He never fell to the bottom of the barrel, where James Taylor, his arch-enemy, or Clyde Choate, the speaker of the House, were, along with all those whose rank fell between 42 and 178, but he also did not retain that rank that he had started out with and that, by temperament, should have had.

It is interesting to look at his voting record in 1975. On three of the votes that the IVI considered critical for the well-being of the people of the state, he simply acknowledged his presence. What were those three issues? (1) No-fault divorce, an issue that was finally passed in the Senate in 1983. The Machine is dominated by Catholics opposed to easy divorce. (2) The restriction of abortion rights, another Catholic issue. (3) The protection of rape victims in trials. The state's attorney's office and the police get the protection of the Machine in Chicago. Washington could not vote against the Machine on those issues. Nor could he vote with it. He studied carefully which issues he would not sacrifice, which he would sacrifice only partly by voting present or by being away during the vote without voting absent, and those he would give up completely. He gave up completely on (1) Congressional reapportionment, (2) the decriminalization of marijuana (a version of which he had fought for earlier, (3) a restriction on police spying (that one truly hurt), and (4) the establishment of a statewide probation system, taking that plum out of the hands of the city and the county.

On five of those critical bills he simply did not vote, not

indicating present or absent but simply not voting. The IVI says, "Some legislators are particularly fond of taking this way out, often disappearing for roll calls." Those issues? (1) A party vote, requiring party enrollment twenty-eight days prior to the primary in order to vote. Now that's a heavy one. A blatant effort by the party to control the election even more closely than it already did. Even a P would look bad there. But how could he vote for such a measure? (2) An exemption of certain public officials from income disclosure. That one's pretty heavy, too. Better to be in the cloakroom for that vote. (3) Provision for hearings before a Judicial Inquiry Board. That's how we control judges. (4) This one is pretty painful for a man who sees himself as a champion of the poor. It prohibits state assistance for abortion to women on public aid. (5) And as a champion of unions, the idiot card vote on this one would have been a disaster. It would prevent collective bargaining for public school employees. This failure to vote is all the more interesting when it is known that, on House Bill 1, the first introduced into that session, a bill permitting collective bargaining for public employees, he voted yes.

This disappearing act is not one invented by Washington nor is it one he learned to use very early. In 1967, he failed to vote only once on one of those bills IVI deemed critical, on an issue that was deadly serious that year. A bill was introduced to ban picketing on public streets—a clear civil liberties issue on which he had always taken a strong stand. It was also a deadly serious issue for Mayor Daley. It would have effectively ended the street demonstrations of the civil rights movement, those terrible assaults on the Mayor. Voting against the Machine on this issue might have been hazardous. Voting with the Machine was impossible.

In 1969, there were apparently no such terrible conflicts, but in 1971, Washington took a powder for seven critical votes; in 1973, for five.

What were the votes he would not sacrifice that earned him a rating of at least 42 instead of 78 or 178 in 1975, certainly not a high ranking for an idealist but one that keeps him out of the ranks of those completely enslaved? Those votes included (1) the Equal Rights Amendment, (2) a bill to strengthen the FEPC,

(3) a bill to entitle those with less than dishonorable discharges from the armed services to equal job opportunity, (4) the creation of a Consumer Advocate, (5) a vote against state aid to parents of private and parochial school children, (6) the lowering to eighteen of the age at which people can serve on school boards, (7) an annual cost-of-living review of public aid, and (8) abolition of capital punishment. Out of forty-three votes selected by the IVI as critical, Washington cast only thirty "correct" ones. Had he been free to vote his conscience entirely, had he been free of the need to select which votes to sacrifice, there is not one among those forty-three that he would not have voted "correctly."

In his first years in the House, many more of his votes were "correct." More important, much of his work was not even reflected in votes because the bills never got out of the committee or were tabled. And his work as a member and later as chairman of the Judiciary Committee is widely admired, Redmond says. "He was very valuable as chairman of the Judiciary." Katz, who headed Judiciary II, which dealt with civil liberties, considered Washington's presence on that committee "very valuable," too. "He was not simply involved with race matters," Katz says. "He was concerned with all other groups, including far-out political types." Like the ones who picket on public streets.

And there was all the maneuvering to stop the "yahoos" and to bring in the legislation he supported. Fiery speeches, Katz says, he made. "He would bollix up the legislature in a proper way, everything according to Hoyle. He wouldn't get up, as others did, in a screaming contest. His anger was always within the restraints of a certain gentility." He was never, Katz says, "the pain in the ass that some people who are dedicated to ideas are. He was never personally obnoxious, never rubbed people the wrong way as some of those people do. He's not a go-along person, he can really crack a few eggs and doesn't hesitate to do it but he's never snarly or nasty. You might get impatient with his ideas or his tactics but you could never get angry because he was always, always affable."

Redmond adds that he was effective as well as affable. "I'm not sure that the medical malpractice business has quieted down since he handled that legislation but it seems likely that it is no longer such a paramount issue because he did such a superb job of a really tough assignment. The whole situation was out of hand. Costs for medical malpractice insurance were skyrocketing. Verdicts were running very high. They held hearings for two years. Then Harold submitted his bills. The whole thing was superbly handled."

Houlihan agrees. "I remember hearing people talk about Harold around that issue," he says. "The doctors and lawyers—there was uniform praise for the way he allowed everybody their say, for the way he directed and monitored a working group to come up with a compromise. He was spoken of very highly by both sides."

The medical malpractice bill was passed in 1975, after the IVI made up its list of critical bills for the year. Perhaps it would not have made that list, however, because it was largely a bill to protect physicians from the greed of lawyers and clients, though it did provide some protection for patients. It was, though, a neutral bill in the politics of race and the Machine. On those other matters, Washington was still in the same trick bag. The black caucus he helped organize in 1969 over Daley's fierce opposition was never a truly unified group because more than half the blacks in the legislature also worked for City Hall and paid total obeisance to Daley, Ray Ewell says. Sometimes they were so splintered among themselves that only three or four of the nearly twenty could hold together on an issue. Ewell describes how only Washington, Caldwell, and he held out on the question of an income tax. "It wasn't because we were opposed to an income tax, we weren't, but everybody else was getting something out of it for their communities but us. They told us, 'You're getting welfare.' We told them, 'Nonsense, everybody gets welfare.'"

It was another nail in the coffin, another guarantee that the leadership he should have had in the legislature, Ewell says, "was denied him because he defied the mayor."

But changes were afoot, rebellion was underway. Back in Chicago, Ralph Metcalfe had called him with a dramatic new development. He wanted to blow the whistle on the Chicago cops and their top boss, the mayor, to expose a long-smoldering problem in the ghetto: police brutality. On a visit to his dentist, Metcalfe learned of the brutal police killing of another dentist, Herbert Odon, who had been stopped for a traffic violation and subsequently been beaten to death by the police. Metcalfe went to the police superintendent. He was ignored. He went to Daley. He was ignored again. He told his young son, Ralph, Jr., who was a product of the sixties and who had been berating his father for several years for "taking the Mayor's shit." Metcalfe called around to black public officials in his bailiwick for support. With Washington, Tyrone Kenner, and Sam Patch, all close associates, he blew the whistle and called hearings in the community. The mayor ordered him to stop. He refused. He emerged as a hero. Not the independent hero he would become a few years later, but a hero in the black community.

In 1975, the following year, Washington and others urged him to take the final step toward independence and really take on the mayor. Run against him. "In the wake of all this positive publicity and the bad press he has had, you've got a chance to beat him," they insisted. William Singer, independent alderman from the Lakefront, had already declared his candidacy. In the three-way primary race, Metcalfe, now a popular hero, could take most of the black votes and a few of the whites and perhaps win. Even if he didn't win, it would be an object lesson to Daley that blacks were finally fed up with the treatment they were receiving from the Machine. There had already been some resistance: as early as 1963 Daley was booed off the platform of the convention of the NAACP. In that year Protest at the Polls had organized. In 1965, they had forced Daley to fire the school superintendent. There had been riots in the streets after the death of Martin Luther King in 1968. There were a few independent aldermanic campaigns against Machine candidates. In 1972, state's attorney Edward Hanrahan was strongly defeated by the black vote that reflected the anger of the community over the death of Black Panthers in an illegal police raid. And there was, in the community, some organizing around specific issues such as welfare rights. But, by and large, following the death of King there was a deep cynicism among blacks. Jesse Jackson's rise to eminence as a media star reflects that cynicism. Jackson never had any support in the community. When he tried to run for mayor, he couldn't even get enough signatures to get on the ballot. He was considered by many to be a loudmouth who could not deliver, but it seemed not to matter. *What difference does it make? If they could kill King, what is my life worth?* Then Metcalfe led what Washington and others thought might be a revolt, a focus for a new spirit that might arise for political organizing and the restoration of political power so grossly removed by Daley nearly twenty years earlier.

Metcalfe declined and threw his support to Singer who, therefore, took a sizeable number of black votes. He refused to run himself and refused to support Richard Newhouse, a state senator who ran against Singer and Daley in the primary. Practical politician that he was, Metcalfe chose to endorse a white liberal who had a slim chance of winning over a black who he thought had not the chance of a feather in a windstorm. While Singer didn't carry even one black ward, his combined vote with Newhouse's carried seven wards and was close in four more. In fact, the white independent Singer did better in the black wards than anywhere else in the city except his own turf, the Lakefront. Had Metcalfe run, Newhouse would not, and he would have taken all those votes. He would have done very well, indeed. Washington was enraged. The final break with Metcalfe was still to come but his refusal to lead the way in that election was a strong beginning.

Meanwhile, in Springfield, there was another rebellion against the Machine. Clyde Choate, Speaker of the House for many years, was a downstater, strongly conservative, not in the mayor's pocket but regularly involved in deals of convenience with him. He ran the House like a private club. Meetings were not posted. There was little opportunity for members to participate in the business of the House. Records were badly kept. Choate's ethics were not so much questioned as his dictatorial methods and his politics. The pressure to unseat him had been growing over the years. In 1975, the Democratic Study Group put Bill Redmond's name in nomination. Caldwell put Washington's name in nomination. Other names were also proposed. Redmond had eleven votes on the first ballot. Washington had two. Redmond is, Houlihan says, "a man for all seasons," a white liberal skilled in all the legislative arts, well-liked, a veteran of sixteen years in the House, a perfect candidate not least because he is not a man who could ever be a dictator, a suburbanite, neither a downstater nor a Chicagoan. After more than a week and about forty ballots, Daley called Springfield to instruct his "boys" to switch to Redmond. It looked like the House would be deadlocked if his boys did not switch, and besides he had been angry at Choate since he embraced Jesse Jackson at the 1972 Democratic convention. His boys did not all cooperate at first. Washington was one of the first. It was a relief to be able to vote for liberal Redmond. One by one, the votes changed. After ninety-three ballots, Redmond was finally elected. Ray Ewell never switched. Not because he didn't prefer Redmond, though he was no flaming liberal himself, but because he had given his word to Choate and he was piqued; he would not follow Daley's orders this time.

Washington was amazed to find himself named, finally, to a position of leadership. Redmond knew his talents; he named him chairman of the prestigious Judiciary Committee.

But Washington's position was becoming more precarious. After his break with Daley over the police brutality issue, Metcalfe lost his patronage army and the support of the party. Washington could no longer rely on Metcalfe's protection, and he had joined Metcalfe on the issue publicly. The year 1975, despite the recognition given him by Redmond, was a dangerous year.

But Washington still had Partee in his corner. Partee had made no breaks with Daley. He had his ear, he had a strong organization as committeeman, he was President of the Senate—a powerful man to deal with, a man who had always respected and admired Washington. A silver-tongued man of infinite political wisdom that he had, for the most part, used to serve the party, Partee had always been in Washington's corner. And he had always received Washington's respect and loyalty. Tim Black recalls going to Springfield to get Washington's assistance on some issue and being told, "Let's go to Cecil and try to put it together."

In 1975, Partee decided to retire from the Senate, to which he had been elected years before, to run for attorney-general. He lost but it was not a major tragedy. He had finished twenty years in the legislature and, at fifty-five, was eligible for the pension. His wife was alone at home after the last child went off to college. He would work in Chicago, then run for city office. Partee proposed that Washington be given his seat. Daley said no. So did Jim Taylor. Partee persisted. He won. Washington was slated and received the support of the party.

It was a new day. A new beginning. Blacks would get leadership slots in this Senate session if Washington had his way. He had his day. It took 188 ballots to elect Majority Leader Thomas Hynes but at the end Washington had successfully won for the blacks in the Senate the right to name their own leadership. He had made the request first. A simple request, it seems. The blacks were to elect their own Senate leader. Daley said no. So they refused to support Hynes until they were given that right. In the process, they also supported the liberals who wanted several important rules changes. Another famous tradeoff.

His failure over the years to get the prized award of the IVI did not prevent him from receiving other awards. Between 1969 and 1977, he was cited fourteen times by a variety of labor, political, and community groups for his legislative ability.

• In '73, he was given the Legislator Award of the Southern Christian Leadership Conference.

• In '74, the Negro Labor Relations League bestowed the William L. Dawson Award.

• A Legislative Excellence Award was given him in 1974 by the Illinois State Federation of Labor-CIO.

• In '77, the Federation of Independent Colleges named him Outstanding Legislator in Higher Education.

In 1977, at the close of the session, the IVI ranked Washington number 6 in the Senate. His score was 18 out of a possible 26. Once again, he was named Best Legislator. He was also named Best Legislator by *Chicago Magazine*. His reputation in the House had preceded him. His colleagues were happy to have him among them. But 1977 was an even more crucial year in the life of Harold Washington. He had been making the break slowly, in his cautious, considered way for fifteen years, a little here, a little there, a step forward, a step backward. Then in the last few years, there had been Metcalfe's police brutality issue and Choate's ouster. In 1976, Metcalfe had finally broken completely and had run, on an IVI endorsement, for re-election to his Congressional seat as an independent after Daley dumped him. Washington was caught in a terrible bind. If he endorsed his old mentor, he would lose all his party support. There was no question about that. Daley was enraged at Metcalfe. Boys who turn on Daley don't get away with it. His vindictive rage was well-known. Metcalfe might have been a power in the black community but without his patronage, his power was, shall we say, diminished. And now Daley was stripping him of his Congressional seat, running a relatively well-respected toady against him.

With the help of the IVI, Metcalfe put together a solid campaign and, after many years of spouting the party line, took strong liberal positions on a wide range of issues: disarmament, abortion, women's rights, racial equality, and so on. He was anathema to Daley. Washington did not endorse him. There was probably no political act in his history that stuck in his craw so badly. He could hardly endure it. Metcalfe won big.

Suddenly, Daley was dead and there was to be a special election to replace him. The Machine had grossly insulted the black community by refusing to permit Wilson Frost, president *pro tem* of the Council, to take his rightful place in the mayor's office even for the few ceremonial weeks before the election. They locked up the Mayor's office and installed guards there.

Roman Pucinski, veteran Polish politician, and Michael

Bilandic, Daley's heir apparent, ran in the special election to replace Daley. Now was the time to make that final break. The insult to Frost, though he was a party hack, was too much. Washington went to some of those with whom he had worked in the legislature and to others, to Don Rose, well-known liberal political strategist who had worked in Metcalfe's campaign, and other liberals, to discuss his candidacy. It was decided he would seek the IVI endorsement. Arlene Rubin, veteran IVIer, recalls vividly the "brilliance" of Robert Mann's speech in behalf of Washington at the organization's endorsement hearing. Washington received the endorsement despite his failure to reject the patronage system, and, though he did not receive the support of most of the IVI North Siders who obviously preferred a Polish party hack to a black. The campaign was late in getting started, had no money, no organization, and, with the resignation of Don Rose, the campaign manager, after Washington had not played it straight with him on the matter of his income tax problems (this matter is discussed in more depth in a later chapter), was not slated for any grand success. That he was running without Metcalfe's prized endorsement—tit for tat—did not help. He took only 11 percent of the vote. But it was a start. It was the first step in building a new political base in the black community. It was not a safe move but it was a helluva lot safer than when Daley had been alive. He had his seat in the Senate. He had, come what may, it seems, the loyalty of Cecil Partee and his strong organization and the following he had built in the mayoral campaign simply strengthened his position.

Shortly after the election, in an address to the IVI Independents Day Dinner, he said,

> There are some people who call themselves my friends who tell me I shouldn't be speaking to this audience. They say "You never lost an election until you started fooling around with those IVIers." I tell them, 'My people are never going to win anything important until they stop fooling around with that Democratic Machine. Both entities are suspect in certain circles.'
>
> In politics, there is obviously no substitute for winning elections. But

I'm sure I do not have to tell this audience that anything worth fighting for in the political arena cannot be won in the first small battle. . ."

For the first time the leaders of the Independent Voters of Illinois, who have often been viewed with suspicion in the black community, indicated to people that they are willing to work for the election of a black political leader to a major citywide office.

That sixty-day campaign also taught us just how far we still have to go to create a winning coalition for change in Chicago. We should take this last election as a trial run and go back to our respective communities to organize for the bigger battles ahead.

In the black community, we weren't defeated by the Machine, we were defeated by rejection of the system. It had been my hope that the Machine would get the votes of fewer than one hundred thousand of the city's half million registered black voters. We succeeded on that count. The Machine got its smallest black vote in recent history. But more than three hundred thousand other black voters stayed home, because they were so disgusted with the electoral process that they couldn't be convinced to go to the polls for *anyone*. In the months and years ahead, I will be going back to those discouraged voters to convince them to join in our efforts for change...

He went further. A few days after the Independents Day Dinner, he took over Mayor Bilandic's conference room on the fifth floor of City Hall to denounce him, to refuse to support him for mayor. He would support no candidate for mayor in that election. He said,

As a lifelong Democrat, I would like nothing better than to be able to support the mayoral candidate of my political party. As a practical politician, I know that any other decision will make my own political future more precarious.

But Michael Bilandic, in the months since he took office, has proved himself to be little more than a third rate Boss Daley. He appears to share all of the late Mayor's weaknesses and blind spots, while bringing to his work as our city's chief executive little of Daley's skill as a balancer of conflicting needs and interests.

I remain as convinced today as I was when I announced for mayor that the Daley Administration policies which Michael Bilandic has promised to carry forward cannot save our neighborhoods, cannot improve our schools, cannot restore our people's confidence in the ability of the police department to serve them efficiently and respectfully. . .

In the conduct of his campaign Bilandic has shown callous disregard

> for the right of Chicagoans to choose their own leaders without manipulation. Like his predecessor, Bilandic amassed a vast war chest of funds obtained from individuals and firms doing business with the city. These facts might be enough to make me turn my back on thirty-nine years in the Democratic party, if only there were another candidate worth supporting.
>
> But Dennis Block proved himself unwilling to work to turn this city around on the day that he enthusiastically seconded the nomination of Michael Bilandic to become acting mayor. Some black members of the Democratic machine may pretend to not remember, but I cannot forget, the insult that was handed to all black people on that day, when the city council walked around Wilson Frost to make Bilandic acting mayor. Mr. Block proved he is not a serious opponent of the Machine by participating in that charade.
>
> So I must—with deep regret because it is not in my nature to stay outside a political battle—announce that I can find no one worth supporting in the current race for mayor. Instead, I urge all people who agree with me that we must fight to make Chicago a city that works for all of its people, to start planning and working now toward the hard political battles ahead of us in 1978, 1979, and beyond.

He did not foresee yet that, beyond, only six years later he would put together that winning coalition to win another mayoral campaign. He did not foresee that Daley's death would leave such excruciating cleavages in the party, intense enough to finally destroy it. Nor did he foresee, on the basis of that run in 1977, the kind of campaign he would have to endure when he was finally a serious contender for the title. But he did foresee that independence from the Democratic Party would now be possible as it had not been in 1965 or even in 1975. The boss was dead and there was no one readily taking his place. Daley had been so dictatorial that he had not prepared his successor.

He also foresaw that there would be a reemergence of black political organization. His thrust at the mayoralty in 1977 was part of a movement that wouldn't be stopped and this time he would be out front. Arlene Rubin didn't need to tell him that she had been unconcerned with his overall campaign, that her interest had been on building an organization in her own ward. "I knew things weren't going so well on the North Side but I wasn't paying any attention. I was too busy," she says. "We had a beautiful campaign. It was a high just like the Metcalfe campaign had been: the development of new people, coalition building, training people who had never done anything political in their lives. It was difficult. We had to function pretty much on our own. The only thing we really needed from the campaign was literature and that wasn't always forthcoming on time but it didn't matter too much. What mattered was the new, fresh blood. When Don left the campaign, it shook us all up. We couldn't decide whether to stay. We even went to O'Rourke's [a saloon on the North Side where Rose goes on Friday nights] to try to talk to him, but we decided that we had such wonderful precinct activity that we would stay if only for that."

"I don't even recall Harold very well from that campaign. He was not grey yet but I just can't recall his personality. I only knew that it was a wonderful opportunity for coalition building and precinct development. As I look back on it now I see that it was all part of the grand movement. We felt wonderful that the independent vote—Pucinski and Washington combined—fell only one percentage point from winning. Except for Metcalfe, the independents had never done that well before. Sure, it was a small victory, but it felt like a real one. Gradually, more and more people were breaking away from what the Machine precinct captain told them to do. Harold carried several wards and it was, wow, we've got those wards in the independent column now."

Washington was now, irretrievably, in the independent column. But the campaign for mayor ended just in time to run for re-election to the Senate. Now he was faced with the wrath of the party, the unrestrained wrath of one of the deceased mayor's favorite toadies, Jim Taylor. Miraculously, he still had Partee in his corner.

Taylor fielded a man never heard of plus two other people whose names were Washington. It was to be a free-for-all. If the Machine candidate couldn't beat him alone, maybe one of those other Washingtons would confuse the voters enough so that he would lose by accident. The Machine allegedly spent $200,000 in that campaign.

Partee moved in his own organization plus one hundred more volunteers to work for Washington. David Canter, a savvy attorney who had worked in his mayoral campaign, managed to knock those two other Washingtons off the ballot. Washington won by 212 votes. Now he could go back to the Senate and take the role he had wanted from his start in politics and which he had dared take only in his first years in the House. His IVI rank in 1979 returned to the 3 it had been in 1967. His score was 11 out of a possible 16, but those votes that were not "correct" were of his own choosing. He still needed some tradeoffs. But he was no longer indebted to the party.

He was indebted to Partee, though, and so he did not interfere in a highly dramatic political event on the South Side. In mid-October, just before the Congressional election, Ralph Metcalfe died suddenly. There was a state funeral—liberals sat beside Machine men, everyone was there. The eulogists praised him as a man of the people. Meanwhile, the Democratic comitteemen were burning up the wires deciding who should replace Metcalfe on the ballot, a duty given them by state law. Sam Ackerman, the state committee chairman, a Hyde Park liberal elected only by a fluke to this den of Machine men, wanted to take no action at all, for which the law also provided, leaving it up to the governor to call a special election later. Allan Dobry, the 5th Ward (Hyde Park) committeeman, agreed. If no action was taken prior to the November election and a special election was called for later, there was time to put together another liberal-black coalition campaign. The regulars were pretty well decided to give the seat to Benny Stewart, a committeeman and alderman whose most outrageous claim to fame was that Ackerman had beaten him for the committeeman's job without even having campaigned—there were hardly any less effective toadies than Stewart. He had served the party well for years and deserved this plum. The committeemen's decision, Dobry says, was made in the office of Ray Donovan, head of the Department of Streets and Sanitation, one of the Machine's most powerful figures. It was one of the most cynical decisions to come out of City Hall for many years. The worst of the toadies replaces the best, the most beloved, of the black political community. Partee seems to have been Donovan's man on the scene.

A meeting was demanded by the Machine. Ackerman acquiesced finally, but insisted it must be an open meeting. The committeemen raged. Ackerman held firm. The meeting was held in a large church which had been the scene of many civil rights and political meetings, the Liberty Baptist Church. Washington did not attend. He owed one to Partee. The meeting was a free-for-all, almost violent. The people wanted to wait for a special election so that they could elect a Congressman who would truly replace the recently liberated and now sadly dead Metcalfe. The Machine would not give up this opportunity to retrieve the seat it had lost to the traitor. Partee tried to head off the free-for-all, asking Ackerman and Dobry to join the others in a "show of unity." They refused. The people would be given their day. The first motion on the floor was Dobry's—to adjourn the meeting and take no action. The committeemen voted no. The meeting went on. And on. And on. And Benny Stewart was named to replace Metcalfe on the ballot. He went to Washington and served the time in the only way he could.

Washington's loyalty to Partee was never quite complete because being so would have meant complete loyalty to the party. He gave him some and withheld some. (In 1982, he backed him for committee chairman; in 1983, he refused him a raise in pay as City Treasurer.) Now he was waiting, biding his time. The next Congressional election was only two years away. Meanwhile, he had a reputation to enhance. There was important work to be done in the Senate. He still had that unfinished business—that stop and frisk law that now needed to be repealed and other significant legislation to win. But the truly big legislation of that last year he was to serve in the State House was to be the Human Rights Act, an omnibus bill that would finally bring together his efforts of fifteen years. It was to be the most exhilarating year in the State House, a dramatic climax of his political career and a stunning finish to fifteen years of dismaying compromise and too many defeats.

It was also to be a year of extraordinary anomaly. If Jim Taylor had shown himself to be a craven toady for the Machine earlier, in 1979 he would emerge as a sickening archetype of that figure—a black man adopting the underlying racism of the worst white political bosses. He was joined by a companion toady, black Gerald Bullock, who, after Washington was elected mayor, was the first to toss his hat into the ring for the Congressional seat. (Washington said of his candidacy, in what may have been his most restrained political judgement, "He's not ready.") But the anomaly didn't stop there. Taylor and Bullock were joined by one of the staunchest white liberals in the House, Susan Catania, who had won several terms handily in a largely black district, running as a Republican, on her liberal credentials. And by Carol Moseley Braun, a black from Hyde Park who was also elected as a civil rights advocate and liberal.

The struggle was over a bill that should have had the wholehearted support of all the blacks and liberals in the State House. The struggle over the bill should have been a strict conservative-liberal one, as the struggle over similar legislation had been for twenty-five or thirty years. But politics makes strange bedfellows, it is said, and so the opposition to the first major civil rights legislation in a generation was a coalition of blacks, liberals, and conservatives. Strange bedfellows, indeed.

The Human Rights Act began, unlikely as it sounds, in the Republican governor's office. The new Illinois Constitution, ratified in 1970, required the reorganization of the various governmental agencies and departments into more efficient, efficacious bodies. In his first session, Governor Thompson's staff put together the reorganization of several low-profile, noncontroversial departments, avoiding the controversial because he had another election to win in '78. In early '79, the staff went to work on the human rights reorganization. Do it first and have it over with early in the term, while the aura of the largest vote for a gubernatorial candidate in the state's history was still aglow. From the start, the bill was heavily political. The Chicago Machine, the staff believed, did not want a truly effective agency to enforce nondiscrimination. It was precisely because of its racist politics that it survived so long, it was believed by the liberals in the governor's office. Further, the bill would consolidate several agencies, collapsing some completely, leaving some people without top political jobs.

There was no question that the conservatives would fight such a bill. And Democrats, considering this issue their private turf—as indeed it had been for many years—would be reluctant to let the Republicans have such a big piece of it. Better to have nothing, many Democrats would reason, than to let Republicans have it. As it turned out in the next several months, all these assessments came true.

It was decided, in view of those suspicions, that the staff would work quietly to produce the reorganization bill and present the finished product to the legislature. They did, though, talk to people all over the country. They rewrote all the human rights bills on record in the state to bring them up to the most recent and highest standards, making their new bill the most stringent and far-reaching in the nation. The bill included strictures against discrimination based on age, sex, race, creed, marital status, national origin, mental and physical handicap, and unfavorable military discharge. It covered housing, employment, credit, and public accommodations. It markedly increased the overall budget for execution and enforcement with a strong appeals provision and brought the new agency into the government as a cabinet level department. They put together the most advanced human rights bill in the nation, by most accounts.

The staff then invited several black legislators, including Washington, to the governor's office to discuss the bill. Washington was thrilled. From that Saturday afternoon in the governor's office in March, he worked steadily and energetically to win approval of the bill. It didn't matter to him that it had a Republican, David Shapiro, president of the Senate, as principal sponsor. It was more important that the bill had as its principal sponsor that president. It didn't matter that the Republican governor would get the biggest share of the praise for the bill. It was a landmark bill, the best piece of legislation for human rights to hit the floor of the legislature in its history. Nothing major had been left out.

The first thing Washington did was to study the bill carefully and suggest changes that would make it more acceptable to both his colleagues—conservatives and liberals alike—and to those pressure groups outside the legislature who would need to support it to assure its passage. A phrase here, a word change here, nothing major. A change of emphasis, a new clause, strengthening it for those who might think it too weak, loosening it for those who might think it too rigid. "He brought to it some political acumen that would help us satisfy the needs of the people who would want to feel that they were part of the process of writing it. He could anticipate so well what others thought."

The Human Rights Act was introduced in the Senate and the House in mid-April. Washington spoke eloquently for it. The struggles began. A staff member who prefers anonymity says that "Washington stands out phenomenally as a man of principle in this struggle. He was always honest and very straightforward about what he was doing, in contradistinction to a lot of others. And he was a man interested in public policy and the principles of government. He did not engage in game-playing or personal agendas that a lot of other people did. The whole experience was characterized by people whose interests were extremely selfish and base and Washington was absolutely beyond all that. I see him as the real hero of the passage of this Act."

As soon as the bill was introduced, there was resistance by the regular Democratic organization, particularly by Taylor and Bullock. It was, they insisted, a bad bill, a Republican plot to foist a non-action bill on the people. Press releases from their offices implied that a Republican governor could not be trusted with civil rights legislation, that Washington was a traitor to the cause, a mere water carrier for the Republicans. The *Chicago Defender*, the black newspaper always on the side of the Machine, published the stories Taylor and Bullock fed them.

Washington fought back. He brought in to Springfield for

hearings and public discussions black and white liberal opinion makers from all over the state to tell them the story of the bill and to get their responses.

When the roll call was taken on the bill in the Senate on May 24, thee were fifty yes's out of fifty-nine, one no, two present, and six absent, an unbelievable vote for civil rights in the traditionally highly conservative Senate, a tribute, according to the staff of the governor's office, to Washington's work on the floor of the chamber, his "calm noncombative presentation." It helped that this was the only vote in the Senate for which Governor Thompson was present. Republicans, too, listen to their leader.

But by the end of the session, June 30, the bill had not been signed into law. The failure was the result of what must now be viewed as a tragi-comedy performed by a foolish woman, a highly political woman, and venal men. Susan Catania had a bill to give women some guarantees in the use of credit cards. Certainly this issue is of paramount importance to women and Catania is one of the most significant advocates of women's rights in the state. Nevertheless, her refusal to support a bill that guarantees wide rights to women unless her own bill was attached as an amendment to the Human Rights Bill and her forming a coalition with Jim Taylor and his buddies in the House to defeat its passage without the amendment has certainly to be seen as the woeful whim of a woman piqued, an unpleasant accusation to make in 1983. Had she been a lesser advocate, it might have been seen simply as a failure to support. Had she been a Democrat, it might have been seen as a political ploy similar to Taylor's and Carol Moseley Braun's. Had she been a racist, it would have been understandable. Being none of the above, it must be seen as pique. If you won't play it my way, I will just have to do you in. Do in the bill, she did. Her clout as an advocate was strong enough to win her victory in the House. The amendment was added. The Senate refused to accept it; it was too controversial.

Meanwhile, Taylor and Bullock were introducing other amendments—over a hundred—simply to stall, to make people waver, especially advocates. Among the amendments they introduced were the first ten amendments to the U.S. Constitution: dilatory tactics designed to make the bill appear to be less than it was, to defeat it to avoid a Republican record on civil rights, to avoid a nondiscriminatory bill with teeth in it that had more application in Chicago than anywhere else in the state with its huge black population, still essentially segregated and discriminated against by the Democratic Machine, and finally, to prevent Washington from adding to the lustre of his own record. Carol Moseley Braun helped them all—an unholy alliance if ever there was one. There were 114 roll calls. The amendment was added. The bill was finally passed in the House. When the Senate refused to accept Catania's amendment, she refused to back down. The bill was deadlocked. The legislature adjourned.

Through the summer and fall, Washington continued to carry the water, talking constantly to everyone and anyone inside and outside the legislature, pushing, pulling, twisting, cajoling. It was crucial to have "a strong, articulate, respected black person to say that this was a good bill," a governor's staffer says. "It took a lot of moxie for an independent from Chicago to stand up like that on the side of a Republican and say this is the right thing to do." But the bill was the culmination of years of struggle in that legislature for Washington. He would not permit it to fail.

Even so, he had his price. The Human Rights Act was a crucial piece of legislation and he would do all in his power to bring it through but the Republicans had to give him his, too, a bill he had been trying to get passed that would guarantee 10 percent of state purchasing for construction to minority contractors. So, in that session of the legislature, Washington brought off two major pieces of civil rights legislation.

On November 8, in a special veto session, the Act was brought up again. This time, because it was a special session, it would require a three-fifths vote. By this time, lots of tradeoffs had been arranged in the House. One vote for the Human Rights Act, one vote for someone else's bill. The Catania amendment was finally removed. The House voted 121 yes's, 24 nays, 1 present, and 31 absent. The governor signed it on December 6. Washington was no longer drinking, but a glass of champagne was in order.

Slate-making, Washington told the committeemen in Partee's office in December, 1979, in a rump meeting called without Ackerman's knowledge, was undemocratic. They did not help the party by giving the people candidates like Benny Stewart. There should be open primaries. They should back worthy candidates. They slated Stewart again. They didn't believe Washington when he warned them of the great gusts of wind blowing through the black community that would blow them all away if they did not change their ways. Sure, they said, the people had defeated the party's nominee for state's attorney in 1972. But Hanrahan had been a big mistake. After that killing of the Black Panthers, slating him had been a grievous insult to the black people of Chicago. A big mistake. Sure, they had voted for some independents but how many and for how many terms. The party always ended up the victor in those wards. Yeh, Byrne had won against the Machine candidate but that was because Bilandic had been so stupid about handling that snowstorm. But this was nothin' like that. Stewart was harmless. Nobody was angry at him. He was a nobody—easy to control, like a paper doll, offensive to no one. Besides, it was a Congressional seat, a plum. Who cared about that? Stewart wanted that plum. He had served the party well for years. Now he deserved the reward. After all, isn't that what it's all about? Rewards and punishment. Washington knew that as well as anyone.

Partee stuck with Stewart. Washington had gone too far. He was being too much of a maverick now. The game was up. So did the black businessmen and the black establishment. It was the kind of campaign for which Washington has since become famous—long on inspiration, commitment, energy, excitement—a people's campaign—short on clean lines of authority and tight organization. He campaigned on the issues: Who would rightfully succeed the independent Metcalfe for this second term? Would it be a party hack or a man long known for his independent streak? He campaigned on his own independent record. He swept the district out of the Machine's control, despite Partee's and Taylor's and the other black committeemen's support for Stewart. His community, as he had tried to tell those committeemen, was very restive, ready for a new politics, a new concept. They would no longer support the old hacks if they had a serious alternative. He gave them that alternative.

In addition to Washington and Stewart, there were two other candidates in that primary: John Stroger, a party loyalist who was trying his hand at some independence, and Ralph Metcalfe, Jr. Young Metcalfe was furious at Washington. This was his rightful seat, he said. There are some who say that perhaps the young man was responsible for his father's death. On the day Ralph, Sr. died, he had convened a meeting of prestigious people including Washington, who would plan his son's career. They would support him for alderman—an independent alderman. Young Ralph had, however, his own ideas and the meeting ended by their agreeing to disagree. Ralph, Sr., got sick. He died the next morning. It was only right, Ralph, Jr. felt, that he should succeed his father in the Congress. His campaign was not conducted at the highest level of debate. Some described him as "distinctly flaky," as if he was on drugs most of the time. John Stroger had been too long associated with the party. The difference between him and Stewart was not too apparent. Washington took a majority of the votes, a wide margin of victory in that four-man race. The general election was a piece of cake. He took 95 percent of the votes.

When he went to Washington, he left behind some debts—not the mountain of campaign debts that the National Democratic Party had accumulated or even those mountains most individual candidates acquire, thousands and thousands of dollars. His debts were, by comparison, piddly amounts: $800 here, $400 there, $200 here, $50 there, debts both from the mayoral and the Congressional campaigns. He hadn't spent a whole lot but you can't run a campaign on pennies and neither campaign was supported by the rich coffers of the Democratic party or by the black businessmen who stayed loyal to the Machine with whom they did business and from whom they always hoped for more business. "They treated him as if he had leprosy," Cecil Troy says. One of the very few businessmen who did support him, Troy donated 75 pounds of potato and other salads and gallons of juice from his Grove Fresh Company for the victory party. "Washington had nothing to feed his workers that night," Troy recalls. "There was hardly money for the basic necessities."

Having licked the regulars in the election, Washington went looking for another victory. The next in line for his Senate seat was Jim Taylor. Neither Washington nor any of the liberals wanted to see Taylor get that seat. In fact, that probability had been an initial issue in his earliest probings on his own candidacy. In late 1979, when he approached 5th Ward Committeeman Allan Dobry to ask for his endorsement, Dobry had said, "But Jim Taylor will get your seat in the Senate." Taylor's voting record was among the worst; his IVI rank was 134 out of a possible 178. He was a poor speaker, of questionable honesty, a toady for the party hierarchy. Washington was concerned, too, and promised Dobry that he would do all in his power to prevent Taylor's getting the seat.

He tried. He refused to resign until he was inaugurated in late January. Partee was furious. It was unethical, he said. And unfair. The man had won. Why didn't he step aside and let someone else have his seat? It wasn't just someone else, though. It was Taylor. He controlled the district committee that, under state law, has the responsibility to replace a legislator when the need arises.

Wasn't that an exercise in futility? Washington had no clout in the party. How could he expect to give his seat in the Senate to someone more estimable? Dobry says, no, it wasn't a futile exercise. "Harold was putting a tremendous amount of pressure on the black committeemen. He had proved that the black community wanted better candidates, that they were no longer willing to stand still for men like Taylor. He believed there was enough rebellion in the community so that he could go to the committeemen and say, 'Look, you better change your ways or else.' Well, they didn't change their ways and here we are two years later. It wasn't futile. This election put Barnett and Shaw out rather ignominiously and the rest are scared out of their minds. Harold understood the situation. He tried to warn them. The trouble is, you can't threaten people with what will happen when they don't believe it will happen."

Well, threats based on what *will* happen are essentially futile, aren't they? On the other hand, Washington, characteristically, had to make that effort. His logical mind could not imagine that people would ignore the obvious signs. He had not won merely because he was a charismatic figure, because of how he spoke, though that always helps; he had won largely because of what he said. Those committeemen had not listened, neither to him nor to those who voted for him. They had been listening to City Hall exclusively for too long. They didn't know how to listen to anyone else. Certainly not the maverick Washington who Daley had clearly dumped years ago, though he had continued to tolerate him. That Washington was no longer a maverick to the voters they did not realize. It would take another upset primary election, this one so much an upset that their political lives would never be the same, might, in fact, end, before they would listen to the man they had been staring at for nearly twenty years. That this crazy idealist, regularly bucking City Hall, would be, only three years later, Chicago's mayor was unthinkable on that day the committeemen ignored Washington's warning and endorsed Benny Stewart for Congress and then again on the day that they gave Jim Taylor the seat in the Senate. They had been saying all their lives, "You can't beat City Hall." That Washington would prove them wrong was beyond credibility. This Congressional win of his—Metcalfe's win in '76—were not signs of the times; they were only flukes. The evil of racism, as Pincham says, is that such dreams are unimaginable for blacks, certainly blacks who have blinded themselves to their own community's voices by tying their souls to the whims of City Hall, by selling their souls for a mess of pottage. Despite the obeisance he had paid to remain in the ranks of the party, Washington never gave up those early, unique and lofty dreams. Patience and persistence were paying off. He was free at last. And he would take to the freedomland all those who the people would permit him to. Some they would reject. But others would be permitted to get on board. Washington understood those men. "It's not easy to be independent," he had said in 1964.

It didn't get any easier for years. When it finally did, when his people finally were ready for him, he was ready and he knew that many of his party colleagues would soon be ready, too. It hadn't been easy for many of them, either. And they had succumbed to that disease of racism that he had, with precious few others, just been able to resist. He emerged from fifteen years of struggle with some scars but a whole man.

Forty Days in Jail

There is pain in John Secaras' voice when he says, "I was terribly disappointed when I heard about Harold's problems with the income tax and taking client's money and not paying his bills. That was not the man who'd been my friend in law school. My friend could never have done those things. He was above reproach."

Lou Roundtree echoes Secaras: "I was shocked when I heard all that stuff. He was the neat, orderly, disciplined guy, Mr. Organized himself at Roosevelt College. I was the disorganized one. Harold always knew exactly what had to be done, when it had to be done, and how. And he did it. What happened to him?"

The echo reverberates once again as Dempsey Travis, lifelong friend, says that he could not have imagined Washington doing the things he was accused of, the things for which he was so severely punished.

What happened to Harold Washington in the twenty years after he graduated from law school is the question asked by everyone who knew him in those years prior to his graduation from law school. He seems to have the same wit and charm, the same impish grin, the same charisma, the same sharp intelligence. He is greyer, heavier, but he seems otherwise unchanged. But it is clear from the revelations of his offenses that something did indeed change. The man people knew in those years was too ethical, too orderly, too smart to commit such offenses. Put aside the fact that a man building a political career knows that his opponents will use everything they can lay their hands on against him. And it was always perfectly clear that he was building a political career. For the young Washington, however, as politically ambitious as he was, honesty and charity were more important. One files one's income tax returns. One doesn't bilk clients, especially poor clients. One pays one's bills, even if one has to borrow money to do it. Not necessarily on time. But in time to avoid the courts. Washington was known as an honest man. His friends are bewildered, shocked by the news of his perfidies. Not because they were such grave crimes. They weren't. He paid his taxes; he simply didn't file the returns—neglect, not fraud. In twenty years, he bilked six clients of a total sum of $265, $60 of which he repaid. Those crimes are not in the class of hundreds of other lawyers who have defrauded their clients of thousands of dollars. His unpaid bills were small by comparison with many that go unpaid a lot longer. Not in the class of the National Democratic Party that still owes Ma Bell over a million dollars, or Governor James Thompson, who still owes $450,000 for his 1982 campaign and $225,000 from the 1978 campaign. It took Bill Singer ten years to pay off his debts from the 1975 Chicago mayoralty campaign.

By comparison with the crime of Ted Kennedy, the dissolute life of Wilbur Mills, the financial crimes of Otto Kerner, Bert Lance, Spiro Agnew, Bobby Baker, Paul Powell to name only a few of the many who profited tremendously from their public offices, and the political crimes of Richard Nixon and his mob, Washington's crimes were infinitesimal. Two years before Nixon was pardoned, Washington served thirty-six days in Cook County Jail for failing to file his tax returns. In 1970, while Nixon was preparing the crimes for which he was pardoned, Washington was suspended from the bar for bilking clients of $205. When, in 1973, the year Watergate was revealed, after his conviction for failing to file his tax returns, the Committee on Inquiry of the Chicago Bar Association voted a new complaint against him and, in 1975, after many delays, the Hearing Board to which the case had been transferred recommended an additional two-year suspension. The Supreme Court Review Board rejected the recommendation because Washington, it said, had effectively been suspended for nearly six years already.

No, they were not grave crimes, but they were illegal acts of omission committed by a man who earlier seemed unlikely ever to be guilty of such acts. They were punishable by law and he knew it. He was, after all, a lawyer and a competent one, though even the most incompetent lawyer knows when he is breaking the law.

John I. McBride, now executive director of the Chicago Bar Association, the secretary for the Committee on Inquiry that processed Washington's case, recalls wondering why "he was so stupid. It wasn't much money. He could easily have paid them off and made his peace." Was he, in fact, stupid? Or was something much more complex going on in his head?

To get at the answer to this major question, we need to ask two others: first, why did this careful, ethical, well-organized man permit these kinds of slovenliness and disregard for the law to occur? And second, how did it happen that Washington was punished so severely for such minor crimes? Was that punishment merely a consequence of his own slovenliness or was there something else operating? Let's review the record.

In November 1966, Washington was reelected to his House seat over the strong objections of Mayor Daley. Only through the intercession of Cecil Partee was he slated again. Perhaps the Mayor went along graciously with Partee's defense of Washington. Perhaps not. He was known to be vindictive and he was quoted by Alderman Tom Keane, one of his most loyal henchmen who was later sent to jail for fraud, as saying that he would never permit a black to have the power that William Dawson had when he cast the vote that gave Daley his first nomination for mayoral candidate and dumped his predecessor from the ticket. No black would ever have the power to dump him as he had dumped Kennelly, he said. Perhaps he was looking for a means to let Partee know who was boss; Partee was gaining power.

McBride insists that he didn't even know Washington was a politician. And in fact there seems to be no one who can connect McBride to the former mayor. Judge Pincham is inclined to believe McBride. "He lived in another world. No downtown lawyers had even the slightest acquaintance with black lawyers or black politics," he says. Well, Pincham certainly knows about that. But Mayor Daley wasn't black and he knew the black politicians. John M. Oswald, chief investigator for the Attorney Registration and Disciplinary Committee of the Supreme Court of Illinois, the agency formed in 1973 to handle the complaints that McBride's committee had previously handled, says that "the disciplinary actions were often 'club' affairs. The attorneys in the big firms seemed to fare better than the others." Club affairs? How about political affairs? Would McBride have acted on a wish expressed by the Mayor? Well, Oswald knows McBride and says, "probably not but you never know about such things." It's only speculation, of course, but the Mayor could have put in a call to McBride. He put in lots of calls to the people in positions of power who could help him maintain control of the political apparatus. Maybe he said, "Listen, Jack, why don't you check out that complaint file to see if you have a little something on one of my boys, a Harold Washington. It wouldn't hurt if you made something out of it." McBride might have ignored his request. His dry point-by-point discussion of the case with me leads me to think there might not have been such a phone call or, if it did come, it was ignored. But it *is* a strange coincidence that Washington was elected to his seat in November 1966 over the Mayor's wishes and, in January '67, the first in a series of letters that ended in his suspension was sent to Washington. Daley was a vindictive man, determined to hold on to and expand his power, and it would have been difficult for almost anyone in the legal profession to ignore him.

Most of the complaints filed with the CBA, it seems, didn't come to much. It was a little like filing a complaint against a policeman. Pincham says, "No one paid any attention to that

Committee." It was rare for a lawyer to have his license lifted, even when he bilked a client of a large sum of money. According to McBride, only about 15-20 of 1,500-1,600 complaints each year ever got to the formal inquiry stage and they resulted, not from bilking clients but from "convictions or outright theft or evasion of taxes." The records of the sixties and early seventies were apparently destroyed when the Supreme Court appointed the new disciplinary agency in 1973, so no exact figures are available for the years in which Washington's case occurred. However, 1981 data are available and some comparisons can be made. In that year, 1,924 new charges against attorneys were docketed. Of those, 43 went beyond the filing drawer stage. Of those, 12 went to and were terminated by the Supreme Court. Two of those 12 ended in disbarrment, six in suspensions, three in censures, and one was dismissed. In addition, among the forty-three cases, six attorneys voluntarily disbarred themselves. Considering the great increase in the number of attorneys (about 2,000 annually), the number of complaints has not risen appreciably. The number of cases that went to the Supreme Court has declined: sixteen in 1979, eleven in 1980, and twelve in 1981, though more cases were pending.

Justice Walter V. Schaefer, who sat on the Supreme Court of Illinois at the time of Washington's suspension, says, "The courts are often too lenient." He recalls the tragedy of Robert Ming, another black attorney for whom the courts showed no leniency and who was sent to federal prison in Minnesota for failure to file his tax returns, one of the rare people ever sent to jail for this offense. Ming had also been disloyal to Mayor Daley. In 1967, in his run for mayor of Gary, Ind., black Richard Hatcher was accused of criminal acts that he denied. He insisted he was innocent, that the accusations were a plot to discredit him. Ming was brought in to investigate the charges. The chairman of the Lake County Democratic Party called Daley to ask that he exert pressure on Ming to pull out. Daley complied. Ming denied. He did uncover a plot. Hatcher was cleared and elected. Shortly after the election, Ming was summoned to appear before the IRS for failure to file his tax returns for several years. He went to Daley, for whom he had served as attorney for the Board of Election Commissioners, to ask for the help he knew the mayor had earlier given people in similar difficulties. Daley was a powerful man. Daley said he could not help. Ming died in prison of heart disease complicated by other ailments developed in jail, according to prison authorities. He was that first black to teach at the University of Chicago Law School. A nationally-known attorney, he had participated in the 1954 Supreme Court desegregation case and several other major civil right cases.

That sort of thing doesn't happen often, Schaefer says. More often, the courts are too lenient. Ming's friends say that his heart disease was more properly described as heartbreak.

McBride insists that the reason Washington's case went so far is because there was such a piling up of complaints—six. Normally, he admits, complaints such as the ones filed against Washington would simply be placed on file with a letter sent to the attorney warning that further action might be taken if more complaints are received. The record indicates, however, that such further action was rarely taken.

• The first complaint against Washington was received by McBride in 1964. Mary Ann Pridgeon, a machine operator in a printing company, needed a divorce. She paid Washington some money in 1963 but he never followed through. Washington says that she gave him $60 toward the $75-100 he requested as a retainer. Only when she was shown the letter she sent to the CBA, did she recall the amount. After paying him the first $60, Washington says, she told him she would pay him no more until he did what she thought he should do. She attempted to "dictate" the conduct of the case, he says. Sometime later, in 1964, she filed a complaint with the CBA. Though he felt he had earned the $60 in his preliminary dealings with her, he returned the money. No action was taken on that complaint.

• Ella Liggins, who was then a housekeeper, paid Washington $50 toward a $175 total fee for a divorce. She claims that she called his office several times but he didn't return her calls. Washington says he made it clear through his secretary that he could not proceed until she gave him more money. Another attorney called him, he says, to tell him he was taking over the case. Washington didn't refund Liggins' money. In 1965, she complained to the CBA. In 1969, she still did not have her divorce. No action was taken against Washington on that complaint, either. McBride explains that this was normal procedure. The Committee didn't act until the complaints began to mount up. It isn't clear, however, why the complaint that started the snowball against Washington started with only one form letter, regarding a complaint filed in December 1966, by Eugene A. Wilcher and subsequently withdrawn. How did it happen that McBride didn't send an omnibus letter to Washington, detailing all three complaints? He says the letter was sent out routinely and then, when Washington didn't respond, the files were searched for earlier complaints. The logic is not entirely clear. Why does a person's failure to respond to a form letter arouse suspicion that there may be other complaints against him? Well, perhaps there is some logic in that. But the coincidence of these events continues to be troublesome.

• Nathan Hudson needed a lawyer because his wife was suing him for divorce. He gave Washington $15 in May 1966 and another $15 in July. He had met Washington at the Holy Name Society in 1964. When the divorce case came up in court, Washington failed to show. The CBA provided Hudson with legal service. Washington offers the same explanation as in the previous cases: Hudson had failed to pay the balance of an agreed-upon fee. Hudson says Washington only asked for $30 to represent him in court.

• Betty Steele still didn't have her divorce in 1970, having hired Washington in 1966. She had met him in the Democratic Hall at 47th and Wabash. She paid him $75 toward his standard fee for divorce, $175. (In 1965, I paid $450 to a black lawyer who was doing a great deal of *pro bono* work for the civil rights movement. My husband paid $1,500 to his white lawyer downtown. Washington seems to have been giving divorces away.) Steele says she never heard from him again. He says he never received the money she had agreed to pay before he would proceed. She filed her complaint in July 1967.

- Early White, a welder, served three and a half years in the Army with Washington. They were both sergeants. He says, "Harold was a brilliant fellow with a wonderful wit." Naturally, when he was in trouble and needed a lawyer, he turned to Washington. He, too, went to the Democratic Hall to meet him and gave him $75 to handle a traffic violation. Three months later, he paid him another $75 to complete the stipulated fee. Washington didn't show up for the court date. The court gave him a continuance. Washington's secretary explained that he had been in Springfield for a vote. At the next court date, Washington was absent again. White says there was a mix-up. Another continuance was granted. White went to Washington's office and brought him to court. The judge granted the jury trial he requested. The date was set for January 11, 1967. White says the judge told him not to come back on that date; only the lawyer need appear. But he had to post a $25 bond. White says, "The mix-up came in," when Washington didn't appear on January 11. According to White, the trial was held on June 10 without notice for him to appear; there was subsequently a warrant for his arrest. White complained to the CBA in June 1967. He was never arrested. He lost his bond money. Washington maintains that there was simply a series of mix-ups and errors and that he had no intention of defrauding White. He did make several court appearances, he insists.

White is the only one of the six complainants who could be found. In response to questions about the complaint and his subsequent appearance at the hearing held by the Committee on Inquiry, he says, "I don't know anything about the Bar Association." Asked whether he made the complaint, he says, "Yes and no. I'm not talking about it. There's no trouble between Harold and me."

Does White mean that his complaint was not all that it seemed from the record, that perhaps something was happening behind the scenes, that his visits to the Democratic Hall were not always to see Washington or to participate in local politics? Or are his remarks simply an effort to avoid further discussion of the matter in an effort to protect Washington, who was now running for mayor? "I know this will be all over the front pages of the paper and I don't want to talk about it," he says. It is difficult to believe that a man who served happily for three and a half years in the South Pacific with Washington would have filed a complaint against his old friend in the matter of $150. On the other hand, he worked hard for his money and Washington had not provided him with the service he had paid for. Still, it is hard to imagine White having made that complaint without a little urging. Most men develop a strong loyalty to their Army buddies. Perhaps there was something else at stake: the Machine was able to offer all kinds of favors to people when they wanted to get something done. And it does seem a strange coincidence that three complaints against Washington were filed so soon after he was elected to a seat in the House over Mayor Daley's objection, on the insistence of a black politician who was becoming very popular. The coincidence is made even stranger by the fact that two of these complainants are known to have had associations at the Democratic Hall.

Mere coincidence? Well, maybe. Wilcher filed a claim in December 1966. McBride sent the following form letter to Washington on Jan. 5, 1967.

> Dear Sir:
>
> Enclosed is a copy of a letter received from Eugene A. Wilcher.
>
> This communication was considered by the Committee on Inquiry, which directed me to advise you that while it is not treating the letter as an inquiry at this time, it is requested that

> you write to the Committee a brief explanation of this matter.
> The Committee will again consider this matter on or about January 19, 1967, and it is suggested that you reply promptly in triplicate so that one copy may be sent to the complainant.

McBride says he usually sent out these letters about a month after the complaint was received. The letter and the complaint were normally then placed on file. In the case of this letter, however, there ensued what must be regarded as a tragicomedy of enormous proportions. Washington did not respond to the letter. McBride does not explain the procedure for discovering whether an attorney responds. On Feb. 24, McBride moved the case forward a bit; it was advanced "from a mere request for information to a formal inquiry." The record on Wilcher seems to be among those records destroyed. Perhaps Washington owed him $200. On March 6, Washington received a notification of the inquiry. Again he did not respond. On April 17, McBride notified Washington that "a hearing on Wilcher's Complaint" would be held on April 24. Washington still didn't reply. On Aug. 28, he was served with a subpoena issued by the Supreme Court. He called on the day of the hearing to request a delay because he was "confined at home." McBride obliged. The new hearing date was Sept. 11. Washington sent a telegram on that day: "Regret cannot respond to subpoena. Legislature in session, two weeks continuance would be adequate." The hearing was postponed again, until Nov. 20. Washington once again failed to show.

McBride took a new path that suddenly opened to him. On Jan. 26, 1967, he sent a new form letter advising Washington of the complaint of Nathan Hudson. Again, no response. On March 6, McBride wrote Washington that a hearing had been set for April 24. Still, Washington ignored the summons. On Aug. 28, he was served with another subpoena. When he didn't appear, the Committee on Inquiry sent him another letter offering a continuance until Sept. 11. Washington called to ask for more time. He got it. The Committee seemed to be endlessly patient. But persistent. It *would* hold a hearing on these complaints. The new hearing was moved up to Nov. 20. A new subpoena was served on Washington on January 21, 1968, after he again failed to appear. What was going on in the man's mind?

The full hearing was finally held. The complainants were requested to appear. Some were subpoenaed. The evidence was heard. Washington was absent. The Commissioners recommended a five-year suspension. Washington was notified of the Committee's recommendation on March 18. A hearing on the report was set for March 21. He did not appear at the hearing. What *was* going on in his head? The case was then turned over to the Board of Managers of the CBA, who sat as commissioners of the Supreme Court. The Board set April 9 as the date on which to file objections to the report. Finally, Washington responded through his attorney. On May 5, 1969, he asked for more time to offer proof of his innocence. The Board granted the time and, on July 10, his attorney appeared before it with Washington's response. The substance of the charges and the responses to Counts 1 through 6 have already been described. Counts VII and VIII state: "Respondent failed to appear at any of the hearings before the Commissioners, and in particular, failed to appear and respond to two Subpoenas *duces tecum* issued by the Clerk of the Supreme Court of Illinois which Subpoenas were duly served upon Respondent in connection with the complaints of Eugene A. Wilcher and Nathan L. Hudson. That the above and foregoing conduct of Respondent tend to bring the bench and bar into disrepute." Washington replied:

> That as to those charges, Affiant was guilty of negligence in not taking advantage of the many opportunities given him to appear and explain his side of the other charges against him, and his reason for not following through evolved around many personal problems that he was having at the time which problems are too numerous to enumerate in a document such as the one being submitted. That he realizes the seriousness of his acts in not properly following through on the charges, and he realizes the number of opportunities given him by this body showed a great effort to hear his side of the story and to not act without so doing. That sometimes personal problems are enlarged out of proportion to the entire life picture at the time and the more important things are abandoned. That this

> section is an appeal to you to permit Affiant a chance to do what you had afforded him before, to explain that there was no effort on his part to convert money of clients and that he has an explanation for the charges, although some of the situations probably could have and should have been handled more judiciously.
>
> And further Affiant sayeth not.

In addition he asked for more time to submit further proof of his innocence—documents that he said were stored away.

The Board of Managers refused his appeal for more time and accepted the verdict of the committee, though it did not accept its recommendation for a five-year suspension but rather reduced the penalty to one year.

Question: Did McBride pursue Washington so relentlessly because he was angered at Washington's failure to respond? Most lawyers who received those initial letters from him did respond, he says. "They might be evasive in their responses but they did reply and they did respond to subpoenas in the rare cases when they were used." Rare? Of the 1,500-1,600 complaints received every year, only 15-20 ever got beyond the form letter. Was it because of that pile-up of complaints? Well, the first letter was sent out on only one complaint. Three others were received after the initial pursuit began. Then there was that sudden onslaught of complaints—three in one year, all of which were received after the initial letter was sent. The case could have been politically motivated, but we can't accuse McBride without more evidence, which seems impossible to locate. Equally impossible to locate, it seems, is any evidence that those three complaints filed in 1967 were made at someone else's urging. But Judge Schaefer says that, for most cases of malpractice, "the courts are often too lenient." How did it happen that the court wasn't lenient with Washington? Perhaps it was because he was so incredibly unresponsive. A couple of lawyers who prefer anonymity suggest that, by his conduct, he insulted the Committee and thus raised their ire. It just may be that simple. Or it may not. Perhaps it was Washington's slovenliness that brought his disgrace upon him. Had he responded to the initial letter of inquiry he might have avoided the whole business. But that coincidence keeps asserting itself. Supposing he had responded to the first letter. What would have happened then? There are those who insist that because the whole affair was politically "rigged," the consequence would have been the same even if he had promptly responded to every communication. Perhaps. Perhaps not. But it couldn't have helped that he failed to respond all those times. The record indicates that those who fail to respond are treated more harshly than those who respond promptly. Oswald says that the failure to respond is considered a sign that the attorney has contempt for the Supreme Court. In fact, the decision of the Court in Washington's case corresponds quite exactly to the other cases that do get go the Court. It is puzzling. If there was one thing Washington knew all too well, it was that, somehow inexplicably, the standards of behavior in this country and especially in Chicago in the sixties, rise when you are black—or Jewish, or Hispanic, or Vietnamese. More is required to stand on the same step. So how could he have put himself in such jeopardy? How could he have ignored those subpoenas? Even if he thought as he did, that the whole business was politically motivated? Even more so if he had that suspicion. Had he never heard or forgotten Supreme Court Justice Cardoza's admonition: "The mere summons to appear at such a disciplinary hearing and make report as to one's conduct may become a slur and a reproach."

By the same measure, how could he have failed to file his tax returns? Sure, the number of people who don't file their tax returns are legion. But they aren't building political careers. And they aren't "uppity" blacks, those who expect to make careers in the white world. Washington forgot, when he failed to respond to those summonses and failed to file his tax returns, that not only must blacks perform better and keep their noses cleaner, but when they get into trouble, they are punished more severely. Though this has improved in recent years, it is still true that more blacks than whites are sentenced to jail for the same crimes across the board—blacks go to jail more often than whites for longer periods for the same crimes.

Failing to file one's taxes gets most people a slap on the wrist and a fine. A jail sentence is practically unheard of, except for a few famous cases, among them Ming and Washington, two black attorneys, one teaching at a prestigious law school, the other a state representative. Examples to the rest of us? Sure. Examples to the blacks that they better not aspire too high? Maybe. Examples to blacks that they better not defy Mayor Daley? You betcha.

Judge Sam Perry, who tried Washington's tax case, asked the state's attorneys whether other legislators who had not filed their tax returns had been prosecuted. "It's a pretty well-known fact that there's been a lot of laxity in that," he said, "and I think I should have some assurance that all the legislators and lawyers are being treated alike. . . I have heard rumors. . . .There may have been some free rides."

But Washington didn't get a free ride. He was not only a black legislator in the Democratic Party being prosecuted by a Republican prosecutor who was digging up violations by Democrats, he was also a maverick Democrat bucking the Machine in Chicago and making waves for the white power structure in the nation. Though he did not take a visible activist role in the civil rights movement of the sixties and though he has always been careful to avoid confrontational politics, there were more than 500 items in his FBI file for activities associated with civil rights and civil liberties. The FBI, through its Cointelpro operation, did not discriminate in their probes between the radicals and the liberals. They were all "subversives." Obviously, Washington was dangerous. Forty days in County Jail, three years probation, and $1,000 fine. For not filing tax returns for four years and consequently owing the government the huge total of $508.

Had Washington fought the case, he probably would have won, several attorneys have said, but he wanted to avoid the publicity of a court battle. He pleaded "no contest," in effect admitting his guilt, guilt for not filing for four years. The prosecutors, to add dash to their case, charged him with not filing for nineteen years but they did not pursue the charge. Obviously, they did not have the evidence. Had they been able to make a case, they surely would. They hoped only to dirty the water enough to get a stiffer sentence by making that baseless charge. It disappeared into the record. But it was on the record for Bernard Epton's lieutenants to unearth and play on as if it were the real thing. But that's another story to be told later.

Washington cannot be credited with ignorance. He knew well these facts of black life and political life. So how could he have let it happen? How could he have let things slide, knowing that as a black public official dedicated to civil liberties and civil rights, he could have no dirty linen at all?

Several explanations have been advanced. David Potter, Washington's press secretary for the campaign, a former editor of the *Chicago Defender* who has known Washington for twenty years, says, "One of the reasons I like the guy so much is because he's a slob with a suit on. I find it endearing. He represents Everyman. He would be more comfortable in a robe and slippers than a suit. His collection of ties is ghastly, not because he doesn't have taste but just because he doesn't give a damn. He just doesn't care. He's all business. Nothing else makes any difference. He's a man who cares, perhaps, too much for people. He is really an all-work, no-play type. I can't imagine him sitting down for ninety minutes to watch a movie. I can easily see him letting things slide that aren't central to his concerns." Pressed, however, Potter isn't sure that he can reconcile the degree of sloppiness involved in the suspension from the bar with the Washington he knows. "He's not that much of a slob. Actually, he's a well-organized guy. Furthermore, he is an honorable man. I can't imagine his ignoring all those letters and subpoenas without some underlying cause." So what was that underlying cause?

Judge Pincham suggests that Washington was "just so damn busy that he didn't even notice what was happening." Besides, he adds, "no one paid any attention to that stuff anyhow." That too-busy-to-notice explanation is commonly heard. It's offered by Washington himself, though he did say that perhaps the answer "can be discovered by a psychiatrist."

Then there's the theory, advanced by someone who prefers anonymity, that Washington might have figured that "he could get away with that stuff because he was in the State House." Is that Washington's style? There is a certain arrogance associated with such an assumption. Is Washington that arrogant? Pressed, this informant says, no, he doesn't think so. Sure, he is stubborn—bull-headed, in fact—but not arrogant. "He's a pretty human guy," he adds. That seems to be the general feeling.

So what is the answer? The too-busy-to-notice explanation won't wash any better than the others. Who is too busy to notice things that can have a devastating effect on his career? He couldn't know of its effect? Nonsense. A man as cautious as he is always calculates the odds. Washington is well-known for such calculations. So why did he permit himself to get into all that tsouras? There is an explanation that rings true. To get it, we must look back over the events of Washington's adult life. Not all the way back. Just to his years at Roosevelt College. Washington says that the happiest time of his life was spent in school. In high school he was a star athlete. His years at Roosevelt need no further explication. Though less well-documented, his years at Northwestern were obviously good ones. He emerged from law school at thirty years old, at the prime of his life, with, it seemed, everything going for him. He could not help but succeed. Those who knew him expected to soon see his name up in lights, so to speak. Instead, for nearly twenty years, his career was largely limited to the reaches of the 3rd Ward and the capitol of Illinois, not exactly the most illustrious, star-filled places in the world, though they did obviously provide great satisfaction.

A closer review of the events of those years shows a man who spends seven years in an integrated world—though being the token black at Northwestern can hardly be described as integration—in which he plays a significant role. He is widely admired and respected. He is his own man—independent, self-reliant, a leader. Then comes graduation. He joins his father's law firm, never an extraordinarily successful one but, with Washington's potential, it can become so. But it doesn't because he can't put his heart in it. He is regularly broke and, though he doesn't care much about money, being truly broke is quite another matter. His father's wealth is helpful in emergencies but not something he wants to have much to do with. Many young lawyers have an uphill struggle, some give up, but for blacks it is even tougher because their clientele is so dreadfully poor. Especially in 1953, blacks are very poor. The sums described in the suspension case give some indication of how poor they are. So Washington struggles to earn a living but spends most of his time at the 3rd Ward office, unable to bear the tedium of simple divorces and house sales. At his father's death, he gets a job in the Corporation Counsel's office. He hates it. He goes to work for the alderman. He hates that. He goes to work for the Industrial Commission. It is tolerable but not much more. Meanwhile, he is spending the better part of his life building Metcalfe's organization, waiting to be slated for that elusive seat somewhere in the city or state government. He knows that Metcalfe will do all he can for him but that Daley will do everything he can to prevent him from being slated. He is too independent, too much of a loudmouth for the mayor. Finally his time comes. He gets that coveted spot in the State House that he has been awaiting so long. At the end of the first term, he gets word that Daley wants to dump him. The Machine just won't tolerate independence. He toes the line on many issues, playing the loyalist, bucking the Machine only on those issues that are crucial to him—race and civil liberties. And all the admiration and respect he enjoyed in college, in law school, and in the 3rd Ward are not so easy to attain in that legislature filled with Daley's boys. Blacks are not admired and respected by the white Daley loyalists and Republicans. Not exactly "boys," Machine loyalists aren't exactly men, either.

Washington remains cheerful, warm, accommodating, energetic. But inside, where it counts, he begins to ache. Not enough to impair his immediate political activities but enough to threaten his future. It is such an uphill struggle, neverendingly frustrating. A man of extraordinary self-control and boundless energy, he manages to keep the balls juggling. His constituency loves him. The YDs still look to him for guidance and work for him in the elections. His colleagues respect him but many are ambivalent—they can't help but like him but they don't trust him. He's not one of them. He's too much of an independent for the regulars and a little too much a race leader for the white liberals. But for Washington, his independence and his race leadership represent painful compromise, too many deals cost so much. He is not truly independent. If he were, the Machine would destroy him. They would fight him and they would win. Though he has built his own election apparatus in the 3rd Ward, he cannot win the rest of the District without the help of the Machine. They have the cards and they will play them against him if he gets too much out of line.

He always does his homework for the legislature, is prepared on the issues as he always has been; he speaks eloquently, does his ward work, and he tends his political patch carefully and assiduously. But there is inside him that ache. Not the pain you take to a doctor or take an aspirin or vitamins for, not even the kind of pain for which you take tranquilizers. It's more like a vague feeling of something missing, like the loss of some of your nerve endings, the connections that keep everything working. It's as if you might come apart unless you concentrate on keeping yourself together.

He drinks a little to ease the pain. Sometimes he drinks more than a little—the great joy of his life, a few years ago, was to discover that he could voluntarily stop drinking, that he was not an alcoholic. And he lets things slide—bills, tax returns, letters and phone calls to people who urgently request an answer, small legal cases for which he has already taken a fee. Sometimes he doesn't turn up for a dinner party, a lunch date, a meeting.

Being beholden to the Democratic Machine, to any machine, is a heavy burden, a depressing burden. What happens when you get depressed? Not clinically depressed, not so depressed that you seek psychiatric help or wind up in a hospital but, as psychiatrists say, situationally depressed. Not blue. Judge Pincham says, "Whites get depressed, blacks get the blues, the down and out blues." Washington didn't have the blues. He appeared to be a happy man. But he had what was described by William H. Grier and Price M. Cobbs years ago as "black rage." He was angry, fearfully angry that he was, because he was black, mired in the servitude that was inescapable for an honest black man who had chosen a political career in Chicago in the fifties. But he was not a man given to expressing anger, having learned the lessons of the middle class—black and white—all too well. Instead, he turned his rage inward. It was converted to depression. If you don't express anger, it must find some other expression, the most common being depression, the feeling of being weighed down by iron balls.

Who of us does not know the experience of letting things slide when we're down? We do the absolute necessities: go to work, diaper and feed the baby, pay the telephone bill when the disconnect notice comes. But anything, anything extra is too much, just too much. Income tax returns? When your taxes are deducted automatically from your paycheck and you don't earn enough to owe the government more than a few dollars? Return phone calls? The easy ones, perhaps. Perhaps. Answer letters? It's just too much. It's enough to do the absolutely necessary things, especially when those things involve constant obligation to others.

Was Washington so depressed? He never appeared to be. He was affable, interested, cheerful, involved. Can it be true that a man who performed as well as he did was actually depressed enough to let some crucial things slide? Listen to his old friend, Cecil Troy, who was poor, too, in the fifties and sixties, so poor that he couldn't contribute more than a few dollars to Washington's campaign funds, though he ardently supported him. "Whatever he did all those years that got him in trouble, he did because he was in a state of depression, starving to death on 47th Street, and then emasculated by that political scene [the Machine]. It's happened to thousands and thousands of young blacks. I've seen my share. Whether they admit it or not, every bastard who is in that scene is emasculated. You don't survive otherwise. That's why I never got involved in politics. I saw what happened. I couldn't stomach it. He has more guts than I could ever have."

Those are strong words. But the analysis rings true to those who have known Washington long enough and have watched his career. His old friends who were bewildered by the revelations of his wrongdoing breathe a sigh of relief when they hear Troy's words. They are relieved to finally understand what seemed to be a tragic contradiction in Washington. "Of course, Harold would only have done such dumb things if he was depressed and couldn't keep everything going."

But there's only hindsight to prove this theory. Washington wasn't even aware himself of this process going on in him, though he knew there was something mighty amiss in his life. He is not a man to feel sorry for himself or to ask for sympathy from others. But he does say, flippantly, "Ask a psychiatrist," when asked for an explanation of those "mistakes."

Is there any more solid evidence? Well, take a look at his record since he broke completely with the Machine. That 1977 run for mayor of Chicago was not designed to win. He knew he couldn't win. He was, instead, announcing to all who would listen, and many did, that he was now his own man, he was free, independent, filled with elation, ready to take on the tigers. He won his State Senate seat again by only 212 votes but it was a heartening win. He knew that he could win a race for Congress against Benny Stewart. He had built his base, the constituency that would give him that seat, independent of the Machine. And his record since 1977? That of an independent, that of a man who has ties only to those he agrees with, to those he serves, a man finally beholden only to those who elected him.

He quit drinking, now takes only an occasional cocktail at a party. Dempsey Travis sees that event as a landmark change in the man. He began to file his income taxes, paid his bills reasonably on time. Oh, he's still late occasionally, still doesn't return every phone call or answer every letter, but he's no more of a slob than many of us. He is, as Potter says, a representative of Everyman. But he is, Potter adds, and dozens agree, an extraordinarily well-organized man with a mind to match that external organization. It's not neatness that counts in life; the test of a well-organized person is whether he or she can locate what they need without a great waste of time. Washington is not neat but he knows where things are.

Which is not to say that there is not in Washington a lingering aftermath of that long ache. One of his followers noted that he sometimes looks "as if he is covered with a layer of dust." There is, regularly, a certain sadness around his eyes. It is a sadness that cannot, will not, go away, the sadness of years spent in partial servitude, of shame for often choosing political expediency over cherished life goals, of damaging mistakes made in the service of that expediency. That pain continues to plague him. His first reluctance to take on the mayoralty contest, with all the problems that it represented, reflects it. But it is also clear from his conduct since 1977 and in his campaign for mayor, that he succeeds most of the time in brushing off the dust, that his ambition, his driving need to serve, his self-confidence and extraordinary ability have once again become the ruling forces in his life.

William Clements, a black artist who has eyes to see better than most of us, who lives in Washington's neighborhood and sees him regularly on the street, observes an angry look in his eyes. "It's a scowl, not a mean look, not as if he would hurt anyone. It's more as if he is thinking angry thoughts. It's the same look that Richard Wright had. We called him, lovingly, 'bitter Richard,' because his face seemed to reflect our own rage at injustice. I see that same expression in Washington's eyes." That expression, worn not for the public nor even in private conversation, but in those moments when he believes he is unobserved, in the grocery store, walking down the street, those private moments he still had before his ascendancy to the mayor's seat may reveal better than anything else his inner motives. He is still angry, but he has at last captured the power and the glory of leadership in the service of ideals that motivated his entire career. He need no longer let things slide. He may yet, at sixty-one, find happiness that equals those days in school.

In the Congress, and Some...

An inauguration is an inauguration is an inauguration except when it is Harold Washington's inauguration and then it is another inauguration. Listen to Judge Charles Freeman tell it:

I would have liked to go to Metcalfe's inauguration. That was in the time when I would have had to plan carefully to make such a trip but I would have sacrificed for it. I was pretty close to him and worked with and for him a long time, but that invitation never came. It went only to the elite blacks. I really liked what Harold did. He arranged plane trips for the few of us who could afford them, Charlie Hayes, Cecil Troy, and about fifty of us and then he got somebody to donate two buses for all the rest—all the people—mostly women—who stood on street corners handing out leaflets and working those precincts, the ordinary folks. One bus broke down along the way and they had to stand up in the other bus the rest of the way but everyone joked about it, they didn't complain.

Ralph invited all the people who raised a couple thousand or more for him. Harold told me I raised more than anyone else—it was only a couple thousand. Most people working for him couldn't get near that kind of money. They were the ordinary, poor folks, and they were the ones he invited.

It was real folksy, maybe too folksy. There was supposed to be a banquet. I asked Clarence McClain, who was handling the whole thing, how they were gonna pay for it. In that hotel, dinner for 200 people would be mighty expensive. McClain said not to worry, he had made an arrangement with a caterer to bring in a banquet.

"But the hotel won't let you do that," I said.

"Don't worry. It'll all work out fine."

Well, of course, it didn't work out fine. The hotel wouldn't let him bring food in from the outside so it was back to cold cuts in the courtesy room. But no one minded much.

Everyone ate a lot of cold cuts that weekend. Most of those folks couldn't afford to go out to restaurants so Harold had this courtesy room open all the time and it was always crowded. It was a three-day party in that hotel. From the time we left Chicago 'til we returned, three whole days, it was a wonderful party atmosphere, a real celebration.

I missed the swearing-in. He had it piped in over closed circuit tv in the hotel but I was so busy talking, it was over before I knew it. Then he made a speech in one of the special rooms in the hotel and everyone was happy.

Then he disappeared. You know the way Harold disappears. Went off to his own suite. He would wander around and talk to people and then he'd go off by himself. That's the way he is and people just seem to accept it. They know him and they don't argue with it.

Washington is, as Mike Robinson, who handles the Illinois delegation for Associated Press and has been a Washington watcher since 1968, says, a hidden person. Knowing him requires watching him for years, watching him in all the various settings in which he puts himself, in all the moods that are only subtly stated, in listening carefully for the words he omits as well as those he says, to his asides, his jokes, his mutterings, to his rhetoric and his careful lawyerly presentations. And then, Robinson says, he will remain hidden. He will talk political issues any time of the day or night but he guards the rest of his life—and many of his thoughts—like a man possessed, though that guarding seems very offhand, not intentional at all.

One of his staff people in Washington proposed that he sit down with him and put together a first-person story about growing up in South Side politics. Washington agreed enthusiastically. He never found time.

Washington estimated in November 1982, just before the election, that he would get 175,000-200,000 votes. When the count was in, he had 176,000, more than any other Congressional candidate in the nation, more than any 1st District candidate in history. It seems he had done his homework well. There are those who wonder whether chalking up such a large vote was necessary at the expense of his House record. To chalk up that vote, he was absent from the House much of the time. He spent every weekend and lots of weekdays in Chicago through his entire first term in Congress, missing many votes. During the 1983 mayoral campaign, his absentee record was used against him.

Well, let's examine that record. For the twenty bills the IVI considered critical to the welfare of the people, he was present and voted "correctly." On the Democratic alternative to the Reagan budget, on the Reagan budget itself, on retaining full power for the Legal Services Corporation (a bill introduced by Reaganites to strip the LSC of much of its power), on tax equity, on a bill to deny health benefits for abortion to federal workers, on the neutron bomb, on the MX and the BIB Bomber, and other such critical legislation, he was present and often spoke for or against the bill. He had the second highest liberal quotient in the House, only five points short of perfect, on a score of 1-100. In the *Chicago Sun-Times,* on his own index, Thomas Moore scored Washington among the three top Illinois representatives and, at the same time, among the most frugal of government spenders, as a consequence of his emphasis on cutting defense spending and farm and nuclear power subsidies. The other two top legislators named by Moore were Cardiss Collins, the woman who inherited the West Side seat when her husband was killed in a plane crash in 1974 and who went on to make a splendid record for herself, and Sidney Yates, long-time representative of Chicago's Lakefront liberals.

He received word that a crucial vote on the Reagan budget would come up late Friday afternoon. Every vote counted. His was mandatory. But he was to address the Black Muslims at a large dinner in Chicago on Friday evening. He couldn't make both. He called Wallace Muhammed to offer a tape of his speech that they could broadcast. Muhammed said no, they wouldn't settle for a tape. Washington's aide tried to ascertain exactly when the vote would come up. Maybe it would be early enough to be present for both. He had to be in Chicago. If he didn't show up at the Muslim dinner, he might lose Muhammed's endorsement and with it 2,000 votes. He would need those votes for reelection.

No one could say when the vote would come up. Washington offered Muhammed Charlie Hayes, a well-known labor leader who was known as a Washington supporter. Muhammed said no again. "We will have no one but you." There was nothing to do but get there. His aides booked him on the last plane to Chicago and scheduled a police escort to the airport. As soon as the vote was cast, he hopped into the waiting limousine, went nonstop under a shrieking police escort to the airport, and arrived an hour late to a cheering crowd of Muslims. An hour wasn't too long to wait, especially since their leader had told them to wait. They endorsed him.

Most often, Washington was on time for his speaking engagements—lunches, dinners, parties, receptions, meetings. Not in Washington. In the Capitol, he rarely went to the receptions and parties that are the social life of the city. Washington went only to receptions and parties where there were votes to be wooed. He went to those affairs because his political career demanded it, not because he enjoyed them, though one would think, watching him, that he enjoys nothing more than those hand-shaking, jovial appearances he puts in as a routine part of his life. And, in fact, he does enjoy them. He simply does not enjoy the appearances that are purely social. Activity has to be career-oriented, political in its purpose. David Riesman called that phenomenon a gyroscope in the inner-directed person, propelling him or her to a useful goal. Such people have no time for play.

It was estimated that, in the year after he had gone to the Capitol, he made about 400 public appearances, about seven per weekend if he campaigned every weekend during the year. He went everywhere where there were votes to be wooed. "From day one, he was running for reelection," David Canter says. It was inevitable that the Machine would run a candidate against him. The party moguls would not put up with another independent stand. He had to prepare to fight off their offensive. It meant building such a strong base that no contender could even be proposed.

Washington had been campaigning so much in the past few years, he would seem to have had little time for anything else—1975 for the Senate, 1977 for the mayoralty, 1978 for the Senate again, 1979 for Congress, and now, even before he settled down in his Washingotn office, he was hitting the trail for reelection again in 1982. Little wonder he had a few campaign bills.

Every Saturday at 12:30, he held a meeting—a rally—in the North Hall of the United Packinghouse Worker's headquarters at 4859 S. Wabash, in the heart of the 1st District, where his political office and the Citizens for Washington offices were located. Food was served, speeches were made. A regular report on the activities of the Congress—Washington's role in those activities—was presented. The issues of the day were discussed. Jane Byrne was criticized. An organization was built. There were constituents to be educated, to be politicized, to be satisfied—hundreds who came every Saturday at noon. There was an election to be won.

Back in the Capitol, Washington's staff were keeping their hands and eyes on the scene for him. William Ware, the chief of staff, a middle-of-the-road black liberal, Tony Gibbs, an aide, a black nationalist, and Steve Askin, a press aide, a white leftist, were sifting the issues, doing the research, preparing the speeches, and briefing Washington on what they saw as the critical problems to which he should devote his long days and nights in Washington. He valued the input of these three highly various people. And he valued the expertise that Ware brought to the political scene. He knew the significant actors in the drama. He made himself valuable enough to move into the top spot of deputy mayor in City Hall.

Is Washington more comfortable—personally and politically—with people like Bill Ware, the cautious, basically conservative type, than with the more flamboyant black nationalist or the fiery-eyed white socialist? Or has he given the top jobs to Ware because he knows that, most often, it is the centrist who can build the biggest constituency?

"I wouldn't begin to guess," a former Washington staff member who prefers anonymity, says, "even though I've known him for a long time. He is a most private person. One thing I will say is that I have to laugh when I see him characterized as a wild-eyed radical. Harold is certainly a militant spokesman for the black community but not at all the kind of radical that some of his white leftist supporters expect him to be. The one thing that is clear to everyone who has been associated with him is that he can and does listen to his constituents. He knows what they are thinking and he knows how to say the things they want to hear. He knows how to be their leader."

One of Washington's closest associates in Washington for the short time before his death was California liberal Phillip Burton, with whom he had formed a relationship years before in the Young Democrats. When Burton was seeking the nomination for Congress, Washington flew a contingent of Young Democrats to California to support him.

Every weekend since the election to Congress, he had been breakfasting with David Canter, chairman of the IVI and longtime participant in independent politics. They talked politics.

"He loves to talk politics, any and all politics," Canter says. Finally, in the fall of 1982, they talked mayoral politics. They met at the Hyde Park Coffee Shop, around the corner from his apartment, an inauspicious enough place, or at the Harper Square Restaurant, a couple blocks away, slightly more auspicious —a big breakfast there might cost $5—or at Canter's house.

Canter's son, Evan, was graduating from St. John's College and seeking a job in Washington's Congressional office. In the fall, after graduation, young Canter went to work for Washington. It wasn't a very high-level job, just above a student intern, but it was what he wanted for the year before he entered law school. In a conversation, Washington told young Canter that he had gone to college on an athletic scholarship. An athletic scholarship? At Roosevelt College? Washington is accused of periodically telling "legends" about his past. What a strange legend that is for a man of his type. He did regret, he has told others, that he was prevented by the school rules from excelling in more than one high school sport. Winning a state championship as a hurdler seems not to have satisfied his ambitions. Ralph Metcalfe had been an Olympic runner, had indeed gone to college on an athletic scholarship.

Canter had the 1983 mayoralty in his head throughout all those weekend breakfasts. But he knew that before any discussion of that election could move beyond idle talk, the '81 campaign for re-election to Congress would have to be won.

It had taken three years to pass a bill in the Illinois legislature making Martin Luther King's birthday a state holiday. In the Congress, John Conyers (D-Mich.), with twenty co-sponsors, was introducing a similar bill for a national holiday. He had first introduced it in 1968, when King died, and again nine more times. Washington joined the list of sponsors as soon as he arrived in

Congress. He was named Illinois coordinator of the National Holiday Committee, an organization designed to carry out a petition drive to support the measure.

Civil rights and civil liberties groups implored the freshman Congressman to take on an additional committee responsibility. The normal assignment for House members is two committees. Washington was on the Education and Labor committee and on Government Operations, assignments he had sought. To add one would require a rule change. But his friends were adamant: sixteen years of experience on the Judiciary Committee in the State House, particularly on issues of voting rights, desegregation, affirmative action should not just be flushed down the drain now. He joined the Judiciary Committee, to focus his efforts on the Civil and Constitutional Rights subcommittee.

Revolution, Richard Lewontin, writing about Darwin in the *New York Review of Books,* says, "is not an event but a process." And to that process many people, in many ways, contribute many different skills. The process takes years to complete, if indeed it is ever complete, continuing in a series of shifts and changes that historians can chart only long after a new revolution has occurred.

The civil rights movement of the fifties and sixties is seen by many as an incomplete revolution, one still to be finished at a future time, one interrupted, off the track. Another view sees the actions of that period as the beginning of a revolution that continues even to this day with the nature of the process changing as one set of demands is met or rejected and another emerges. In that earlier period, it was necessary to attain the basic civil rights for blacks; access to the institutions and services, both public and private, of the nation. The Voting Rights Act was the central accomplishment in that attainment. Millions of blacks, as a consequence of that Act, voted for the first time and have elected thousands of public officials since then. But because a revolution is a process, it is subject to be turned back, to be overturned by those forces that fought from the first to resist it.

So it was that in 1980 the pivotal accomplishment of the civil rights movement—the 1965 Voting Rights Act—was under attack. It also happened that Harold Washington went to Congress in 1980. Having won the fight on the floor of the Illinois Senate for the Human Rights Act, to further the revolution in his own state, Washington now took on, with his colleagues in the Judiciary Committee and the Congressional Black Caucus, the extension of the Voting Rights Act.

The liberals in Congress in 1965 had failed to get a bill passed that would provide blacks permanent protection of their vote. The bill was seen only as an emergency measure that would not be needed in fifteen years. In 1980, it was said, federal marshals would no longer need to supervise voter registration and voting in the South. Whites would not attempt to once again wrest away the voting rights of blacks. An optimistic view? There are those who maintain that it was rather the belief and hope of white southerners that, once the revolution was over, once blacks had "quieted down," the Voting Rights Act would run out and things would return to "normal."

There was strong sentiment in the Reagan Congress against the extension of the bill. It was said that it was no longer needed. But the NAACP, the SCLC, the Southern Poverty Center, and other organizations and individuals offered strong testimony that, without those federal marshals in the South, things would, indeed, return to "normal."

Blacks did not vote for Reagan. He hadn't asked for their votes. He owed them nothing. Neither did Henry Hyde (R-Ill.) who, with others in the Congress, attached amendments that would have grievously diluted the effectiveness of the bill.

First, he had held on to his state Senate seat, something unheard of in the halls of Congress. "They just didn't understand Chicago politics," Mike Robinson says. There was talk of voiding his election, of barring him from his seat.

Then, having finished with that business, Washington took to the floor of the House with flamboyant speeches against Reagan, calling the President "crazy" for having sent down to Congress the budget he did, cutting social services to the core.

This freshman Congressman was fast establishing himself as a bit of a nut. Then the mood changed. It was time to settle down for the hard work of getting through a strong version of the Voting Rights Act. The prudent, careful, lawyerly Washington emerged to conduct hearings in the South, to ask piercing questions, sift and weigh evidence, present arguments. Unlike the ordinary freshman Congressman who, Robinson says, "sits around and listens and occasionally comes up with some off the wall idea," Washington worked quietly and thoughtfully beside the veterans to get the job done.

Henry Hyde, who had been at the southern hearings with Washington, withdrew his amendment to submit a couple more that were not nearly so restrictive. He had, he said, seen evidence in those hearings of widespread activity to prevent blacks from registering and voting—the old-fashioned tactics, closing registration early, literacy tests, gerrymandering, and so on, Robinson reports.

When it was time to fight the amendments, Washington, Robinson adds, made every effort to "avoid grandstanding"—he made reasonable, carefully prepared speeches that addressed the issues and avoided rhetoric.

All six amendments were defeated.

"It was a team effort," Robinson says. "Washington is as astute in the cloakroom as any politician I've ever seen and I've been in this business for seventeen years." He insists that the Voting Rights Act Extension is due to the efforts of all those—Conyers, Washington, and the rest, who worked together to pass the bill untethered by restrictive amendments.

"What made Washington special in that scene was that he was a freshman who participated as an equal with the experienced legislators, unheard-of."

Thirty members of Congress, among them Harold Washington, sued Ronald Reagan in Federal District Court to challenge the President's right to send military aid and equipment to El Salvador. The suit charged that Reagan, Secretary of State Alexander Haig, and Defense Secretary Caspar Weinberger violated the War Powers Resolution, the Foreign Assistance Act, the Universal Declaration of Human Rights, the Geneva Convention. "The evidence is overwhelming that the President has certified more to what he wishes were the case in El Salvador than to what is actually taking place," Washington said.

Evan Canter was the point man on the nuclear freeze issue, to prepare background for speeches, for an insertion into the *Congressional Record,* for legislation. Washington was the major speaker at the April, 1982, rally at Kluczinski Plaza in downtown Chicago. He had been speaking out on the issue since he went to the Capitol, according to Bernice Bild, coordinator for the Illinois Nuclear Weapons Freeze Campaign. He was honored by the Chicago Peace Council in 1982 for his contribution to world peace. These were his new constituents, the peaceniks of Hyde Park-Kenwood. It was an issue he had long been sympathetic to but had stayed clear of earlier in his career—the local Democratic Party was not even a scant inch to the left of the most hawkish elements in the national party. Till the end, the Vietnam War was a just, sane war in the Central Committee of the local Democrats. Daley was most famous nationally for ordering a police attack against the antiwar demonstrators at the Democratic Convention in 1968 in Chicago and for his own behavior at that convention.

On nuclear power, too, Washington's Congressional opposition was not the favored position. Illinois has more nuclear power plants than any state in the nation. Most of his votes on defense issues and on other national issues flew in the face of the local Machine. Byrne had given the same "honeymoon" to Reagan that others had. It was left to the minorities and a few white liberals to criticize his budget, his social spending cuts, his defense spending increases, and the series of anti-black measures he introduced in the first two years of his term. Washington's speeches back home matched those he made in Congress. His re-election statement is typical:

> I want to continue the fight in the Congress and in the community against the dangerous troubling assaults upon our people.
>
> I am angered by the assaults on domestic justice, civil liberties and world peace launched by the rampant Reagan administration and its allies in Congress.
>
> I am angered by the needless suffering already inflicted on our community by inflation, by cutbacks in human survival programs, by elimination of jobs and training programs in our community. I am further angered by the slashing of federal programs for stimulation of Black business.
>
> I want to return to Congress to fight against a totally unprincipled Reagan and his ministerial minions who have set out to undermine the living standards of the Black community by quite deliberately creating unemployment on a scale that can never be tolerated in a civilized society and for which there is only one remedy—fight back and fight back until the battle is won.
>
> I want to return to Congress to fight the disease of Reagonomics—which is sweeping the country and threatening to devastate the working people of Illinois and kill the city of Chicago.
>
> I want to return to silence the drumbeats of war. To solve problems at home, we must stop squandering hundreds of billions of dollars on war programs, the neutron bomb and other massive weapon systems.
>
> I want to stop the secret shipments of hazardous nuclear waste on the busy highways where you and your family travel.

Washington fought Reagan on big issues and small ones. As he had in the State House, he raised the race issue wherever it was appropriate. On Reagan's effort to get tax exemptions for private clubs, Washington proposed that the exemption be limited to those clubs that do not discriminate against women and minorities.

At 7801 S. Wabash, Washington maintained his district office much as the 3rd Ward office had been run in the old days, though there were not the funds to provide the services that the Democratic Party had offered. In the first year, over 100 meetings were held there and over 5,000 names were logged in as having requested some service.

In December, 1981, the *Forge,* the Citizens for Washington newspaper, was launched and distributed throughout the district. Canter had proposed the paper in June but Washington had hesitated for several months. Where would the money come from? Campaign funds are not easy to collect six months after re-election. The weekend trips back to the district, the Saturday afternoon lunches, the three offices all cost money. But by early winter, he had decided to risk it. Once again, he would take a chance. The money would be found. The first issue appeared in December. Largely put together by Canter, the newspaper was a powerful campaign tool, with eight pages of photos and stories about Washington's efforts on behalf of the community and his stands on various issues. Printed in large red and black headlines with lots of photos, what it lacked in professional journalism it more than made up in zeal, the purpose of a campaign tool, after all. The four issues published from December through March added lustre to Washington's early bid for re-election, a testimony to his ambition.

"The First Congressional District has turned into one of the most vocal districts in the nation," he is quoted as saying. "If I am seen as a fighter, it is because I believe that the interests and concerns of our community are worth fighting for." Campaign rhetoric backed up with photos of the candidate at the front, with union leaders and workers, at hearings, on the streets.

In the March issue, on the front page, appears a message from Martin Luther King, Jr., urging people in Chicago to vote: "Think about the power of your vote. Join together with your friends and vote for civil rights candidates. If we can elect Negro sheriffs in Alabama, we can certainly elect civil rights candidates on the South Side of Chicago." Washington had come a long way from party discipline. King didn't realize how long it would take for South Siders to follow his advice.

The fight was on. Or so Jane Byrne thought. She floated the names of Gerald Bullock, state rep.; Lenora Cartright, her head of the Department of Human Services; Partee, and State Senator Richard Newhouse. Bullock told Byrne it would be suicidal to run against Washington. Cartright called Washington to deny that she was in the race. Partee was equivocal. He owed Byrne nothing but then she owed him nothing, either. In the primary that she had won, he had run on her opponent's ticket, the incumbent's ticket. Partee was a cautious politician. Newhouse refused to run.

There was no way out. Washington clearly had the nomination. Even Jim Taylor had announced his support. The slate-making committee, mindful of the meeting two years earlier at the Liberty Baptist Church, called an open meeting at a massive ballroom in McCormick Inn, a large near South Side hotel. Washington packed the hall with his people. Charlie Hayes rose to say, "The community demands that Washington be reslated." The sentiment was overwhelming. This time, they would not ignore the wishes of the people.

Washington arrived. "We are all Democrats," he said. "I am proud to have your nomination."

He couldn't miss. He had collected 250,000 signatures instead of the 610 (one-half of one percent of the voters in the previous election) he needed to get on the ballot. Why 250,000? Well, it was a lot safer that way. Who would dare contest a candidate who could round up that many signatures for a mere petition to get on the ballot? Obviously, a formidable organization was out there in the streets.

The election would be a shoo-in. Now it was time for Canter to start talking mayoral politics. Washington resisted. "I like the Congress. I'm having a ball. I'm secretary of the black caucus. I might even be elected chairman. What makes you think it should be me?"

"Ok, Ok, Harold. So it won't be you."

"Well, that's better. Now let's talk about the election. First, how do you know you've got the votes?"

Canter had the figures all ready. He had been reciting them to anyone who would listen. The votes were almost all in place. All that was needed was a registration drive to boost the black vote. Washington maintained, Canter says, "his charade. He still wasn't interested. Except, 'show me the figures,' he says."

Canter showed him. Assuming Washington, Daley, and Byrne in the race, and assuming an 80 percent black turnout with 80 percent of that number voting for Washington (258,000 votes), and assuming one-half of the Lakefront votes (32,000), and 9,000 Hispanics, the total was 299,000, or 32 percent of the total.

"Not good enough," Washington says.

"You're right. What we need is a larger registration of black voters."

It is June. The goal is 100,000 new black voters. Added to the 32 percent, this will produce 41 percent of the total vote, enough to win in a three-way race. If the new registrations can be gotten, the election can be won.

There were lots of people out there who wanted to win that election. A loose confederation of community groups—PUSH, POWER, TWO, and others—was formed in July and the registration drive was underway. It received a big boost from Edward Gardner, a black businessman, who gave $50,000 and by black radio station owners who donated time to push the campaign. Slim Coleman had the brilliant idea of getting permission from the Board of Election Commissioners to set up registration tables at local libraries, supermarkets, welfare offices, shopping malls. By October 5, the closing date for registration, there were over 100,000 new black voters on the rolls. The probability of a win was in place.

Meanwhile, Canter kept talking to Washington, listening to his demurs, ignoring them. In September, Washington went to Rome to the meeting of the Interparliamentary Union. As he was leaving, Canter handed him a 200-page plan for the mayoral campaign: budget, personnel, timetable, committees, literature.

When he returned, Washington called Canter to invite him to his house to discuss the plan. Late into the night, over cocktails, they talked. When Canter left, Washington walked out with him, to the all-night grocery to pick up a pack of cigarettes. As they parted, he said, "Dave, I'm game," and smiled his broadest grin.

Game, but not quite ready. "You and I can't do it alone. We need lots of help." He went back to Washington and thought some more. He called state treasurer Roland Burris and asked him to run. Burris turned him down. He was running for re-election; it was a sure thing. So Washington started, very quietly, out of sight of the press, in Canter's living room, to meet with businessmen, community leaders, political leaders, the organizers of the registration drive. There were questions. There was wild enthusiasm. There were doubts. There was elation. There was hesitation. There was support. There were promises of support—later. There was, however, enough to begin to put it together.

First, a campaign manager had to be found. There were hard qualifications: he had to know Chicago, from Howard Street to 130th Street and all the politicians between those two farflung boundaries. There would be no outsider who didn't know "Fast Eddie" Vrdolyak and Martin Oberman, and other slippery eels of Chicago politics. He must know them and have his own contacts in the wards.

The campaign manager also had to be loyal, "not a little bit loyal, not partially loyal, absolutely loyal. He has to be committed

1,000 percent to independent politics and to Harold Washington. No one with any connections with the Machine, with Daley, with any traditional Chicago politics need apply."

None of the candidates measured up. Renault Robinson, loyal, energetic, enthusiastic, who had been a major spearhead in the registration drive but who was largely inexperienced in city politics, was chosen.

True, the campaign was ready to go but Washington was still in doubt. He stayed in Washington for two weeks, was not heard from by either Canter or Robinson. Canter didn't give up. He sat in his living room every night for two weeks briefing Robinson. And, at his own expense, he printed petitions to be circulated in time to insure that Washington's name would be placed on the ballot.

Finally, Washington called. "Ok, Dave, I'm ready to go." He had still told no one, not even his own staff. But he had talked to a lot of people, asking for secrecy. How many people can keep a secret, especially such a secret? Rumors spread all over town. Washington would enter the race.

It wasn't a hard election. He had no competition. He got 176,000 votes, the largest vote for a Congressional candidate in the country. The new voters turned out at the polls and the turnout was higher than it had been in years. Adlai Stevenson, running for governor, the clear underdog, predicted to lose heavily, won a massive vote in the black community and lost the race by less than a percentage point. Washington had endorsed twelve candidates. All did well in the 1st District. It was a test run. There were, in his own district, some 175,000 votes for him to look forward to in the February mayoral primary.

On November 9, seven days after the Congressional election, a luncheon was held at the Hyde Park Hilton, the poshest spot on the South Side. Charlie Hayes was the chairman. Bankers, labor leaders, financiers, community leaders, every black "top dog" and a few whites—the hoi polloi. It was closed to the press. Canter presented his figures. A black could win the mayoralty. Everybody was shocked. Washington made his announcement: he would run for mayor.

On November 10, a press conference was held. With Washington, press conferences are as different from the usual as are inaugurations. Paul McGrath describes it in a November 26, 1982, issue of the *Reader:*

> The place was so packed that even those who got there on time couldn't all get in. By a couple of minutes after 11 there wasn't even any more room on the podium for the microphones of the press. "This is the last one to set up," shouted a black man from the dais. Another man added, "The rest of you are going to have to hold your microphones in your hands."
>
> Many big Chicago journalists were there, but this time they did not dominate the scene. Today they were just a few white faces in a big black crowd. Hugh Hill, the political editor of WLS TV, was standing toward the back of the crowd with his raincoat on looking vaguely uneasy.
>
> The journalists had come to hear Harold Washington declare his candidacy for mayor of Chicago, but they were not prepared for this most unusual of press conferences. The room was so packed that I couldn't get close enough to the wall to read the little sign that says, "Occupancy above ______ is prohibited." Whatever the legal limit was, it had been passed long ago.
>
> It took a big event to get the media stars out to the Hyde Park Hilton for a press conference. But most of the people there were not reporters. There were many recognizable faces—the Reverend Jesse Jackson, Slim Coleman, the Uptown community organizer, looking respectable in a Sunday-go-to-meeting navy blue overcoat, his hands jammed into the pockets. Bob Mann, former state representative and Hyde Park liberal. The Reverend Jorge Morales, head of the Westtown Coalition, a Latino group that has specialized in needling Mayor Byrne.
>
> But even this group of celebrities was outnumbered by black ministers, black lawyers, black doctors, black nationalists.
>
> The place was jammed and noisy. Periodically excitement would sweep the room when it was thought that Washington's arrival was imminent. "Ready?" said a guy on the platform. "All right. He's going to come in. We have to clear out the center." The call was picked up by

others. "We have to clear out the center so the working press can see."

Fat chance. No one was moving anywhere. You couldn't move, even when the humorless black security guys with sunglasses and lapel pins joined hands and pushed.

There were a lot of bosses and a lot of shouters. Gradually Renault Robinson took over. "OK, why don't you start your machines," he suggested to the reporters over the PA system. "Start all your machines."

This precipitated a crush as reporters tried to get to their equipment in the little forest of microphones taped to the podium. "All right, we're getting ready to start," said Robinson. "Let's go. Quiet please."

But there was another surprise for the minority of journalists in the crowd. "We'd like very much to bring on a gentleman that we've all been waiting for," said Robinson, who had by now taken command. "But first of all we'd like to have a quick opening with a prayer."

A prayer! What was this? The white media stars looked at each other. A black minister moved to the podium. "Let us pray," he commanded. "Gracious God we thank You that the man and the moment and the movement have met. We thank You that we have a man here who is a man not only for all seasons but a man for all of the people of Chicago." Here and there in the crowd black people responded, "Yeah," or "Amen."

On the following Saturday, Canter went to Washington's regular meeting. It was held not in the North Hall but the huge South Hall. It was jammed—about 2,000 people. He distributed those petitions he had kept in readiness. He had only had 25,000 printed. Those 2,000 people wanted a dozen apiece. There weren't enough to go around. They insisted on duplicating them then and there on any machine available. Canter protested, "The election board will toss them all out if they're not uniform."

250,000 signatures were ready to be filed. More had been collected but they had been put on the computer and the bad ones weeded out. Those 250,000 signatures, however, were divided. Half were filed on December 13, for Washington as a candidate in the Democratic primary; half were held for filing on December 31 as an independent candidate to run in the general election. The decision about whether the second half would be filed had to wait for Richard Daley's decision about how *he* would file. Every day, the press reported another shift. He couldn't make up his mind. If he ran as a Democrat in the primary, and Byrne won, he would be locked out of the general election. You can't run in both. If he waited and ran as an independent in the general election, he might stand a better chance because, though Republicans never take a big chunk of the vote, it is a three-way race. On the other hand, with Washington in the primary, it, too, was a three-way race, though there was little likelihood, his advisors assured him, that Washington would make much of a dent. Still, it would be a three-way race. And Washington's votes would be taken from Byrne, not Daley. She was the one they were angry at. Without the whole black vote and without the Daley loyalists, Byrne was a sure loser. Washington, too, was a sure loser. The word was out that Washington would follow Daley into the general election if he went. Washington, too, needed a three-way race. Daley didn't need to wait for the general election. He clearly had it tied up. Washington and Canter took no chances. They waited for him until 4:59 in the office adjoining the Board of Election Commissioners on December 31. He didn't show. As one of his followers in Bridgeport said, "Richie didn't do his paper work."

There is disbelief. Can it be true? Are they truly standing here in this massive crowd waiting to hear the victory speech of the first black mayor of Chicago? There are some in this crowd who feel as if they are sleepwalking. They will wake, they are sure, to find that this balmy night in February is only a lovely dream, that there is actually a huge snowstorm blowing outside their windows and that Mayor Byrne has been re-elected. They are smiling absently, as if in a daze. They are amazed at the crowds of young people around them who are so confident, so self-satisfied. These youngsters are not in a state of shock. They have not waited as long to see this dream come true.

There is jubilation, almost delirious joy. They did it. They pulled it off. It's not a dream. There are 15,000 jammed into the ballrooms, corridors and lobbies of the first two floors of the McCormick Inn, singing, dancing, talking, laughing, waiting patiently for Congressman Harold Washington to come to the speaker's platform to tell them that the word is official. He really is the Democratic nominee for mayor. A cautious man, he will not emerge from the twenty-third floor to make that announcement until 98 percent of the vote is counted.

There is watchfulness. What will happen in this city known so long as the most segregated city in America, this city where the Mayor's lieutenants, desperate to win, threatened whites that a vote for Richard Daley, Jr., would mean a "disastrous" vote for Harold Washington and where Richard Daley, seeking black votes, distributed only cartoons on the South and West sides, while he blanketed the white communities with expensively prepared literature explaining his candidacy.

There is cynicism. "We elected a reform candidate last time, too, remember?"—the cynicism that has so long been the stance of Chicago blacks who have been betrayed over and over again by white and black politicians alike.

There are elegantly dressed business and professional men and women—more than a few of the men with paunches, grey, lined, a little stiff—the lawyers, doctors, dentists who have prospered as the black community has prospered in the last twenty years. And there are elegantly dressed young professionals for whom the civil rights movement created opportunities their parents only imagined.

There are working people—steel workers, waitresses, machin-

ists, janitors, old and young. There are the unemployed, from Wisconsin Steel and from all the other plants that have been hard hit by Reaganomics. And there are the youth, the unemployed youth, the kids in college, and the kids in high school. All ages, all stages, all points of view, a few whites, mostly blacks.

Some are jammed into the ballroom on the second floor of McCormick Inn, where Morris Ellis's band is playing and where the television crews are doing what they can to provide some interesting news from Washington's victory celebration for the people at home, the people who, like those at the hotel, are waiting up to hear Washington claim his victory. The ballroom is surprisingly quiet, considering the number of people there. They are talking softly, laughing a little, struggling to maintain a little space to breathe, to lift an arm to scratch a brow. Occasionally a cry rises in the air: "We want Harold." No one dares to smoke. No one boos Jesse Jackson as he clings tenaciously to the microphone on the speaker's platform for what seems like hours, and the crowd follows him as he leads them in endless verses of "We Shall Overcome" and "We Won't Let Anyone Turn Us Around," but there are many who wish the floor would suddenly swallow him up. "What's he doing up there?" is asked throughout the ballroom. This is serious politics here and there is no place for Jesse Jackson.

The hours creep by. Some people arrived at seven when the polls closed. A few, a mere handful, tired of waiting, exhausted by the strain of the day's tension, leave at midnight, one, one-thirty. Finally, at a quarter to two, Washington appears to make his statement. There is no doubt left. Ninety-eight percent of the vote is in. He would not have risked an embarrassment. He is a cautious man.

It is a blend of cautious conservatism, hopeful optimism, and capacity for rage, sweeping back and forth across the black community for many years, that has created this spectacular victory for Congressman Harold Washington.

There are in this hall tonight cynics who are saying that it wasn't a true victory but one that merely fell to Washington in the internecine warfare that the elder Richard Daley bequeathed to this city. Of course, Washington benefitted by that white power struggle, but it is patently untrue that black victory was automatic. Even with the 100,000 new black voters registered with the hope of unseating Jane Byrne, the victory was not assured. Those new voters rejected several anti-Machine aldermanic candidates in November 1982. They did so well for the Machine, in fact, that "Fast Eddie" Vrdolyak, party chairman, claimed credit for that registration drive. The Machine aldermen probably only did so well because they came in on the coattails of gubernatorial candidate Adlai Stevenson III, and he only did as well as he did because blacks would have voted for any decent Democrat to register a vote against Reaganomics.

No, this victory is no win by default. It represents the sheer power of the candidate's appeal to the voters, to their deep wariness and intense hopefulness. He spoke to their legitimate aspirations to political power with his simple, straightforward description of the disparities between black and white in the city. Some people, naive about the process of politics in Chicago, are accusing him of making racist appeals in his promises of equity for blacks. A mayoral candidate has to address the whole city, they say. Washington concentrated most of his efforts on blacks. Racism, they shout.

They don't understand Chicago. They don't understand that most politicians here have built their bases in their own racial and ethnic communities. Before Washington could hope to go to the white community as a serious contender for the mayoralty, he had to win big in his own community.

While they appreciate Washington's deep concern for the welfare of his people, it is clear from the remarks being made tonight that his audience also applauds his appeals for racial unity. They believe that with him in City Hall they will get fair representation, a fair distribution of the goods, but no more. With their longstanding cautiousness comes a certain hard sense of reality. They know what is possible.

At the same time, it seems clear in this sea of faces tonight that Washington has met the hopes and the aspirations of his people. The crowd here at McCormick Inn looks much like the one that assembled in 1963 in Washington, D.C., for the first great Civil Rights March. At the march, inspired by the joy and excitement emanating from the crowds in front of him, Martin Luther King, Jr., improvised his "I Had a Dream" speech that has annually rung out of our television sets since his death. He said, "I have a dream that, one day, on the red hills of Georgia the sons of former slaves and the sons of former slaveowners will be able to sit down together at the table of brotherhood. . . . Now is the time to lift our nation from the quicksands of racial injustice to the solid rock of brotherhood." It is perfectly plain to all who listen to him tonight that Harold Washington also has a dream, that he, too, is improvising a speech for the occasion. It isn't one of those great Biblical speeches that King made. But he is no slouch with the language. He has become famous in the campaign for his colorful alliteration—"ministerial minions"—and his lofty metaphors. The kids in the ghetto call him "Harold Skytalkin'" and some people think his language pretentious. They resent the fact that they don't always understand all the words he uses.

King was inspiring his own people and appealing to the consciences of whites. Twenty years later, Washington is extending that message. At 1:45 A.M. tonight, he joins the cheering crowd to say, "Let us heal the wounds of this city. . . ."

To those who have opposed us, we open our arms . . . and invite you to join our movement. . . . Our concern is to build.

Our concern is to heal. Our concern is to bring together. Our concern is to make the Chicago economic base a much more fruitful oasis that has open doors for all its citizens. . . . We have to build, we have institutions to maintain, we have taxes to raise, we have crime to get rid of. We have neighborhoods to build, and with the help of God and you, the good citizens of Chicago, we will do exactly that. Thank you, thank you, thank you.

The Campaign

Saturday night following the Tuesday election: Schaller's Pump is a neighborhood institution in Bridgeport, on Halsted and 36th St, part of the large Southwest Side, across from the 11th Ward Democratic Party headquarters, an Irish stronghold, the Daley stronghold. Politicians have been coming here to eat and drink for fifty years. Many layers of paint are encrusted on the ancient walls with their black oval panels and dim wall lamps, bare of any other decoration. The chandeliers are the same ones installed some hundred years ago. The tables and chairs are the same. The boiled ribs and baked potato are edible—$9.95. The pickled beets and cole slaw are fresh but bland. One waitress, Colleen, rushes about serving a dozen tables. I pay for but never receive my second glass of cheap bar wine. The bar extends the full length of the room and is lined, by nine o'clock, with people who have come just to drink and visit. A few drink cocktails; most drink beer. It is amazing how little hard liquor there is on the bar in this Irish saloon. The tables are filled with diners. Bridgeport is well-represented: the expensively coiffed and dressed middle-class businessmen and professionals, the men who run the Department of Streets and Sanitation and their wives and children, the men who drive the garbage trucks and repair the streets, with their families (Streets and Sanitation is largely staffed by Bridgeport). The precinct captains and the handyman at Sox Park. There are still some poor in Bridgeport but there are many who are no longer poor. Mayor Daley took good care of his neighbors. They live in the neat yellow and brown brick bungalows that line so many streets in their neighborhood.

Some patrons are dressed for a night on the town—suits, dresses, jewelry, freshly coiffed. Some wear plaid flannel shirts and work shoes, some windbreakers and t-shirts. There are no class distinctions. Everybody knows everybody, everybody talks to everybody.

Joe Mahoney, from Sox Park, says Tony will arrive on the stroke of 9:30. Sure enough, at precisely 9:30, the door opens and Tony enters, to the glee of patrons. Short, middle-aged, happily smiling, he moves through the saloon greeting friends, kisses for the ladies, handshakes for the men. Fifteen minutes later, he takes his place on a stool at the back of the room and opens with "Seems Like Old Times," his theme song, and goes on to songs from the twenties and thirties, accompanying himself on the accordian which has a mike attached to it. The crowd sings along. I request Stardust. "I love it," he says but never sings it. I'm a stranger.

Schaller's is your classic corner saloon. The lights are bright, the crowd is noisy—laughing, singing, visiting with each other up and down the bar and at the tables. The bitter election of four days ago is over. Their man had lost the primary and they are nervous about the future with that black man in office but it doesn't interfere with their good time Saturday night at Schaller's.

A couple of young men walk by us. "The 'Epton, Epton, he's our man, we don't want no Af-ri-can!' types," I say to my friend. Black leather jackets, tight jeans, hard sullen faces, dull eyes, long hair and sideburns, loping down the aisle, cowboy-style. They sit down to eat, order a beer. My friend observes that they are quietly talking, eating neatly, seem quite respectable. "In Bridgeport, it's respectable to hate blacks." I respond. "You don't have to be an ox at the dinner table to yell obscenities." Still, it is hard to imagine the people at the next table in their tweeds and corduroys yelling, "Attaboy, Jewboy, go get 'im."

The couple next to us at the bar are planning their daughter's wedding. The wife, in her striped acrylic dress, string of pearls, and heavily sprayed reddish hair, drinking whiskey and soda, suggests that they hire Tony to sing for the cocktail hour before dinner. Her husband, greying, neat in a sports shirt and jacket, drinking Hamm's from a can, agrees. They are quietly, contentedly going over the plans: a large sit-down dinner, a band for dancing afterward. But politics is never far from their minds.

"Richie's not like the old man. He shouldn't kiss the ass of the niggers," he tells his wife. To me he says, "The city is gonna get darker. We're not the right shade."

While the election does not interfere with the good times at Schaller's, it is not far from anyone's thoughts. "The nigger" drifts across the bar regularly, somehow louder and stronger than the other words in the sentences. Perhaps it is actually louder. Perhaps we are more sensitive to its sound.

Before Tony arrives, the jukebox is played steadily. Somebody plays Louis Armstrong singing "Jack, the Knife," right after somebody else plays Al Jolson singing "Mammie." Louie played for the Russians and for Queen Elizabeth, too.

Schaller's has no listing with the telephone company. You have to be in the inner circle to get the number.

At 10, the white-haired, paunchy precinct captain says goodnight and goes home with three six-packs.

At 31st and Shields, about a mile from Schaller's, in the Italian section of Bridgeport, near Sox Park, the ABC Tap is another corner saloon. Like most of the others in Bridgeport, its lighted sign above the entrance says, "Beer, cans and bottles." Its name is on an unlighted sign in the window which is completely covered and dark. Most saloons in Bridgeport are inconspicuous except for that bottles and cans sign. Unlike Schaller's, the ABC Tap is dimly lit and the juke box is for young people, with records by white singers of the Elvis Presley vintage. A dozen young men, swarthy, with dark hair, worn long, mustaches, wearing windbreakers and leather jackets, line the bar. They, too, all know each other and visit back and forth along the bar. They are friendly to us. The short, balding, greying, sweet-faced bartender sells us one beer, puts a shot glass upside down on the bar and says, "The next one's on me."

"How come you don't have a picture of Jane Byrne up there beside old man Daley and Richie?" I ask naively after we have exchanged pleasantries.

"Are you kidding? This is Bridgeport. She hates us. She starved us. No one with a Bridgeport address could get a job with the city in the last four years." He tried to return to the police force after a short absence, having served ten years. "The girl told me, confidentially, that I should fake an address outside of Bridgeport."

"Bridgeport will never forgive Richie Daley," the bartender says later. "He'll never get another shot at the mayor. He coulda had it in four years, but he hadda do it now and look what we've got."

"Did you think he had a pretty good shot at it last fall?"

"Sure. He was a shoo-in."

"He must have thought so, too."

"He did. But then things changed. He didn't do his paper work. He didn't sit down and figure it out. [He does not say, as many Chicago pundits say, that Richie Daley is not his father's true heir; he isn't very smart.] No one here will ever forgive him for splitting the white vote. Byrne would have won by a landslide if he hadn't split the vote."

If Byrne starved them, if they hate her so, why would they prefer her for another four years to Harold Washington? In Bridgeport, any white is preferable to any black. Even a white you hate.

"Will you support Richie when he runs for state's attorney again?"

"Oh sure. We ain't gonna take everything away from him." (Washington will also support Daley in his bid for re-election in 1984, he announced shortly after the election. After having made a graceful concession speech throwing his support to Washington, Daley stayed quietly away from the campaign, not wanting to further alienate his constituents. But he was the first white to support Washington and he was among the first to condemn the St. Pascal's bigots who attacked Washington on Palm Sunday. Washington supported Daley's opponent in 1982, a reform Republican. But politics is a matter of compromise. His support for Daley is gracious and may win him four votes in the City Council, which will help strengthen his hand. Besides, Daley did a creditable job as state's attorney, by most accounts. He instituted a victim assistance program, for instance, and hired a feminist attorney to develop better handling of rape and domestic violence cases.)

The second bartender serves us our second beer and he sets up his own upside down shot glass. He is a Vietnam veteran. He left half of his left leg on the battlefield. He has decorated one long wall of the ABC with government posters depicting the war—some of them recruiting posters. Some maimed vets get even more patriotic.

Someone puts a quarter in the jukebox for Elvis Presley to sing "America the Beautiful."

The little green paper turtles with a name attached that are tacked to the walls just below the low ceilings all around the room signify that patrons have donated a dollar to the favorite charity of the owner of the ABC. "He doesn't take a penny for himself," the bartender explains. "I've been there when he donates the money to the crippled children or the retarded kids. It's a beautiful sight." Those turtles don't indicate, as they say in fund-raising circles, a "high level of giving," but rather wide spread support. The people who drink and eat in the ABC don't have much money but they are generous—except to blacks. As Washington would say, "Crazy, crazy, crazy."

Above the bar at the ABC is a television monitoring camera. Another is in the back room. The owner lives above and he can watch what is going on. "They have to have it," a patron explains. "During the games, it gets very crowded in here, before and after, and a lot of blacks come in."

For Richard M. Daley

Say a prayer for Richie
Take a moment out
It doesn't make a difference who you love
For God's the biggest clout.

(A stanza from a poem framed and hanging above the bar at the ABC)

The people in Bridgeport aren't the only ones in Chicago who hate Jane Byrne. Many of the white liberals who helped elect her on a reform platform were furious when she abandoned that platform soon after she was elected, to embrace the Machine politicians whom she had called "the evil cabal." She soon became their handmaiden, on the one hand, and, on the other, became erratic, insulting, power hungry, and greedy, greedy for the huge campaign contributions that were the prerequisite for city contracts, some worthy and some without merit, given only to get a contribution. At the start of the primary, she had the largest campaign fund ever accumulated for any mayoral campaign, over $10 million. (It would be interesting to know whether any of the money destined for that campaign fund found its way into a private bank account somewhere.)

But those most angry at Byrne were the blacks. The same coalition of white liberals and blacks that put Washington in office put Byrne in office. The blacks were the major reform voters in the city. They were altogether through with the Democratic Machine. She then not only turned her back on her largest constituency but grievously insulted them by naming white ethnics to positions formerly held by blacks on the school board and the Chicago Housing Authority—the schools and the CHA are most heavily populated by blacks—and by passing over a local black for school superintendent and another for police chief, in the latter case installing a white, though she did bring in a black school chief.

In 1981, the infant mortality rate in Chicago rose to double the national average—the third highest in the nation—and continued to rise. Early in her administration, Byrne closed down all the well-baby clinics in Chicago and replaced free service in the Board of Health clinics with a sliding scale fee, which greatly reduced the amount of prenatal care poor women would receive. The costs of collecting those fees were about $700,000 annually, an expense not covered by the fees collected. The planning? The logic? Who knows? The effect? Blacks and other poor people deprived of urgent medical care; huge rises in illness and infant mortality.

To defeat Byrne, the blacks put together a campaign beginning in the summer of 1982 with a boycott of Byrne's biggest summer festival, ChicagoFest. There were street demonstrations, too, and then, most important, in the fall there was the voter registration drive. Dozens of people, individuals and organizations ranging from the Chicago Urban League and Jesse Jackson's PUSH to welfare mothers in the projects, cooperated to get blacks registered. By the close of the registration, they added 100,000 people to the rolls (after the primary, they added another 13,000), bringing the total of black registered voters to 640,000 out of 1.625 million voters in the city.

Chicago blacks don't vote for blacks traditionally. They have voted overwhelmingly for local Democrats since 1955 and for national Democrats since Roosevelt. But in recent years, they have voted, as they did for Byrne, for reform candidates, black and white, when they had the opportunity. A month after his candidacy the *Defender* took a poll of Washington's support in the black community. Only 20 percent of blacks said they would vote for him. Washington was little-known outside his own district, despite his run for mayor in 1977. He had not been a community leader. He had, after all, spent most of his years keeping his nose clean in the Democratic Machine. But he was taking his reform message to the community and then he appeared on three televised debates with the other two candidates. He said what blacks wanted to hear: a new slate—reform across the board. No more patronage, equal opportunity, open government. And he said it eloquently. He was clearly the superior candidate for his people. That 20 percent swelled to 80. Some still went for Byrne and Daley. They believed in the patronage system, they had profited by it, or they had some other complex motive.

Midafternoon, primary election day: Attorney, former judge, Mark Jones is at the legal command post for Washington. He goes into the Board of Election Commissioners where he finds a huge crowd of people complaining that they had registered to vote but, when they went to their polling places, they found that their names were not in the binder. By accident or by design, those registrations were "lost." But the people have receipts. They demand to vote. The Board refuses. Jones, in one short hour, puts together a suit against the Board and goes to court. The crowd follows. They pack a courtroom.

"Are you going to tell these people that if they do the right thing, if they register to vote, they can't because of somebody's negligence? Are you going to tell these people the system doesn't work?" Jones asks the judge. "No," the judge says. Then to the crowd he says, "You can vote. Just go over to the Board of Election Commissioners and sign an affidavit and take it out to your polling place."

The crowd cheers, returns to City Hall and lines up to sign the affidavits. One woman is weeping. She tore up her receipt when she was told she couldn't vote.

"Isn't there something you can do?" she asks Jones.

"Nope. If you don't have a receipt, I can't help you." She walks out, still weeping. Ten minutes later she returns, stalks up to the man behind the desk who had told her she couldn't vote.

"You told me I couldn't vote. You saw me tear up that receipt and throw it in your wastebasket. Now you find it and fix it for me." A few minutes later, jubilant, with her receipt and her affidavit, she is on her way out of City Hall. It is 6:15. The polls close at 7.

"Where do you live?" Jones asks.

"114th Street," she says.

"You'll never make it," he says sadly.

"I've got $43 in my purse. If it takes every one of them to take a taxi, I'm going to vote today."

The race was close. Daley conceded first. Byrne couldn't believe she had lost. She told her workers to go home, maybe they would still win. The next day, she called a press conference and graciously conceded and promised her support to Washington. (A couple of weeks later she would try to conduct a write-in campaign against the advice of almost everyone.) The Chairman of the Cook County Democratic Committee, Alderman Edward Vrdolyak, followed suit and promised his support, unenthusiastically, and then worked behind the scenes for Washington's opponent. The President of the Cook County Board, George Dunne, was enthusiastic in his endorsement and was one of the few party stalwarts to help Washington. Three independent alderman were also enthusiastic, two of them had supported him in the primary. Two more independents, who had supported Daley, waited a couple of weeks and finally saw the handwriting on the wall and gave him their enthusiastic support. Every black public official in town rushed to support him. Cecil Partee led the pack. One regular Democratic alderman announced his support. A few followed. Finally, a meeting of the Central Committee was held and all but eight gave him an endorsement. Most worked quietly for Bernard Epton, the Republican sacrificial lamb in Democratic Chicago who had taken 11,000 votes out of 1.6 million votes in the primary and who had announced that he would retire to Florida as soon as the election was over.

Snap, crackle, pop! This election was suddenly now another game entirely. Within a couple of days, Bernard Epton—former state representative, 61, rich Jewish Republican who resigned from his synagogue earlier in the year when his rabbi, Arnold Wolf, after the Conference gave the same award to Ronald Reagan, sent back to the American Conference of Christians and Jews a brotherhood award given him a few years earlier—was catapulted from a candidate who no one had ever heard of to a serious challenger to the Democratic candidate for mayor. In fifty-two years there had been only one serious Republican contender. But there was a new ingredient in 1983: Epton was white. It didn't matter to the overwhelmingly Democratic white electorate in Chicago that Epton was a Republican, nor that he was a Jew, nor that he had no campaign funds, no organization, nor that no one had ever heard of him outside liberal integrated Hyde Park where he had lived most of his life and served as state representative for fourteen years. It mattered not that his record on abortion, equal rights, and civil rights was similar to Washington's. Nor did it matter that he seemed a bit flaky, given to wisecracks instead of serious answers to most questions. He was white. Therefore, the money poured in. Citizens for Epton offices opened all over white Chicago—he never bothered with black Chicago—and the crowds at his campaign stops grew massively and enthusiastically.

While he had support all over white Chicago, including the traditionally liberal Lakefront, his strongest support came from the ethnic wards on the South and Northwest sides of the city. There was a feeling—strong in those parts of the city—that Epton could defeat Washington. He had to, was the feeling. Any other possibility was unthinkable. It wasn't so different from the 1970 election in Newark, N.J. when black Kenneth Gibson ran against the incumbent who was on trial for extortion and tax evasion. That didn't make any difference to the whites of Newark; he was white. Gibson won in heavily black Newark but took only 11 percent of the white vote.

• An Epton supporter in Marquette Park cheering on his candidate: "Attaboy, Jewboy, go get 'im."

• John Madigan, WBBM-radio commentator on the Palm Sunday attack on Washington and Walter Mondale at St. Pascal's Church: "It wouldn't have happened if he hadn't gone there."

• An Epton enthusiast: "I'm voting for that guy, Epstein."

• Black spray paint graffiti on the side entrance to St. Pascal's Church on Palm Sunday: "Harold sucks. Nigger die."

• A Northwest side housewife overheard in a beauty shop: "The first thing he'll do is move them niggers in here."

• A man on the street on the Southwest Side interviewed by CBS-TV: "He's nothing but a crook."

• Another man interviewed by CBS-TV on the day after the election: "I don't like it."

"Why?"

"Because he's black."

• A television commercial aired by Epton: "Bernard Epton: Before It's Too Late."

• Two young men in a yellow Chevie stop at a street corner to address a young woman, tall, striking, with the curly remnants of a kinky permanent framing her face and wearing a Washington button: "I hope he rapes you. Maybe he'll molest your child. Maybe you're already married to a nigger." The speaker turns to his companion and says, "Look, she's even got nigger hair."

• A button: "Educated People To Oust Niggers—EPTON."

• An official leaflet: "If you do not vote, the real loser will be our community as we now know it."

Harold Washington
Alias: “Brother Mayor”
“Campaign Promises”

1. Raise Whitey’s Taxes!
2. Ban Democratic machine—replace with El Rukins and Black Disciples!
3. Move City Hall to 63rd & King Drive
4. Change donation bureau to “Leon’s Rib Basket.”
5. Move to “Bridgeport”—3500 S. Lowe.
6. Change City Flag Emblem to “Black Fist.”
7. Replace Supt. of Police with “Shaft!”
8. Replace CTA Buses with Eldorados!
9. Change State St. to Amos & Andy Drive!
10. New campaign headquarters to “Cabrini Green.”
11. Issue more riot permits.
12. Pay gas bill with city funds.
13. New song for city—“We Are Family.”
14. Dedicate my campaign to “ALL MY CHILLINS.”
15. Campaign funds paid by “Mastuh Charge!”

    Special thanks to the Master Puppeteer—The Rev. Jesse Jackson.”

BEFORE YOU VOTE YOU HAVE THE RIGHT TO SOME ANSWERS. MUCH HAS BEEN SAID ABOUT THE BACKGROUND OF THE TWO MEN WHO ARE CANDIDATES FOR MAYOR.

A RUMOR HAS BEEN CIRCULATED THAT HAROLD WASHINGTON WAS ARRESTED FOR SODOMY WITH A 10 YEAR OLD. IS THIS TRUTH OR FICTION? WE SHOULD KNOW THE FACTS BEFORE WE VOTE. THE CHICAGO TRIBUNE HAS COMPLETED AN INVESTIGATION OF THIS STORY AND SO FAR FAILED TO RELEASE THE RESULTS -- WHY HAVEN'T WE BEEN TOLD? IS THIS RUMOR, TRUTH OR FICTION. WE HAVE A RIGHT TO KNOW THE TRUTH BEFORE WE VOTE - CALL THE TRIBUNE AND ASK ABOUT THIS.
CALL 222-3232 AND DEMAND THAT THEY RELEASE THE RESULTS OF THEIR INVESTIGATION THE CITIZENS OF CHICAGO MUST KNOW!! ROYKO AND KAY WHAT DO YOU KNOW ABOUT THIS? WE HAVE KNOW THE TRUTH ABOUT HAROLD WASHINGTON.

WHY WON'T YOU TELL US?

CBS - CHANNEL 2 944-6000 NBC - CHANNEL 5 861-5555
ABC - CHANNEL 7 263-0800 WGN - CHANNEL 9 528-2311

YOUR VOTE FOR MR.EPTON

WILL STOP.....CONTAMINATION AND OCCUPATION OFTHE CITY HALL,BY A MR.B A B O O N...ELE
RACIALY WITH THE VOTES OF THOUSANDS B A B O O N S ....NONPRODUCTIVE,I
PONSIBLE AMERICANS,AMERICAN BABOONS WHO CANNOT CARE LESS FOR THEIR DUT
WARDS AMERICA.THOUSANDS OF BABOONS WHO HAVE NEVER WORKED ONE SINGLE DA
THEIR LIFE,NEVER BOTHER TO PAY A SINGLE PENNY TAX,USING AND MISSUSING
MONEY OF THE WORKING AMERICANS.
HOW MANY THOUSANDS OF DRUG ADDICTS,GANG MEMBERS,PROSTITUES,ALKOHOLICS ,
NALS AND LIKES,WERE BUSSED TO THE POLES TO ELECT YOUR MAYOR......HOW M
BE BUSSED IN THE FUTURE TO ELECT YOUR GOVERNER,,YOUR PRESIDENT.

WILL STOP.....TRANSFORMATION OF THE CITY HALL....IN A NEW PUBLIC HOUSING PROJECT.DO
WE HAVE AND SUPPORT ENOUGH OF THOSE????

WILL STOP.....THIS NATIONAL DISGRACE..THIS UNBELIEVABLE GIVEAWAY...PERMITTING BABOON
DIES TO BEAR DOZEN OF CHILDRENS FATHERED BY TWO DOZEN OF DIFFERENT FATH
PAID IN FULL WITH THE TAX MONEY OF THE WORKING AMERICANS...THUS PRODUCI
MORE RACIAL VOTES ..FOR FUTURE ELECTION OF YOUR REPRESENTATIVES ,
ARE YOU READY TO PERMITT TAKE OVER BY THOSE WHO DO NOT CONTRIBUTE TO TH
BEING OF AMERICA,BY THOSE WHO MISSUSE OUR DEMOCRACY.
WILL STOP..... A SICKENNING EGO-POWER TRIP OF A "SUPERBABOON" KNOWN AS MESSY-JESSE A
MILITANT FOLLOWERS.
THING ABOUT THE FUTURE OF AMERICA.THING ABOUT THE FUTURE OF YOUR CHILDR
WILL ELECT....A WHITE MAYOR...A REPRESENTATIVE OF THE WORKING AMERICANS,AMERICANS DEV
TO AMERICA,AMERICANS WHO RESPECT AND FULLFILL THEIR DUTIES TOWARD AMERI
AMERICANSWORKING FOR PROSPERITY OF AMERICA
DO NOT PERMITT IRRESPONSIBLE AND UNPRODUCTIVE AMERICANS TO DICTATE THE
OF YOUR CHILDREN.
WE ALL KNOW THAT ELECTION OF HARALD WASHINGTOM WAS...IS ,..AND WILL BE
RASISTS VICTORY AND MOVE BY UNITED BLACKS.
WHAT IS WRONG IF WE WHITES UNITE.WHAT IS WRONG IF WE STILL IN GREAT MAJ
UNITE AND PROTECT WORK OF OUR FOREFATHERS,WE DID NOT SUPPORT AND FINANC
PROMISCUITY,PROSTITUTION,DRUGS,ALCOHOL AND VARIETY OF VICES WE DEARLY P
FOR WITH OUR TAX MONEY.
YOUR VOTE FOR EPTON
IS A VOTE FOR WORKING AMERICA,BY WORKING AMERICANS.IT IS A VOTE AGAINST GIVEAWAYS,MIS
OF CITIZEN RIGHTS AND DUTIES,AND AGAINS..THE VERY BLACK FUTURE OF AMERICA.
YOUR VOTE FOR EPTON
IS A MUST ..FOR THE FUTURE OF ALL OF US,FOR THE FUTURE OF OUR WORKING AND PROSPEROUS A
RICA..IS A VOTE AGAINST WELFARE AMERICA,PUBLIC HOUSING AMERICA,FOODSTAMPS AMERICA.

THINKS ABOUT IT FELLOW AMERICANS...VOTE REGARDLESS YOUR POLITICAL PARTY...VOTE "WHITE"
TO PREVENT BEING OUTVOTED"BLACK":DO NOT FORGET THAT ....
99% BLACKS WILL VOTE FOR WASHINGTON,BECAUSE HE IS BLACK
HAVE IN MIND THAT YOUR VOTE WILL KEEP THOSE B A B O O N S OUT THE CITY HALL,OUT OF
POWER FOR NOW AND FOR EVER.

RETYPE...COPY...DISTRIBUTE...DISCUSS....AND AS A "WHITE"
VOTE "WHITE....

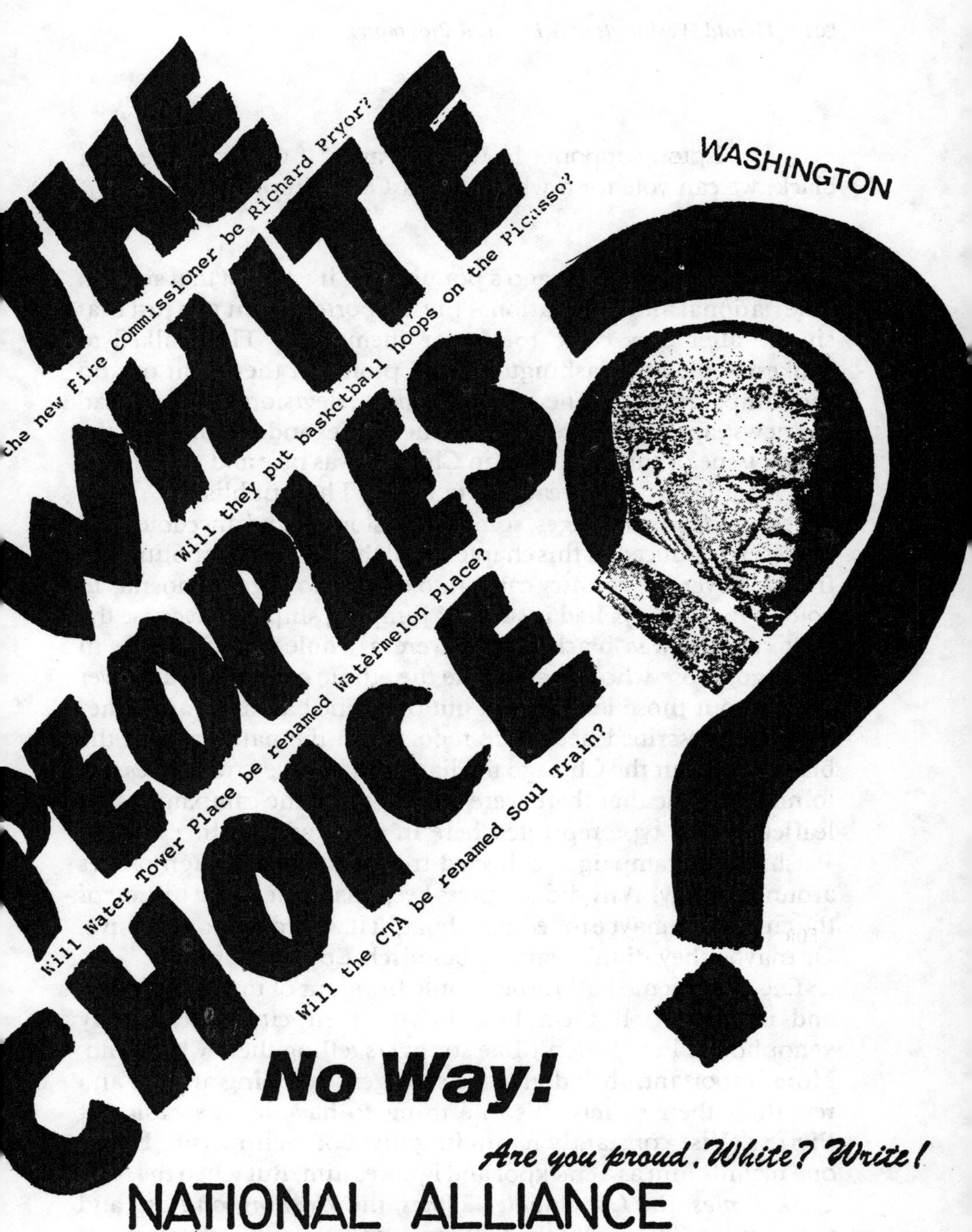

NATIONAL ALLIANCE

606 W. Barry St., Rm. 196 Chgo, IL 60657

- Epton supporter in Rogers Park: "If they can vote for a black, we can vote for a white. It's just that simple."

For 48 percent of Chicago's population, it was just that simple. The national and international press reported that it was just that simple after they came to see for themselves. They talked to spokespeople for Washington and Epton and they went out on the campaign trail. They watched local television and they read the newspapers. They reported to their cities and nations that the major issue of the campaign in Chicago was race and that Epton was regarded as the Great White Hope. They published, sometimes on their front pages, some of the slogans and anecdotes and leaflets reproduced in this chapter. And the Democratic politicians from all over the country came into the city to urge Democrats to vote as they always had instead of jumping ship just because the new captain was black. There were a whole lot of people in Chicago, those who lived outside the ethnic enclaves, who never knew about those leaflets and buttons. The handbills and other materials described here were reported in the national and the black press, but the Chicago media didn't believe it was necessary to make public that there were by the end of the campaign sixty leaflets of the type reprinted here in a file at the offices of the Washington campaign, collected from Epton campaign offices around the city. Why did the press keep that secret from the rest of the city? Well, maybe the editors thought it would be too explosive. Or maybe they didn't want to besmirch Epton's name.

The city resented all those people from out of town coming in and trying to tell them how to run their city. Not entirely xenophobic. People don't like strangers telling them what to do. More important, they don't like strangers snooping around and revealing their secrets. It's one thing to have local sociologist Pierre deVise constantly reminding them of their racism. Everyone regards him as a crackpot and ignores him. But when the *New York Times*, the *Los Angeles Times*, the *Washington Post*, and the *London Times* all take that message home with them, that's another story. Not since Mayor Daley ordered his police to "shoot to kill" has the city's bigotry been broadcast so widely.

The local press called foul. Anne Keegan, a popular columnist for the *Chicago Tribune,* pointed out proudly that Chicago had elected a woman mayor (she neglected to say the first woman mayor, which certainly did redound to Chicago's credit) four years ago, which she somehow believed proved that Chicago is not racist. She then got closer to the issue by stating that half of the six major candidates for top city jobs are black. That many major cities have had black mayors for a score of years and that those black candidates were Machine loyalists, she failed to say. Perhaps she doesn't know. Few white journalists know anything about black politics, as was clearly evidenced by their shock at Washington's primary win.

More important, however, Keegan says that the reason all those whites are campaigning so hard for Epton is because Washington has committed those crimes. "The fact [of those crimes] is something that is skimmed over by the outside press. But it is not looked upon lightly by many people in Chicago. The average homeowner takes his taxes seriously. . . . he is scared to death of the IRS. . . . the average citizen has learned to take his bills seriously because he must. And if *he* must, he expects it to be the same for others, no matter their position, elected official or not." The fact that Washington's actual crimes occurred fifteen years ago and that most of the other charges levelled against him by Epton proved spurious, she does not credit. (Douglas Frantz, a *Tribune* reporter, believes that "Keegan's biases should have prevented her from writing about the campaign." Another *Tribune* man reports that the newspaper "only printed her better stuff. Other more rancid columns were pulled.")

Keegan was not alone in defending the white citizens of Chicago against the charges of racism levelled by the national press. There was a virtual cavalcade of stories in the newspapers and comments by the broadcasters protesting the heinous charge. Bill Grainger, another *Tribune* columnist, says on April 7, "the out-of-town press has hanged Chicago for bias without admitting there is probably not a major city in this racially divided country that does not practice racial bias on a large scale." That 233 cities in this racially divided country already had black mayors, that there were 21 black congressmen, over 340 state legislators and 5,000 elected black officials in this racially divided country, he fails to mention.

Probably the strangest statement made to prove that Chicago is not a racist city and that the election was not based on race came from Brian J. Kelly, a reporter, and Basil Talbott, Jr., political editor of the *Sun-Times,* the day after the election. They sum it all up under the headline: "How white vote spelled victory." They write, "Harold Washington won Chicago's mayoral election by getting a bigger slice of the white vote than in similar black-white mayoral elections in all but one U.S. city, according to an analysis of vote tallies." An analysis of vote tallies? Which vote tallies? Those in Spokane, Wash., Little Rock, Ark., Pasadena, Cal.? Following is a list of seven cities with 100,000 population, except Tallahassee which has 82,000, which had black mayors in 1980. The list gives the percentage of blacks in the population.

Spokane, Wash.	1.6% black
Little Rock, Ark.	32.2% black
Hartford, Conn.	33.9% black
Pasadena, Cal.	20.6% black
Berkeley, Cal.	20.1% black
Roanoke, Va.	22.0% black
Tallahassee, Fla.	31.8% black

It should be immediately evident, as Roger Fox of the Chicago Urban League says, that in all of these cities a black mayor would need a minimum of 27 percent of the white vote to get elected. Washington took 16-18 percent of the white vote, though that includes a heavy proportion of Hispanics, who are estimated to have given as much as two-thirds of their 95,000 votes to Washington. (Since voters are not identified by race and, even if they were, since individual votes are not counted, this figure is only an approximation based on the general racial composition of the ward. Some wards are known to be all-white or all-black but, especially on the Lakefront, there are blacks in predominantly white wards and an occasional white in what are viewed as all-black wards. The latter is not considered important, but on the Lakefront the black vote, though small, must be considered as contributing to the total, thus raising a question about that 16-18 percent white, since the non-Hispanic part of it came largely from that section of the city.) The question that emerges is: are Kelly and Talbott such poor journalists that they would grace the front page of their paper with a completely uninformed statement, or were they so caught up in the racial struggle in Chicago that their normally adequate skills failed them? Intent on proving that Chicago is not a racist city, their vision became clouded, their skills sank into the morass that racism creates. Deep in their story, Kelly and Talbott state that "*Several* [my emphasis] national election experts noted that only when Cleveland elected Carl Stokes mayor in 1967 did whites in a major northern city give a non-incumbent black more votes—20 percent—than the 18 percent of Chicago whites, including Hispanics, who turned out for Washington."

Who were those national experts? Well, it turns out to be one—Paul Maslin, an associate of Patrick Caddell, who was Jimmy Carter's, and Washington's, pollster. Maslin says that Talbott and Kelly "got it a little wrong;" he was quick to point out that "New Orleans and Atlanta were in the same ballpark." He did say that "Washington got a bigger white vote than the black mayors in Newark in 1970 and in Detroit in 1973, both cities with large ethnic enclaves that have longstanding ties to the Democratic Party." In Philadelphia, shortly after Washington's win in Chicago, Wilson Goode took 22 percent of the white vote, and in all the seven cities mentioned earlier, the white vote was at least 27 percent. In March, during Goode's primary campaign, the *Philadelphia News* published a poll that showed that 37 percent of the white registered voters in the city said they would vote for W. Wilson Goode. That he did not get that much of the white vote is attributed in part to a racist campaign by his opponent but in part to his own lack-lustre campaign. Goode did win, however, five predominately white wards, including the prestigious and wealthy Chestnut Hill, while Rizzo, an avowed and strident racist, took 2 percent of the black vote. In California, though he lost, Tom Bradley took 40 percent of the white vote in the gubernatorial election and lost by less than 1 percent.

Maslin speculates that cities with larger black populations vote less readily for a black candidate than those with fewer blacks because the whites "fear the loss of their political power. In Spokane, Wash., for instance, the black candidate can appeal purely on his own qualifications. He does not represent a large black community that is seen as a threat to the power of those who have always had it and don't want to give it up."

Sounds reasonable. Maslin insists that this fear is not racist. Other fears—of crime, housing deterioration, invasion, sexual fear—get closer to that racist source, particularly since they have proved unfounded in other cities with black mayors. But fear of the loss of political power? No, that isn't racist. It's natural, Maslin insists. Who wants to give up longheld power? Well, let's look a little more closely at that equation in Chicago. Let's look solely at Bridgeport, which we have seen a bit of earlier. Mayor Byrne had stripped Bridgeport of its political power, not because she hated the Irish, Poles, and Italians in Bridgeport but because she wanted for herself the power formally held by the 11th Ward. Only by stripping it of its patronage could she remove its power. She was successful.

The folks in Bridgeport, in 1983, were in the same position as the blacks in Chicago—no patronage, no clout, only their votes. But they will never give their former favorite son, Richie Daley, a shot at the mayoral again because he split the white vote and permitted a black to win. Daley didn't reckon with the fervor of the racism in his precious 11th Ward. He didn't realize that his people would have preferred not to take a shot at winning back the mayor's office if it meant risking the election of a black candidate. In Bridgeport, at least, the ethnics would have preferred their powerlessness under a white mayor than any condition under a black one. Maslin's theory might benefit from a trip to Bridgeport.

Maslin also forgets that Jane Byrne ran four years ago on the same reform platform Washington was running on. She threatened to break up the Machine and, in fact, her primary election did defeat the Machine. After the primary, however, the Democrats quickly lined up beside her to win the race as they had done for their candidates for fifty years.

Talbott wrote earlier, on April 10, two days before the election, "The nation's suitcase journalists are portraying Chicago as a national capital of hate, racism, and ugliness. Their case against Chicago is skewed, flawed, and more inciting than insightful." He then went on to describe the techniques of the journalists from around the country—poor selection, quick assumptions, shortcuts, preconceived notions. Then, as his final shot, he pointed out that "Many suitcase journalists came from the more severely segregated District of Columbia area ... violence-stained Boston, burned-out Bronx. Has God put the worst racists in Chicago's Portage Park while sending tolerant, thoughtful whites to lily-white suburbs around the nation's capital?" Boston is certainly violence-stained, the Bronx is certainly burned out, but has Talbott been to Chicago's West Madison Street lately? To call Washington D.C. segregated, however, is slanderous. It is 70 percent black, but to the extent possible with only 30 percent of the city white, it is an integrated city. Very stringent fair housing laws are enforced. And, while there are certainly some all-black sections in a 70 percent black city, most neighborhoods are well integrated. Nor are the suburbs lily-white. Both blacks and whites have been abandoning the city for years, first because it was badly managed under the federal mandate and then because, after decades of neglect, city services were poor and, more important, living costs became prohibitive. Cheaper, better housing was available outside the city. Did Talbott bother to check his facts? Did he check out St. George County? Or, as in the story on the day after election, did he write what he thought, regardless of the facts, in order to make that crucial point: Chicago is not racist.

Is Chicago racist? Are those incidents and trophies of the campaign cited earlier enough evidence to condemn the whole white population of a city? Let's look further at the press coverage. James Squires, executive vice-president and editor of the *Tribune* said in a staff meeting, on the subject of covering the primary campaign, ". . . Byrne, Daley, and that black guy." Squires couldn't remember the name of that black guy, the third contender in the primary contest. The staff was aghast.

The objections to anchorman Walter Jacobson's election coverage on CBS-TV Nightly News were intense. One white viewer describes his behavior as "a man who seems to be deathly afraid to have a black man in City Hall. He kept raising the issue of race, out of context, unnecessarily, implying that Washington was only in the race because he was black. He came across as a terrible bigot."

James Ylisela, Jr., discussing in *The Chicago Reporter* the press coverage of the primary, says,

> There is evidence that the *Tribune* had little faith in its minority staff [to cover the campaign]. The editors there chose to [bring in two white Washington reporters and] deny its black reporters a role in the election coverage of the mayoral campaign. Ironically, it was Munroe Anderson, one of the *Tribune's* three black general assignment reporters who broke the story of Washington's decision to run for mayor. The article appeared Nov. 8, along with [a piece], written weeks earlier by Anderson on how a black candidate could beat conventional Chicago political wisdom and win the race for City Hall. That was the last significant piece Anderson would write on the [primary] campaign.

Reporters on both dailies told Ylisela that they were surprised that Anderson was not covering the campaign. "The *Tribune* reporters often checked with Anderson when they needed black contacts. If anyone knows the pulse of the black community, it's Munroe," one of his colleagues on the *Tribune* told Ylisela. "Indeed, Anderson discussed the campaign nearly everywhere but in his own newspaper, appearing on many radio and television programs to analyze Washington's candidacy." Ylisela quotes Squires as saying that he favors "experience in political reporting over local contacts. I would have been very reluctant to put an inexperienced reporter out there—black or white. We didn't make any decisions on who covered this campaign on the basis of race." Anderson has been at the *Tribune* nine years, as a general assignment reporter, which means he covers everything from fires to funerals.

Well, perhaps Squires was right not to put a reporter who has worked in general assignment for nine years out there in the fray of a political campaign. Perhaps an old hand at campaigns is better. The question is: why were Douglas Frantz and Tom Shanker, both general assignment reporters, assigned to the campaign? And it does seem strange that, after Ylisela's story appeared on the street in Chicago, and after pressure was put on Squires by the staff, Anderson's byline appeared regularly over stories during the campaign for the general election. Is a primary election more difficult to handle than a general election? Or did Squires decide that, after all, local contacts are worth something in the coverage of a story? Getting those contacts has always been the prime goal of most reporters, whatever their beat.

The *Sun-Times* did much better in this regard. Lillian Williams, a black with many contacts in the Washington camp, was assigned to the story along with three white reporters who had extensive contacts among the candidates' people, Ylisela reports. He quotes Williams as saying, "I wasn't lucky or fortunate . . . I developed the sources and earned the assignment."

Well, apparently at the *Sun-Times* having the sources can earn a reporter an assignment. One reporter at the *Tribune* is quoted by Ylisela as saying, "I think they started off on the basis that Washington couldn't win and that had a lot to do with how he was covered. The editors and higher-ups who planned the coverage never made any attempts to get the views of the black reporters." Instead the "higher-ups" brought in two Washington correspondents to handle the campaign with three local white reporters.

Among the combined staffs of the *Tribune* and *Sun-Times*, numbering more than 750, there are not twenty blacks.

Chicago is one of the few large cities in the nation that has no black anchorpeople in prime time news slots.

A large number of Chicagoans, black and white, wondered how the *Tribune* and the *Sun-Times* would have handled the campaign if they had not endorsed Washington. The *Tribune* endorsement which came on March 13, two weeks after the primary election, was one of the most eloquent editorials to appear in any newspaper, obviously carefully drafted. It began:

> For the first time in 52 years, a Republican has a real chance to be elected mayor of Chicago. And for the first time in its long history this newspaper finds that prospect regrettable.
>
> Heaven knows *The Tribune* has nothing against Republicans, or for that matter, specifically against former State Rep. Bernard Epton, the party's nominee. We have endorsed him for government office with no regrets, and under normal circumstances might even be recommending him for election next month.
>
> But the circumstances under which Mr. Epton aspires to the mayor's office are not normal. They are extraordinary. And they are, sorry to say, distressing.
>
> Mr. Epton has a chance to be mayor not because he is a Republican, or because he has outstanding qualifications, or because he has an unbeatable campaign organization. He is a legitimate contender for one reason only—because he is white and because the Democratic nominee, Rep. Harold Washington, is black.

It went on to say:

> The Republican Party, what there was of it to begin with, considered him something of a joke. And its members for the most part supported Democrats. North Shore liberals hooted at the mention of his name. And to the rank and file of Chicago's voting masses, his party was an absolute disqualification for the office of mayor . . . .

And then the editorial said:

> Mr. Washington was not our choice in the primary, mainly because he did not seem to be able to organize his campaign or draw to it the kind of sound and respected fiscal advisors and political operatives needed for a successful administration. He has now begun to do these things.
>
> Another reason was that Mr. Washington's campaign was having a polarizing effect on Chicago citizens. It still is, but Mr. Washington is trying to do something about it. A man of galvanizing presence, he has reached out to the business community and to supporters of his opponents in the primary to broaden his political base and begin bringing this divided city together.

The editorial ended by saying:

> Meanwhile, the Democrats for Epton movement, complete with a bag over its head and a thinly-disguised racist appeal, would have set this city's social progress back a decade and sharpened the divisions for years to come. And the Republicans could claim some credit for it if they wished.
>
> It is understandable why some segments of this city fear the kind of change the election of Harold Washington as mayor signifies. It was the same fear felt by the South during the civil rights struggle 20 years ago and in cities all over this country in the years since.
>
> But it is a fear unfounded, one that must be met and defeated in Chicago today, tomorrow or some day down the road. And it might as well be today.

The *Sun-Times* editorial, which came a few days later, said much the same.

The campaigns were well underway. The endorsements were unexpected. There was nothing in the press coverage to lead people to expect them. The betting was that the two papers would endorse Epton with loud apologies for the slap in the face to blacks, since neither paper had endorsed a Republican for mayor for many, many years. But as the endorsements stated, the circumstances of Epton's campaign were simply too outrageous. They had no choice. As thoughtful, intelligent, rational people, they had to endorse Washington.

On March 27, the *Tribune* ran another editorial entitled, "The Constituency of Fear."

> If Chicago doesn't wise up soon, its 1983 mayoral election may go down in history as evidence that MLK's dream of a racially tolerant nation is still just that . . . .
>
> The outpouring of protest over this newspaper's endorsement of Mr. Washington, examples of which appear on the opposite page, is a disturbing illustration of what everyone already knew, that fear of a black mayor would become a searing issue with a substantial number of white Chicagoans . . . .

The question is: why did the *Tribune* print that page full of letters? It could have printed the usual three or four or five letters to the editor and ignored the rest, as it does every other day, selecting the most interesting, most topical. Instead, it chose to dignify the attacks on Washington by printing the letters while they kept under hat the more scurrilous materials that would have revealed the depth of racism that prompted those more temperate letters.

The next day, the *Tribune* ran another editorial: "Lightweights in a high wind," and though the editors were far tougher on Epton than on Washington in this contest for who carried the least ballast, the remarks about Washington could hardly have been written by someone who had a strong commitment to his candidacy:

> By most measurements Congressman Washington, who could make a good mayor and whose candidacy carries the endorsement of this news-

paper, should not be the first black man with a chance to get elected. He does not possess the impeccable qualifications needed for such an uphill battle. His record as a legislator in Springfield and in Washington is adequate but not exceptional. Before this campaign, he was virtually unknown to white Chicago.

Of more significance are his past troubles with the law. Overcoming a jail sentence for failing to file income tax returns and losing a law license for professional misconduct is tough enough for any candidate. For a man trying to overcome racial prejudice as well, it can become an albatross. And for Washington, it has.

Since he rode the wave of black voter independence to an upset victory over Mayor Byrne and Richard Daley in the Democratic primary last month, Mr. Washington has been on the defensive, unable to do much beyond explaining his past transgressions. Although an outstanding speaker and a skilled politician savvy enough to run this city, his campaign continues to play into the hands of those who seek to defeat him.

A few days later, the *Tribune* rose to defend Washington against the most scurrilous of the almost daily attacks by Epton on Washington: he had been arrested as a child molester. How does the editorial writer choose to introduce his defense?

The mayoral campaign may be setting a record in mean-spiritedness. It began with racial appeals, and it has deteriorated from there. Charge and countercharge: unpaid bills, conflicts of interest, tax conviction, psychological problems. And this represents the high ground of the campaign, the part that takes place out in the open. Beneath it things are even uglier.

It ends by saying:

Most people in this city will see this kind of rumor for what it is. But the purveyors of it know that there are some who have become so afraid or so confused by the drumbeat of nastiness on all sides that they may just give it some credence. And that is the pity of this kind of thing. It preys on people. It victimizes them. And it distorts a political process that has already been terribly disfigured.

The implication is clear. While this charge against Washington is particularly scurrilous, both candidates are guilty of "disfiguring" the political process with innuendos and "mean-spiritedness."

Epton: "Harold will . . . if he can read."

David Deardourff, Epton's media man: "Washington engineered that scene at St. Pascal's [where Washington and Walter Mondale were booed by a crowd outside the church on Palm Sunday]."

The editorial writer didn't say that for every charge levelled against Epton, there were a dozen coming out of the Epton headquarters against Washington. He or she didn't say that the two major charges against Epton—a questionable history of mental health and a conflict of interest while he was in the State House—were well-documented. Douglas Frantz, covering the Epton campaign for the *Tribune,* says he hated reading the hospital records of Epton's psychiatric history—records that were apparently stolen from Michael Reese Hospital by an employee supporter of Washington—and hoped not to have to write about it but was forced to by the TV broadcasters who broke the story first. Epton's behavior on election night, in which he screamed at his followers, stalked off without so much as a thank you to his workers, refused to concede long after it was clear he had lost, and then, the next day, on his way to Florida, fired a parting shot that he hoped Washington would learn to pay his bills, lent some credence to the introduction into the campaign of his psychiatric history. It was a performance that could not even be dignified by calling him a poor loser. It made people shudder that he might have been elected mayor of the city.

A few days after the campaign, Epton was interviewed in his Florida condominium by Mike Flannery of CBS-TV regarding his possible purchase of the *Sun-Times,* which was for sale. Would he retain the leading columnists on the paper—Mike Royko, Basil Talbott, and Roger Simon? "No," Epton said flatly, and went on to call them incompetents and liars.

The next night, the former champion of blacks told Flannery that he felt he had disappointed the hundreds of thousands who had voted for him because he was "the hope of their children and grandchildren." He wished Washington the best, he said, but had a great rage in him. Rage? At having lost an election in which he was the candidate of the worst racist elements in the city and the most corrupt politicians? Perhaps he should once again hospitalize himself in the psychiatric ward where he sought help earlier. He explained his rage several weeks later by saying that the press—the "slime"—had grossly misinterpreted his post-election behavior. All his actions had rational explanations, he said.

Epton's rage was a sad befuddlement. He consistently denied the accusations of Washington and the media that he was conducting a racist campaign, appealing to the basest emotions of the white ethnic community. His "Before It's Too Late" slogan, for instance, referred to Washington's criminal record, not his color, he insisted. His daughter, who was his primary campaign manager, asked "What *is* this?" of the slogan, warning of its clear implications. She was ignored. His wife, Audrey, in a TV interview, was insulted that her husband, whose record in civil rights was so clear, was being accused of racism. There are those who claim that Epton simply did not know what he was doing. His innocent words, they say, backfired on him. He insisted he was misunderstood. He did, on rare occasions, attempt to separate himself from the grossest racism of his supporters. At the start of the campaign, he said he did not want the votes of those who would vote only on the basis of race. But throughout the six weeks of campaigning, as his followers became shriller and shriller, he was never heard to make such a disclaimer again, or was he heard to tell his supporters to desist from their ugly race baiting.

Perhaps he truly did not understood. Perhaps the cheering crowds obliterated his ability to judge events intelligently. He had not been a serious contender for the office. He had retired from the legislature "for reasons of health." Those crowds made him a contender. Perhaps it "went to his head" and he was not able to resist the idea of winning, under any circumstances.

There is reason to think, however, that he never actually believed he could win, that he was simply enjoying the adulation of the crowds. While he went among the cheering crowds almost daily until two days before the election, when he suddenly disappeared, he did not take the serious steps toward taking office that a man who believes he is winning makes. No transition team was ever announced, though he did say regularly he was putting one together. There are some who say that he made no such announcement because he could not recruit any blacks to a team. Perhaps his efforts to recruit a team all resembled the one he made to recruit Dr. Quentin Young, an active supporter of Washington.

Young has been a civil rights activist in Chicago for thirty years, having founded The Medical Committee for Human Rights in the sixties. In 1980, to quiet a tumultous revolt among the medical and nursing staff at Cook County Hospital, he was named medical director.

On April 4, eight days before the election, Epton wrote to Young:

> Dear Dr. Young:
>
> Although I know that you are busily engaged in trying to elect Harold Washington as Mayor, it certainly in know [sic] way detracts from my admiration from you both as an individual and a learned physician.
>
> I do not know what the outcome of the election will be on April 12, but in any event, the people of Chicago would be well served if you would be willing to place your services at their disposal for the next four years.
>
> I do not have any particular position in mind although obviously it would be in the health field.
>
> If I am fortunate to be elected Mayor on April 12, I wonder if you would give consideration to serving with me during the forthcoming four years. Regardless of the results on April 12, the people of Chicago need and deserve your advice and counsel. I hope you will consider this seriously and respond to me at your convenience.
>
> Kindest personal regards.

Young replied:

> Dear Mr. Epton:
>
> I have your letter of April 4 inviting me to serve in your administration should you be elected next Tuesday.

The complimentary tone of the request would normally elicit from me a simple polite response, yea or nay. Given the conduct of your campaign, that is not possible.

Self evidently your right to seek office is unimpeachable. Similarly, your campaign against Mr. Washington or any other opponent can be as aggressive and challenging as you want.

That said, I must convey my conviction that you have chosen a course which has already hurt our city badly, how deeply and how irreparably we will learn with time.

Were you youthful, ignorant, provincial, unsophisticated or impoverished, your embrace of the politics of segregation and racial fears would still be unconscionable.

But, in fact, you are an educated, erudite, mature millionaire who was privileged to serve for many years as representative of an integrated politically progressive district.

You know better. So your choices—from the "Before it's too late" slogan to your equivocation when roaring mobs of your supporters changed Chicago's public political morality—your choices are execrable.

The people of our city are pulling free of the Machine clutch of a half century. It is a paradox that the Black voters, hitherto the more tightly controlled, broke loose ahead of the rest of us.

At this critical moment, you would rescue the political bosses by plugging into the mindless hatreds of many in our city. No one of our awesome problems will be mitigated by these passions. Indeed, they may become insoluble thereby.

If you are lucky, you will lose the election and Mr. Washington, unfortunately, will have a harder task because of the nature of your campaign. If you win, history may find that the latent schisms threatening our country tore wide open starting in Chicago with your victory.

In a letter dated April 12, Election Day, Epton replied:

Dear Dr. Young,

I'm sorry that my schedule prevented an earlier reply to your April 6 letter but I can only say that I feel sorry for you. You have been effectively brainwashed, but in America, that is certainly everyones [sic] privilege and you see fit to think ill of me, that is also your privilege.

Naturally, I will not utilize your name again. I can only state that I entered this race with pride and integrity and I leave the campaign with my pride and integrity untouched.

Very truly yours,

Did Epton, in fact, know what he was doing?

As for the charge against Epton of a conflict of interest, the Illinois Public Action Council investigated his record in the legislature and the profits made by his insurance company and revealed some damaging facts.

In 1978-82, while he was the chairman of the Illinois Insurance Law Study Commission, which he founded, and chief Republican spokesman on the Insurance Committee, his firm received more than $1.3 million in fees from the insurance industry. Seventy-five percent of the legislation he introduced in his fourteen years in the legislature dealt with the insurance industry. One of his fellow Republicans in the legislature says that the only time he appeared on the floor was when insurance matters arose. Much of the time he was ill, nursing the migraine headaches for which he was famous in the legislature. "There was very little question," Robert Creamer, director of IPAC, says, "that he sold his seat to the insurance lobby. Everybody understood that he was there to do business for the insurance companies and that was about all. If you wanted to do business with the insurance lobby, you talked to Bernie Epton. That's the way it was for many years." Curiously, very little attention was paid by the media to that conflict of interest.

Compare the coverage of Washington's misdeeds. Take the page 1 story that the *Sun-Times* broke on April 6 under the byline of one of its best-known reporters, stating, "Mayoral candidate Harold Washington and two other people failed to pay more than $2,200 in real estate taxes they owed on a building whose tenants were evicted by the city for safety reasons in 1977, the *Sun-Times* learned Monday."

The next day, the *Tribune* reported that the story had emanated from Epton headquarters. The *Sun-Times,* it seemed, had learned of the story from Washington's opponent, not always considered, in election campaigns, the most reliable of sources, but had failed to say so, and, when I inquired, refused to name the source, according to standard journalistic practices. There was silent embarrassment when I quoted the *Tribune* story and asked why the *Sun-Times* had not also revealed that questionable source.

While Washington's name was on the deed of the building in question—one of the properties he inherited from his father—he had never taken any role in the building operation and had received no income from it or from the sale of it. The *Sun-Times* also failed to make clear that the building was sold in 1978 and that the new owners agreed but failed to pay the back taxes, assuming the quite ordinary obligations of many real estate purchases. In addition, Art Petacque, the *Sun-Times'* popular reporter and his co-writer, Lynn Sweet, added a little spice to their story by writing that the unsuccessful efforts of process servers to reach Washington when suits against the building were filed were the same as the difficulties "encountered by Peoples Gas when it was involved in a dispute with Washington."

That latter dispute was over a gas bill left unpaid by Washington's campaign headquarters, one of the unpaid bills with which he was constantly charged by Epton, charges repeated over and over again by the media—campaign bills that were tiny by comparison with the unpaid campaign bills of other candidates, a fact not alluded to in the media. As Washington said, "If you owe $425 you're a deadbeat, but if you owe $450,000 you're a great fiscal giant. Crazy, crazy, crazy." Was the campaign equally disfigured by both candidates? One can't tell from that *Tribune* editorial only four days before the election. Creamer insists that the contrary is true. Washington refused to attack Epton. The press conference to release the foregoing facts about Epton's conflict of interest was to be held jointly by Washington and Creamer. At 1:30 in the morning, before the press conference the next day, Creamer got a call from Washington's office "You handle it," the aide said, "Harold doesn't want to take part." Consistently, Washington refused to attack Epton while he was being barraged by attacks by Epton. George Dunne had said, "Don't get down in the mud." He didn't know who he was talking to. Washington wouldn't step in the mud if it meant losing the election, though he admitted later that he would have taken a larger percentage of the white vote if he had attacked Epton more. But it was a game he wouldn't play. He is a proud man, a stubborn man.

And what about the issue of Epton's relationship to the insurance industry? Epton did seem to have a serious conflict of interest. It didn't seem to be merely a personal attack. Why didn't the media pursue it? Were they protecting Epton? Or were they simply overwhelmed by Epton's attacks on Washington, unable to think clearly about the problems of this filthy campaign?

Munroe Anderson suggests that they were confused and a little bewildered because they were "grappling with their own demons." Ylisela points out that Washington severely criticized the press for what he viewed as racist coverage in describing him as articulate and bright, as if somehow he were the lone black with these qualities. "His criticism forced reporters to become more sensitive to the issue of race," Ylisela says and goes on to quote some reporters who said they watched their copy carefully for evidence of racism—"their own demons." It was easier, safer, it seems, to discuss Washington's early errors in the conduct of his personal life than to grapple seriously with the issues he was raising in the campaign—issues of reform, issues concerning the lack of fair government in Chicago—and with the central issue: racism. Anderson adds a light but ironic touch when he says, "they really didn't want him to win. They would lose all their normal access to power. They aren't gonna be hanging out on the South Side drinking with blacks to get their stories."

Anderson may be right that white reporters dread what he calls "a transfer of power," but the chances are probably better than average that the City Hall sources under Washington will be hanging around Counsellor's Row and the other downtown saloons that City Hall politicians have always frequented. There certainly is a transfer of power both to whites who have been excluded and to blacks but, once they are in power, they will no doubt take over all the places of power, including the saloons.

The media complained steadily that neither candidate was addressing the issues but instead was only regaling each other with personal attacks. There is general agreement among the reporters who covered Epton that he rarely addressed himself to issues and when he did, it was the issue, veiled though it often was, of race: "We will save our neighborhoods." Those who covered Washington also agree: he *did* cover the issues. Munroe Anderson says that the problem with Washington's campaign was that his approach was too general, too idealistic. He spoke on all the issues but did not discuss specific reforms, which made it difficult to write a new story every day. Lillian Williams, of the *Sun-Times*, says that while he covered the issues, his charges against Epton sometimes overshadowed his discussions of the issues. Overshadowed? Compare Washington's remarks made on April 10 to a group of Jewish supporters to Williams' story of that speech. Williams writes: "Belittling Bernard E. Epton's vow to be a one-term mayor, Harold Washington told national television audiences Sunday that his Republican opponent is just a rich man who wants to play with the city like a 'toy.'"

It appears, from her story, to be simply another personal attack—"belittling" Epton. Washington actually said:

> "Epton has said, 'I only want one term as mayor.' How can he say something like that? He's not a serious candidate. I have the impression of a rich man who wants to use the city of Chicago as a toy in his declining years and then resign after four years of inaction . . . *He has no transition team, has made no effort to put one together* and do you know why? *Because the Democratic Party leaders have supplied his transition team*. He doesn't need one. *They will transition him right into the City Council where he has no base, doesn't know anyone, where there are no Republicans, where he has no stake with the people there. He would be a puppet for four years. He couldn't even sustain a veto if he ever tried* [my emphasis]. This city would not be run by an executive. There would be no separation of powers. The system of strong council/weak mayor would emerge and we would have four years of what we had back when Kennelly was mayor—totally inept, not knowing how to handle those barracudas [the aldermen], not knowing how to relate to them, and city government would be in the hands of [applause] . . . . I will go into the City Council if not with, approximating very closely, a majority of the council with me. I helped elect a lot of those guys. We will elect another five this coming Tuesday. Those who have worked with me in the past know my ability to put coalitions together and if I have twenty-three [of fifty] you can bet your life I'll get the next three to make that majority. Not only would I go into government with an equal basis with the City Council, but I'm also

> putting together an awesome transition team. In other words, we're ready to govern this city. And we are opposed by an individual who thinks it's a play toy.

Washington's words do not constitute a personal attack; they are a political attack, an attempt to show that his opponent is not a realistic alternative for a city needing to be governed. Andrew Malcolm, in the *New York Times* April 17, says,

> Mayor Byrne's weak political base forced her to deal with the same aging politicians who had divvied up the spoils under her mentor, the late Mayor Richard J. Daley. Spotting the same lack of support for Mr. Epton, many of these Democrats openly or secretly worked for the election of a Republican who needed them most.

But in Williams' story, this strong, significant political attack is reduced to a personal attack by Washington against his opponent. Williams can't be charged with racism. She's black. But she can be charged with not understanding the issues in the race and how to handle them. Even a black could be bewildered by the barrage. Williams says that she did not write any stories that her editor rejected because they were too supportive of Washington, as Anderson charges his editors. Small wonder. She also insists that the press coverage was fair. It was simply that Washington, by his "tone, inflection, manner," made his charges against Epton seem to take precedence over his other remarks. Well, reporters are human, I suppose. Perhaps I'm idealistic. I have always assumed that reporters ignored the histrionics of a speaker and directed themselves to the issues.

Douglas Frantz, at the *Tribune*, also insists the coverage was fair and that his editors were scrupulous in their fairness. In fact, he says, it was Jim Squires who asked him to do a piece two days before the election distinguishing fact from fiction because the allegations had become so confused with reality. It seems Squires recognized, late in the campaign, that the coverage in the papers had not clearly enough made the distinction between fact and fiction.

Washington's conviction for failing to file his tax returns was, in the way that stories tend to get distorted, drastically altered to a charge that he didn't pay his taxes. That conversion became so pervasive that even his press secretary, late at night, exhausted from too little sleep for several weeks, slipped and referred to Washington not paying his taxes while discussing the charges.

Almost every day, a new charge came out of Epton's offices. Even when the reporters attributed their stories to the Epton headquarters, another had to be written the next day explaining that the charge was baseless. Take the one that stated that Washington had not paid the water bills on his campaign headquarters. There simply is not a rental building in Chicago in which the landlord is not responsible for the water bill. (Perhaps all the journalists live in condos.) By some error—it may have been, instead, an attempt by the landlord to pass this bill onto Washington—the bill was in Washington's name. He responded to the charge by saying that the landlord was responsible. The papers printed the story; the TV news broadcast the story. Washington had not paid still another bill. And one more crime was added to an already long list. Except that the landlord confessed his responsibility the next day. It had been an error. That Epton spent most of his time on the campaign trail impugning Washington's character is one thing; that the media printed and broadcast his charges as front page news was probably the worst case of yellow journalism in many years and helped to create the smokescreen that was used to hide racism. Then, that smokescreen that they created was used to deny the racism that lay behind it.

Even the well-meaning exceptions ended badly. Roger Simon, in his daily *Sun-Times* column, wrote what he called, "The anatomy of a smear," in which he dissected a charge levelled by Epton against Washington and showed it to be phony—perhaps based on doctored evidence. Simon ends by saying:

> This does not make Harold Washington an angel.
> The fact is he *should* have been in court that day. He had been sent a notice demanding his appearance.
> The fact is he *didn't* pay that gas bill until it was revealed in the newspapers.
> The fact is he *didn't* pay the other two bills Epton brought up Wednesday.
> But Washington *is* innocent of Epton's most scandalous charge: that in order to get out of paying a bill, he claimed to be unemployed.
> I have just two more questions:
> First, how come Bernard Epton doesn't check his facts before he shoots off his mouth?
> Second, is there anyone in this election we can trust?

Perhaps Washington should, indeed, have paid that gas bill. But it was one of those campaign debts—$800—that are so often owed for so long. It is a truism that no one wants to do business with candidates running for office. It is estimated that politicians' creditors often have to settle for ten cents on the dollar. For Simon, however, as for nearly all those writing about Washington during the campaign, that debt made him untrustworthy.

Even Mike Royko, syndicated *Sun-Times* columnist who wrote the most eloquent column of the campaign supporting Washington on the day after the primary and continued to write friendly columns for several weeks, was finally overwhelmed by the Epton barrage as it was printed in the press and broadcast on television. On March 23, a month after the primary Royko wrote a characteristically ironic column placing Washington's tax conviction in the context of the rampant tax evasion in this country. He ends with:

> It makes me wonder if Washington is really going to lose many votes because of his tax conviction.

> Maybe the opposite will happen. If there's as much routine tax cheating going on as *Time* magazine says, there could be a huge groundswell of support for him.
>
> Maybe people will look into their cheating souls and say:
>
> "Hey, he's a kindred spirit."

Two days before the campaign, however, Royko wrote what was probably the most damaging piece of the whole campaign, so damaging that my phone rang all day with people wondering whether it would kill off Washington's possibility of winning. In more space than he usually has, Royko delineated all the problems of Washington's campaign in his usual skillful style. On the financial matters, he says:

> Beginning a campaign with a tax conviction was bad enough. But then came the drip, drip, drip of all the other goofy disclosures. The unpaid water bills, the electric bills, the real estate tax bills, the eviction notice, and on and on.
>
> Many of them were explainable. Some were bills from earlier campaign offices—not bills from Washington's home.
>
> Fine. But *who the hell* was in charge of explaining them—and getting the explanations out to the voters fast? Not his staff, that's for sure.
>
> And why weren't the disclosures anticipated? When you run for office, you frisk yourself in the beginning. Or you have smart advisers who do it. If you have an unpaid parking ticket in your background, you'd better remember it and be ready to explain it. Or better yet, pay it before it surfaces. You don't wait until somebody digs it up and runs it on the front page, then slap your brow, and say: "Gee, I forgot."
>
> And you don't dismiss them as trivial matters. They might be trivial to a candidate and his advisers. But to people who routinely pay all their bills, they're something to wonder about.
>
> That could be the ruin of Washington's campaign. There may have been too many things to wonder about. And too many people who couldn't help but wonder.

Fortunately for Washington, Royko, who is the most powerful columnist in Chicago, wrote another column on Election Day. Also longer than usual, he did not urge people to vote for

Washington, but he made such a fool of Epton that the choice was clear. A choice bit:

> Then there was the time Epton was almost thrown out of a federal judge's chambers because he showed up—unannounced and uninvited—to hold a private conversation with the judge about a case involving a huge chunk of Epton's personal fortune.
>
> The judge sternly lectured Epton about how it wasn't proper for somebody to come around his chambers to chitchat that way.
>
> When this came out during the campaign, and Epton was asked about it, he gave this explanation. He was just concerned that the judge had too many cases on his calendar, and he had thought of a way to speed up that particular case, and just wanted to help the judge out.
>
> In other words, he wasn't worried about his millions of dollars—he was concerned that the judge might be overworked.
>
> Well, I guess that's better than saying he went in the judge's chambers to wait for a bus.

The whole problem might have been eased slightly if Anderson's proposal to write a piece on racism had been considered by his editors. He would have made explicit some of the fears whites have and why they have them and how those fears tend to distort the relationships between whites and blacks and the perceptions that whites have of blacks. But his editors turned down his suggestion. They had enough copy already, they said.

Just before the election, both papers reaffirmed their endorsement of Washington. On the same page that Talbott wrote of "suitcase journalists," the editors said:

> We do not excuse Washington for his failure to file federal income tax returns and perform legal work for clients. Those were serious offenses and they disturb us greatly. But Washington paid for them—with a jail sentence and a suspension from the bar.
>
> Moreover, his past personal wrongdoing has not affected his performance as a public official. Even Epton has failed to turn up evidence that Washington ever benefitted financially from legislation he supported, cut deals with shady politicians or sold out to special interests.
>
> When all the issues, including his past, are considered, Washington

> still emerges as the better-qualified candidate. Hardly anyone is really *for* Epton. Few of his supporters knew who he was until six weeks ago. He is an accidental candidate beholden to politicians who hope to increase their own power under a figurehead mayor . . .
>
> Epton, too, has issued good position papers, but the important difference is that Washington might be able to put his ideas into practice. [Washington] is not an ideal candidate—few politicians are—but he is better qualified than Epton to lead Chicago for the next four years.

The *Tribune* said essentially the same thing.

And what about the coverage in Chicago's black newspapers? In 1965, John Sengstacke fired his editor, Chuck Stone, after he published a front page story in the *Chicago Defender* about the fire-bombing of a black family that moved into Bridgeport. The *Defender* was the major black newspaper in the midwest. One would have expected such an event to be front page news in it. But Sengstacke was so deeply embroiled with the Machine that Stone's consistent anti-Daley stance had forced him into a prizefight with the publisher. Sengstacke had expressly forbidden anti-Daley stories. The firebombing piece was the last straw. Mayor Daley was already furious enough; Bridgeport was his town. Letters and telegrams poured into Sengstacke protesting Stone's firing but the publisher's loyalty to the Machine had priority. The paper has never recovered from Stone's absence. He brought a brilliance and wit to it that had never been there before and Sengstacke has never hired a real replacement for him. Circulation rose under Stone but has declined steadily from 50,000 to 20,000 and the paper's journalistic and publishing standards are, by the lowest standards, pretty tawdry. Typical of the quality of the paper was the front page headline the day after the election: "Dirtiest election in history," when, in fact, it was the cleanest election in Chicago's history, with the help of about ninety attorneys out of the U.S. Attorney's office, about 720 out of the state's attorney's office, hundreds more out of the Board of Election Commissioners, and thousands of poll watchers for dozens of organizations.

The *Defender's* position on the Washington campaign was

consistent with its long history of subservience to the Machine. When Washington announced his candidacy, a front-page editorial "welcomed" him into the race, but the paper continued to support Byrne. As the momentum in the black community grew and with it pressure on Sengstacke, especially from the Black Task Force, a ministerial organization operating parallel to the campaign organization, the *Defender* could no longer maintain its stance. On Feb. 12, an editorial appeared, stating: "Watch Jane run. Mayor Jane Byrne is running again. Our question is WHO RUNS JANE BYRNE? . . . Some months ago, those who run Mayor Jane Byrne wanted to compromise the Defender for its Editorial support. During our 77 years in existence, the Defender's endorsement has never been for sale, and it is not for sale now. If Jane Byrne does not know what her bosses are doing, she ought to know now." The editorial then went on to endorse Washington ten days before the primary. It is likely that what Byrne offered was more of the city's official advertising, a not insignificant offer because the *Defender* is in shaky financial shape. There is little advertising and the circulation continues to drop. It does bring a chuckle to Sengstacke watchers that he could not simply endorse the highly popular black candidate but had to make it appear that he was forced to by the illegal shenanigans of the candidate to whom he had obviously pledged his loyalty. Only because she had tried to buy him off had he endorsed his community's clear favorite. Pressure from the community didn't count. After Washington won the primary, however, the reporters who had always supported him were able to write more of the kind of stories they wanted, offering balance to the stories appearing in the downtown papers and the television broadcasts, ignoring the most questionable stories emanating out of Epton headquarters and reprinting the racist handbills and other materials distributed by the Epton people.

There is, in the black community, in addition to the daily *Defender*, a number of small weeklies, all of which maintained a strongly supportive position. They, too, reprinted the racist literature coming out of the Epton camp, plus human interest stories of people involved in the "crusade." Though none of the black papers has any sizeable circulation, their combined impact did tend to offset some of the impact of the mainstream media.

Does all of the preceding prove that the white-dominated press in Chicago is racist, that it is only one highly visible racist institution in a city that is more bigotted than others in the U.S., that Talbott, Squires, Simon, et al, are racists, though they are struggling, as Anderson says, "with their demons," wanting to be fair to Washington because they are well-intentioned, honorable journalists, but unable to overcome the feelings that arose in the ugly atmosphere that besieged this city like a heavy storm? Did it become impossible for these journalists, under the pressure of less well-intentioned racists, to do their jobs as they would have six months earlier? Clarence Petersen, a feature writer at the *Tribune,* says he was aghast at the leaflets slipped under his door in a Near North Side high rise. "Horrid stuff." Petersen didn't have to write about the campaign. If he had, could he have resisted the insidious effects of all those leaflets? Certainly, he did not "believe all that stuff," but they did, he admits, create doubts. When there's smoke, there's fire. That this fire was arson was never made completely clear because Washington refused to call it that.

In the end, it must be said that Washington's failure to call that fire arson was certainly a large factor in the racism exhibited by the press. He might not have quenched the fire by anything he said but more people—including those in the media—would have had the opportunity to know its source and better evaluate their own attitudes toward it.

But the very question over whether Chicago is *more* racist than other cities cannot be seen as anything but a subtle reflection of Chicago's racism. Is it important to know whether a fire is bigger than another fire raging elsewhere if they are both destroying life and property? That comparison is made routinely. This accident was worse than that. This volcanic eruption was worse than that one. We cannot resist these comparisons, they seem to be as natural to our thinking processes as the questions we ask about why an event happened. But we do not excuse an airplane crash because it is not as bad as one three years earlier. Reporters and columnists do not write apologies for an airline because its crash wasn't as horrible as another airline's. They do not make those comparisons to diminish the impact of the current event. Those comparisons are not devices used to clean up a dirtied reputation. The comparisons of Interior Secretary James Watt's giveaways to the coal industry with similar infractions were not made to whitewash Watt. The comparison between Chicago's racism and that of other American cities was an obvious attempt to make Chicago appear less invidious.

Were those defenses of their city made by journalists out of racism or merely out of civic pride, as some insist? Well, maybe the motive was pride. Understandable. The trouble with pride, however, is that it often creates monsters of us, endowing us with characteristics we would normally eschew but characteristics we succumb to, perhaps unwittingly, in the service of that great god, pride.

Whether Chicago is more racist than other cities is irrelevant. The campaign against Washington was one of the dirtiest in history. But let's for a moment consider the comparison. To which cities do we compare ourselves? Certainly, Chicagoans are not still bombing black churches as they are in Boston. But there are also all those towns and cities across the country that elected black mayors without the kind of campaign that was conducted in Chicago. That there are so many black mayors is no insignificant fact. The job of mayor of the city, more than any other elective job, reflects an electorate's confidence and trust of a candidate to handle their affairs. Unlike other elective posts, the mayoralty is close to the people, affects their daily lives, their futures. Garbage disposal, public transit, education, street maintenance, the nitty gritty of daily living are governed by the mayor. Of the fifty largest cities in the U.S., nine have black mayors. While 233 mayors represents only a token number in the larger picture of thousands of municipalities, the fact that only twenty years ago there were none represents a dramatic rise in the ability of blacks to elect this highly significant public figure. That many of those cities are heavily black does not diminish that fact, for, traditionally, blacks have voted for whites. It is only in recent years that this equation has changed—that blacks have, on the one hand, been able to challenge whites for those seats of power and that their fellow blacks, on the other hand, have been willing to support them. At the same time, while many black mayors govern largely black cities, there is a sizeable number that govern largely white cities. Not since Carl Stokes' bid for the mayoralty in Cleveland in 1967 has the national press taken such notice of a local election. Nor would so much notice have been paid had not Chicago been widely recognized as one of the last strongholds of white power. If a black can win in Chicago, the wisdom said, he can win anywhere—a bellwether for national and local politics of the future.

It was the failure to see their city in that realistic light, to put it into a realistic national context—a failure of sophistication and wit—that led Chicago's journalists astray. They were the victims of Chicago's racism even as they were its perpetuators, if racism can be viewed at least in part as the consequence of xenophobia, of cultural ignorance, of political unsophistication.

But that failure must be seen in the particular context of the mightily divided city that Chicago is and the greater failure of the media to fully understand and deal with that division. There is no journalist in the city who does not know that Chicago is a series of ethnic enclaves that serve as a mountainous backdrop for the Lakefront. White ethnics, Hispanics, and blacks live, as Isaac Rosenfeld described in an essay in *Commentary* in the early fifties, inland. There are the landed folks in Chicago, he said, and the water people. While it is an oversimplification to say that he attributed the greater sophistication and liberality of the water people to their life on the water, it is, in fact, the heart of his argument. Living on water is powerfully energizing and vitalizing. It provides an element of universality that is denied those who live in tight landlocked urban settings. And that energy, vitality, and universality creates in those privileged to live on the Lakefront a liberality and sophistication that does not occur elsewhere in the city. Not only liberality in politics, but in art, theater, and music. When Rosenfeld wrote his prophetic essay, the Lakefront population was still quite small and exclusive—it was in the days before the massive high-rises were erected from one end of the city to the other along the lake. That burgeoning community has transformed Chicago from the hog butcher of the world that Sandburg described in the twenties and the cultural wasteland that A. J. Liebling described in the forties to a town bursting with theaters, jazz clubs, art galleries, dance groups, with the best symphony orchestra in the nation, a leading opera company, the only free jazz festival in the world, the most advanced architecture in the nation. Once a provincial city known for its criminals and its stockyards, for its intensely guarded ethnic enclaves, Chicago can now be described as a highly sophisticated city that exports its cultural products to the world. The largest part of that work is done by Lakefront people.

The city's journalists live almost exclusively on the Lakefront. They are proud of their community, its cultural activities, and its liberality. That there is only a sprinkling of blacks and a handful of Hispanics among them does not deter them. Any minority person with money and credentials is welcome. That the money and credentials are harder to come by for minority people is seen by most on the Lakefront as a sorry state and some contribute generously to try to change that condition. But most ignore it. They are universalisitic in their attitudes but they are also, like most people, content to live their own lives unmindful of the plight of others. When it is time to vote, they usually vote for reform because it is one of the universalistic goals. On the other hand, voting for a black mayor was, in the primary, for more than three-quarters of the Lakefront liberals, a bit much. Almost half of them voted for Washington in the general election but that is a considerable drop from the vote they normally give reform candidates.

Lakefront liberals are not only unmindful of the plight of most minority people in the city, they are also unmindful of the majority of most of the whites in the city, those workers who live out there on the land who fear change, who fear the encroachment of minorities into their tight little communities, and who are unaware that Chicago has become a major cultural metropolis. They bowl, drink beer, watch television, go to an occasional movie, go to church, take care of their little houses, and try to get along on a small paycheck. They don't like the rich Jews and others who live along the Lakefront but they don't mix with them. They go to Schaller's Pump for dinner, not to George's or Ambria or Gordon. They don't even know those restaurants exist. They live in another world, miles away from the lake, locked into the land. The young people go to the public beaches that crown the city from one end to the other and then they go home. They also go occasionally to Rush Street, a tourist strip of clubs where they mostly meet their own types.

For a Lakefronter to go to Schaller's Pump is an excursion into the boondocks, into forbidden territory where they are not welcome.

That this division should be mostly ignored by the Lakefronters, that they should live their own somewhat complacent, often smug lives, unmindful of the rest of the city is hardly surprising or noteworthy. How many of us take any detailed note of our distant neighbors? If we do, it is the exotic we note, those in El Salvador and South Africa, not the working people in our own backyards. But that this division is not closely watched and understood by the city's journalists who, of course, live on the Lakefront, is quite another story, a story that accounts for the failure of the media to interpret the facts of the campaign. It was, for the city's journalists, a case of their Lakefront xenophobia opposed to the rest of the city, to the massive political changes in the black community, and the resistance to that change in the white landed people, along with not just a few of the Lakefronters. Isaac Rosenfeld would have loved to be an observer of this scene. His untimely death deprived us of the shrewd judgments he would have made.

Despite what Don Rose, the political strategist who engineered Jane Byrne's upset victory in 1979 and campaign commentator for ABC-TV, calls "the most inept large scale campaign I've ever seen," Washington pulled it off with 16-18 percent of the "white" vote and a tremendous outpouring—97 percent—of the black vote. Rose isn't alone in calling the campaign inept. Most observers, inside and outside the staff, agree. They say: Washington did not trust his staff, perhaps justifiably. He knows more about campaigning than ten of them together. He hired a campaign manager and then undercut him regularly and finally eased him out. He arbitrarily changed scheduled dates without consultation with those in charge of the schedules. He intimidated his press staff so that they didn't feel safe speaking for him. He permitted chaos to reign by never permitting anyone to pull together the various centers of influence. He did not create a strategy group until close to the end of the campaign. So go the charges. Some are documented.

The veteran campaigner, Rose, volunteered to work for nothing. He could prepare the media materials. He could handle the press. He could even be campaign manager. His offer was rejected. Friends in the campaign offered two explanations: Washington resented Rose's resignation from the '77 campaign. (Rose resigned when he was made to look foolish by failing to deliver the tax returns for nineteen years preceding the ones in which Washington failed to file. Washington promised Rose the earlier returns but failed to produce them.) "Apparently, he thought my resignation was disloyal," Rose says, "but I had no choice." Was Rose correct to resign and should Washington have realized that he could not do otherwise? Or was Rose hotheaded and impetuous, proudly resigning instead of simply admitting that Washington had failed to produce the materials? Rose insists his integrity was at stake.

The second reason suggested to Rose for Washington's rejection of his offer is that he is so visible in Chicago that he would be credited with the victory that would legitimately be a black peoples' victory. This explanation carries some strong credibility. Rose is, as indicated previously, generally credited with Byrne's 1979 victory and with the victories of other candidates for whom he has worked. There is no reason to believe that the same credit would not devolve on him again when, in fact, Washington's victory is the consequence of intensive and extensive work by hundreds of blacks. Engineered by the candidate himself, of course, but accomplished by the incredibly dedicated work of hundreds of people working long hours seven days a week.

There is no question that most of those charges against Washington are true. He did try to run the show himself and thus created the chaos that Al Raby, his campaign manager, described every time he was asked about the campaign. Washington did create his own chaos by contermanding the orders of those supposedly in charge of things. He did reorganize the staff several times, sending some very competent people off to Siberia and elevating some incompetents to positions of power to placate others. Furthermore, many of those on the staff were inexperienced, often downright incompetent. Young blacks, with no prior experience in politics, often did not know what to do or how to do it. But this was their crusade. There was enormous jockeying for positions of power, planning for the future instead of concentrating on the job at hand. And there was what whites who have worked in black political activities since the late sixties have come to expect: resentment and suspicion of them among blacks. Not, of course, by Washington, who has worked with whites all of his adult life, but those on the staff, many of them without any prior experience in political activity or in day-to-day (very long days) contact with whites.

One of the nearly disastrous results of the chaos in Washington's headquarters was the failure to visit enough, until almost the end of the campaign, the white sections of the city. Several explanations are advanced. "He liked to go where he was loved," one pundit says. "He owed favors to those who had won the primary for him," says another. "He thought he could just win it off the black vote. Until he realized that was impossible." A staff person has another explanation: "There were only so many white votes he could get. As it was, he took more than any other first-time black candidate except Tom Bradley [that story was hard not to believe]. He had to get the numbers which means that he had to get every black vote he could." That explanation is the first that sounds credible, even if it was wrong-headed. To say that he liked to go where he is loved is an impossibly naive estimate of the practical politician, Harold Washington. To say that he was repaying favors is too cynical but it also is based on the naive assumption that Washington was actually "drafted." In fact, he was waiting impatiently in the wings for the black community to organize itself well enough for him to run a successful campaign. To say that he thought he could win it simply with the black vote implies that Washington can't count, hardly a reasonable assumption. But to say that he was unsure about what that white vote would be, knowing the composition of the city, and believing that he could count on the 6 percent who had voted for him in the primary plus another 4 or 5 percent, it may have seemed reasonable to concentrate on getting out every possible black vote to assure the numbers. Too late to capture a bigger white vote but in time to take the 16-18 percent he did get, Washington finally, in the last weeks of the campaign, went north to the liberals who were his other natural constituency but who, like the media, as a consequence of the media's handling of the campaign, were beginning to waver. The response to him was warmly enthusiastic. Large crowds turned out—much bigger than expected—and they cheered him just as blacks cheered him. There is no guarantee, of course, that, had he made more effort to win the liberal Lakefront, he would have taken 75 percent instead of 45 percent. But those who worked for him worked hard—and spent money. To draw people to the main North Side event, a page ad was taken in the papers to announce the rally and listing 750 sponsors. Just before the election, another support ad appeared. Ron Stevens, the director of the Lakefront campaign, refused to say that Washington had not appeared in his community often enough but would say,

> The more time we have him up here, the better it is to do our job because he's the best thing we've got. The more people see him, the more they hear him, the more convinced they are of his intelligence, his charm, and his humanity. Because of that, the more we have him the better and the less we have him, the harder it is. And now that he has come up here more often, this last week, I think it will help a lot. Especially the press coverage. The press has not covered his appearances on the north side all that well. I certainly would have liked to have him here more.

A footnote to the discussion on media coverage emerges here. It seemed to those who watched that the television people preferred to show Washington's meetings with blacks. While he did not spend enough time on the north side, by all accounts, the time he did spend there was hardly covered by the broadcasters. And his appearance at the biggest rally on the north side as it appeared on CBS-TV showed him speaking first and, then, for a crowd shot, in the foreground, strangely, one of the few blacks who attended that rally, with whites as hazy faces in the background. When, in the last few days of the campaign, he appeared in both the black and white communities, the broadcasters chose to show him only in the black communities. Watching the television coverage, one could not know that Washington spent any time among whites. Stevens says, "Everyone agrees that the story this week [the last week] is happening on the Lakefront. That's where it's going to happen. Then those very people who say this don't show footage of the Lakefront." Knowing that the television people choose to show the most spectacular of events covered, was the footage seen on TV more spectacular than what appeared on the Lakefront, thus releasing the television people of selecting footage to air for political reasons? One of the most dramatic events of the campaign was a 6:45 AM meeting of about 100 whites who crowded into a restaurant to listen to Washington before going out to leaflet trains and bus stops. The crowd was tremendously enthusiastic—at 6:45 in the morning. The TV news that evening showed Washington shaking hands at a train stop in the black community. No mention was made of the early morning appearance before a mostly white audience. The message? Washington is the candidate of the blacks, Epton the candidate of the whites.

Stevens was disappointed with the 45 percent that Washington took on the Lakefront. "I thought at the beginning it was possible to carry the Lakefront. But given the circumstances, I guess we did all right." The circumstances? His candidate did not conduct his campaign in a way designed to help Stevens carry the Lakefront.

Does it make any difference? He won. Isn't that all that's

important? No, that's not all that's important. In this racially divided city, had he taken a larger white vote, he would have carried a larger unified mandate into City Hall, which would have made governing the city easier. Had the candidate early on established a strategy committee to plan ahead instead of working day to day, hit and miss, the vote would most likely have been larger in the white community, enlarging Washington's mandate and creating a picture of greater unity, less racial division, than the actual vote provided.

All that said, Robert Creamer adds,

> It's true there was no one in charge, Harold ran it all. There seems to have been no campaign manager. It's true that not enough was done to attack Epton on the issues, on insurance, on redlining, on toxic wastes, property tax relief. It never came together as it should have. It's true that Harold didn't show up for many white scenes as a result of a very amateurish scheduling operation. It's true that there was no clear strategy about message delivery, particularly to the white community. But all that is minor in the larger scheme of things. The fact is the man won. It is an extraordinary event in Illinois political history. It is basically a spectacular political movement. Furthermore, we see this all the time. The candidate runs his own campaign, doesn't allow anyone else to make real decisions. Apparently Harold didn't have anyone he trusted enough to give up the reins. But that's a two-way street. On the other hand, you can say he's not willing to delegate authority. On the other hand, he's a very savvy and experienced political person and it's hard to find somebody to match him. This was the big stakes. Who's to say that he didn't make the right political decisions and if he'd turned them over, somebody else might have made the wrong ones. The fact is, he won. Furthermore, I don't think he anticipated that Epton would be able to whip up the racist fervor he did or that the Machine group would fight him to the last.
>
> But in the end, the extraordinary thing about that campaign was the energy. Compared to the Stevenson campaign, which occupied the same space, the energy and excitement was enormous. And I'd trade that any day for all the organizational things the campaign lacked.

Energy?

6 P.M.: "Dave, is the schedule out yet?"

"No, call back in an hour."

7 P.M. "Dave, got the schedule yet?"
"No, call back after the 10 o'clock news."
11 P.M. "Dave, how about the schedule?"
"Here it is."

"Roz, can I go through the clip file?"
"Sure. But it's better to come either late at night or early in the morning when there's not so much activity going on."
"Fine. How about 10 tonight?"
"I'll be here."
10 P.M.: This is less activity? The press room is filled with people: staff and volunteers. Everybody is either working or conferring.
"Florence, could you make something of this?"
"What is it?"
"A speech on veteran's rights."
"I'll try."
11 P.M. The press room is emptying out. Roz Marovitz has retyped and xeroxed the speech I've written. We settle down to the file cabinets that house the clip file.
1 A.M. "Florence, I have an offer of a ride home. Would you mind if I leave you here? If you need my help again, I'll be here early in the morning."
Roz Marovitz was not unique. And she was a volunteer. The entire staff at 53 W. Jackson, in the renovated landmark Monadnock Building,—paid and volunteer—were there from early in the morning til late at night. They might be difficult to reach; meetings abounded though it's not clear how many decisions reached in those meetings were approved by Washington and carried out. The staff was notorious for not returning phone calls; some were notorious for their rudeness. But I knew, if I was persistent, I could reach the person I wanted. He or she would always be there.

As so often happens, because I was writing a book about the

candidate, I became an instant expert on the election. In the closing days of the campaign, as some pollsters predicted a very close margin and some pundits said it was too close to call, my phone rang constantly with people asking, "What's going to happen?" *Perhaps I have a misplaced faith in this city that I love, but I think there are enough whites out there who are wise enough to rise above the bigotry and hatred to realize that Harold is clearly the only possible choice. I believe there are enough white people in this city who can rise above their own personal racism to put the welfare of the city first. And I believe that there are enough whites who, while we all have some racism deep in us that we find it difficult to erase, are sufficiently well-intentioned toward blacks that they understand and even agree that it truly is time for those who represent 40 percent of the population of this city to have a turn at governing it. Especially since Harold is the most qualified man ever to run for the office of mayor in this town, it seems to me that there will be enough whites voting for him to elect him.*

That answer was not entirely personal. It was based on what I had seen on the campaign trail and on what I had heard from people on the streets, in saloons, at parties in the last twenty years. On the campaign trail I saw about 1,500 whites, including Hispanics, cheering wildly when Washington spoke. One has to extrapolate from those who go to the rallies to the many more who don't. I figured, quite unscientifically, that for every one person who went to listen and cheer, there were twenty or twenty-five people sitting in front of their television sets quietly cheering their candidate and another similar group who had some misgivings because of his legal problems but who could not vote for the inept Epton. And I did not attend all the meetings that Washington held with whites.

The margin would not be large, I knew, because Epton's smear campaign had taken hold. Washington's lead had slipped badly since the beginning of the campaign when Epton was just getting his strategy together. And I was certain that Washington had made a strategic mistake in waiting until the last two weeks to begin seriously campaigning on the Lakefront. But when I heard his speech at the Belmont Hotel ten days before the election, I said,

"He will win. These people will go out and get the votes for him. He has said just what they wanted to hear, the way they wanted to hear it. If only he had started earlier."

The national press that carried its message around the country that the Chicago mayoral race was simply a matter of racism were correct. It is probably correct to say that most blacks voted for Washington because he had become their great hero, and that most whites voted for Epton because he was their Great White Hope. There were a few whites who voted against Washington, not because they were bigots but because the smear campaign worked. Three percent of blacks also voted against him for that or other, more complex, reasons. A small but highly significant number of whites voted for Washington for all the reasons I predicted they would. The city's image in the world was saved by these people.

On The Campaign Trail

In the middle of the primary campaign, Washington went to the Second Baptist Church in Evanston, a suburb adjacent to Chicago that has a large middle-class black community, to raise funds and gather supporters. To his all-black audience, he explained his campaign:

There are some people who ask me why I would abandon the fight against Reagan, which I have waged for the past two years, and have been dubbed as the person who is the most anti-Reaganite in Congress. I deserve the accolade. I appreciate that accolade. I have worked for it (applause). I cherish it. And even though I will leave the Congress this coming April and take on another responsibility, it will not be to shirk my job of fighting Reagan and whatever he stands for. I can continue to do that, and I think I can do it just as effectively if not more so, by marshalling local forces and getting them ready to fight Mr. Reagan, because what he stands for is obviously something that is anathema to us and something which must cease and he must be stopped. And also, in case we don't know it, there are Reaganites all over this country. One is now the Mayor of the city, and it is my purpose to weed out Reaganism wherever I find it (applause) and so having locked horns with the major Reaganite I feel it only necessary that I lock horns with some of the saturns and flunkeys and so for that reason and if for no other reason, I come back to Chicago to replace that Reaganite, because she has wreaked havoc in our community, there is no question about it. . . .

I think Congress has gotten the message. And if I have any regrets about leaving Congress, it will be because the new Congress will have some degree of sanity to it and I would like to be known not as just a person who fought Mr. Reagan the hardest, but one of those who helped beat the liver out of him the hardest (applause).

But duty calls, and I must respond. I am not the grandson of a Methodist minister, and the son of a Methodist minister for nothing. They left me a legacy and part of that legacy was a deep-seated concern about my fellow man, so I am into the area of public service, and even though I didn't feel I was a good enough man to follow in my granddaddy and father's footsteps and religion, I felt that my feet were big enough to move into politics and give it a breath of fresh air, having been raised in a spiritual environment. And I think it has been good for politics and for the city and this country.

So I come back to Chicago, to do a job which the people in Chicago have asked me to do. I was not reluctant in running, contrary to what people said. I was only a reluctant prospect. I am not a reluctant candidate (applause). . . . I have approached this campaign with gusto, verve and vigor. We have put together in Chicago something many people thought would never happen. We have put together one of the most powerful independent political machines that ever existed in any city in this country. It is well staffed. It is well peopled. We have people in the field in the area of maybe 6,000 and we hope to get around 10,000 on Election Day. All self-starters. If literature is late, they put together their own. If they don't have poll sheets, they go door to door and get the names of the mailboxes. They don't waste time. They don't look for directions, they just move. They are all salesmen. And they are satisfied that they have a good product, like Campbell's soup on the shelf. So they don't have any problem going out and selling it (applause).

So we are not impressed with those phony statistics based on phony polls that you see. We know something that they evidently don't know. You don't poll our people through the use of telephone. I mean, that is elementary psychology. We didn't exist in this country 400 years for nothing. We have a healthy paranoia (applause). If some stranger calls you on the phone with a Caucasian voice and asks you who you are going to vote for, you know what you are going to tell him: well, I don't know. I haven't made up my mind. Or you are going to tell him something you think he wants to hear. I mean that is the whole ball game. We are not stupid people. So those polls don't mean anything. When it comes to white folks, I take their word for it what they poll. But when it comes to my community, or Hispanics, or even a lot of poor whites, those polls don't mean one doodly squat (laughter). The example of it was this last November election. Gallup, the master of all polls, just came into Chicago and he is going to do a job. He did a job on the *Sun-Times,* he sold them a bill of goods, so he goes to . . . and he says . . . "35 percent of the black folks in the city of Chicago will vote for Jim Thompson. When anybody walking the street knew better than that (laughter). Thirty-five percent! Jim Thompson got seven percent of the black vote. And anybody who had any sense at all had to read into the terrific black registration in Chicago, which was twice as great as the white registration for the first time in history of the city, that that was an anti-Reagan vote, and that they were going to vote the straight Democratic ticket, not because they loved Democrats necessarily, not because they were particularly enamored with Stevenson, although I endorsed him, but because they wanted to strike at Mr. Reagan and the only way to do so was to vote his opposite party. So these polls don't mean anything. . . .

We know that we are going to win this campaign. And we are not making any excuses to anybody. I resent the media, time after time after time, trying to impose upon us some rationale for black people wanting to have a black mayor. That is insane. We have supported unstintingly, not just in Chicago, but throughout the entire country, not just in large urban areas, but everywhere, we have supported candidates of all views, races, and sexes but our own. We have had faith in them. We have listened to them. We have mulled over their propositions. We have supported them. And we have got the same thing every time. I submit to you that there isn't a black politician in the city of Chicago that has a thimbleful of political power. Not a one. Not a one. They talk about our twenty-four judges. Big deal. Should be forty, fifty. Of the 200 and some odd judges we have in Chicago, with Irish being 5 percent of the population, you have got over 110 Irish judges. What manner of men are they that they should be born in a world with a better judicious temperament than anybody else? You know what that game is all about (applause). There is nothing written in the heavens that says that all the mayors must be Irish, or that they should all go to non-public schools. Do you know that I would be the first mayor in modern history, in Chicago, who went to a Chicago public school system. The first (applause). They don't even send their children to a public school. None of them. Kennelly, Kelly, Daley, Cermak, Bilandic, the present mayor.

Now this is not a demagogic speech. I am not trying to elicit hate and meanness. But I am saying that the mayors of the city of Chicago have not been relevant to the city, or to most of the people of the city. They have had their own narrow strident attitude. We are not out to penalize anybody. We are not out to punish anybody. All we said is that we want a fair government. We want decision making to come from the people of the city in all its constituent parts. I have said such revolutionary things as, for example, Chicago should have a Freedom of Information Act so people can run in and see what the Sanitary District does with their money, what the Department of Personnel does, what all these agencies do. How can you monitor and make government accountable unless you can see? I said that we should have a budgetary process to give the people enough time to testify about the budget. To give enough time for some of those concrete-headed aldermen to look at the budget. This is not revolutionary. This is common sense. I said that I will issue an affirmative action program in the city of Chicago for every city job and that the city will be a rainbow and that Hispanics and women, and blacks will have their pro rata share of jobs, based upon their qualifications and . . . and everybody gets uptight about it. I am not going in there and fire everybody, but I am going to make it clear that if you work for the city you don't have to pay any political dues to anybody.

Give me a day's work, you get a day's pay, and your political business is your own. I would hope you would support me, but if you don't you won't get fired. You would just be classified as stupid. That's all (applause). And if that don't get you, firing won't help. And that is the bottom of the barrel. I am not only going to do that, but I am going to open my contracts so that everybody can have their fair share. . . .

I am not going to be like past mayors to sit on top of all that power in Chicago, arrogant, frowning out at the people, half scared and half frightened to deal with it, and the net result is that Chicago has become an isolated island of high taxation and low delivery and a monolith and a reputation all over the world which has reduced us to pure clear laughter. I go through the halls of Congress and Chicago is a joke. It's the city not of the big bang, but the big buck. You buy what you need. You pay under the table. Businessmen are pushed around, shoved, grabbed, blackmailed. They don't treat people right, they don't treat business right, they don't treat their citizens right. They don't treat anybody right. It is a graft-ridden city, corrupt with crime because we have a Police Department led by a police superintendent who thinks his main responsibility is to campaign for a mayor, give out false statistics (applause) and try to muscle people (applause). Then you wonder why business leaves Chicago. It hasn't left because it had a black mayor, unless somebody has been in the closet all these years (laughter). It has left because they have been mistreated. There's no inventory, there's no relationship, it has no concern, just bleed, bleed, bleed, take, take, take, buy and sell. . .

I didn't come here to knock the city and its people, I came here to knock the leaders. That monolith that calls itself the Democratic Party leadership is going to be moved aside and out of the way of municipal administration in the city of Chicago. I believe in party politics. But I don't believe in any party controlling every movement, every dime, every discretion of a community, and I particularly don't believe it when that oppressive Machine has used my community as a submachine with no rights that they are bound to respect, none they do respect. . . .

This campaign has come down to two things. Is it winnable?

The answer is yes. So it comes down to one thing. How can we convince the few naysayers in our comunity that it is winnable? Because 90 percent of the black people in the city of Chicago say that they will support us, but only 65 percent think it is winnable. That is going to erode their confidence. They don't have all these sophisticated facts that you have. They are not aware of the fact that we have over 200 black mayors. They don't understand these things. They work hard, they're busy. They have problems. They don't concentrate. We have only twenty-one days to get that message out. It is going to be hard. It is going to be tough. You here in Evanston, in a sense, and this is not a putdown, are an extension of black people in Chicago. Wherever you can reach them, I wish you would. I wish you would talk to the sister who is tired, who thinks that the world is just totally and completely white and you can't find your way into it. You have got to let her know that the Civil Rights movement was not successful in emancipating us, but it pushed us in some directions. You have got to talk to that old jaded black gentleman who gets every dime he has ever made from the white community and feels that he owes something back. You have got to let him know that he owes something to black people and to black youth. You have got to talk to those young people (applause), you have got to talk to those young people in our community who are so hip, so out of it, so sophisticated, so worldly, so knowledgeable, that they are in the way. They are a problem (applause). You have got to let them know, "Listen, man, you can't afford to go sit your feet under that table and eat those grits and do nothing, take the faith and take the word of a lot of other people who think this must be done. Get on up and get on out there and vote, don't just vote, talk to your fellow young boys and girls and get them to vote. We need all the help we can get because the campaign is winnable, we have got to break down that little naysaying resistance in the black community. *We have all the white votes we are going to get. We open the door, ask them to come in, they can still come, we aren't wasting any more time on them, we are going to cultivate the turf.* We need you to help cultivate that turf. We need you to help operate from Evanston. A radio program, a telephone bank that will reach into Chicago and talk to them. We will have Congressional black caucus members down, we are going to have black mayors down. We are going to have all the entertainers down. We are going to do all those things, but we need a tremendous network moving from the suburbs and from the state wherever black folks are, descending upon Chicago like locusts, focusing upon the head of every black person and saying, "Listen, up off your . . . baby, this is no time to pray, because this job is done" (applause). Because if this job is done it will have reverberations all over the world. Chicago is the . . . of the Antilles. It is desired, it is a powerful market. If we win this campaign the reverberations will be so loud and clear that there will be drums in Zaire. Thank you very much (applause).

About 1,000 people overflowing the ballroom of the Belmont Hotel chant "We want Harold" as he enters behind the barrage of television cameramen, photographers, and reporters. A long list of North Side political figures have just finished their tributes.

We have covered so much in this campaign and there are so many issues, side issues, more side issues and complicated issues, that we have gotten bogged down and lost sight of what is really involved in this campaign. Obviously, and clearly, if you like it or not, certainly we didn't perpetrate it, but it is there, it is insidious and sinuous and has warped this campaign and . . . it, it has caught the attention of the national press and brought it to this city and it has been embarrassing, but it is there and has been discussed by all polls, and that is the question of racism. It has been raised primarily, if not exclusively, by the kind of campaign my opponent is conducting.

We are in the process of talking about that but I propose not to add any more. I have tried to avoid it throughout this campaign, not because I am afraid to deal with the issue, not because I couldn't add anything constructive to the discussion of that issue, but I just don't think it is time to deal with that issue because there is another more fundamental issue which uses that issue as a cloud and smoke screen to keep people from focusing upon the real problems in the campaign.

There is an old saying which has reverberated throughout this country ever since the day of the padded balls and you know what it is. "Chicago ain't ready for reform." I submit to you that in 1983 Chicago is ready for reform (applause and cheers) and one reason why some of these voices are so . . . strident in dealing with base subjects is because they want to cover up, confuse and get away from the focus of this campaign and the focus of this campaign as of day one, which is Chicago's political reform. It needs reform, and the overwhelming number of people in this city not only want reform but insist upon reform, and those who are opposing us, in the main, no matter what tactics they are using, know it and don't want that reform. It is just that simple.

What is this reform all about? We are not talking about changing the basic form of democracy. We are not talking about that. We have it, we are proud of it. What we are talking about is a phrase I used earlier in the campaign, which was deliberately misconstrued to make it seem I was trying to destroy the Democratic Party. That has never been my purpose. I was born and bred in it. I am of the manor born. My dad was one of the first black Democrats in Chicago. He had a good day if he brought in twenty-five Democrats back in the days when blacks were lopsided Republicans, as they are now Democrats. My old man couldn't even get my mother to vote Democrat! (laughter). No way! She was a hidebound Republican.

I have worked within the Democratic Party for years, I think too many, but worked within it. I have always felt that on balance it represented the best of a lesser of two evils and the one place where there was a chance for people in this country, independents, aggressive people, poor people, black people, most of the ethnics to escalate themselves. Even though it is not perfect, far from perfect, back in the realm of perfection maybe it was ranked as a "10," but in the realm of perfection the Republican Party was ranked a sub-zero (more laughter). I propose as Mayor of this City to lift the Democratic Party up intact and lift it over and place it to the side and let it be that which is supposed to be: an interest group, a legitimate interest group, which rallies for candidates and tries to get them elected, but does not penetrate deeply into the bowels of government (applause). . . .

Those defectors are gone, thank God, they may be gone forever (applause and cheers) and now we Democrats (cheers) who really need a vehicle to get things done can recast the Democratic Party in an image more to the liking of the people and all these neighborhoods who want it and who don't want any Mayor using tax dollars to browbeat workers back into a state of feudalism, sending him out into the boondocks everywhere (laughter).

Don't lose sight of what we are talking about. We are talking about reforming municipal government in the City of Chicago and . . . those men of greed and avarice who don't want a change in the pattern, who want to maintain a tight hold on this city, who want to have control of the city workers, they are the ones who are destroying the Democratic Party (applause and cheers).

Here is what really flipped their minds: I said this: that I will take no more than a reasonable amount by way of campaign contributions from any person who has a contract with the city. That sent a signal up, they knew darn well that I was not going to do like my predecessor immediately has done, which is to sell this city for the next four years. Look at the campaign disclosures of this mayor and you will see page after page, 10, 15, 20, 30, 40, 60, 80 thousands, of course the laundered money is there, too. It goes up, up, up. Of individuals who do business with this city. What are you saying? Or what am I saying? In effect this whole business of economic development and planning has been skewed out of proportion. The money goes to those who pay the campaign contributions. And what we see is the spectacle of this city giving a million dollars to a liquor store to expand when you can't get capital development money to rehab your home (cheers and applause). . . .

The point is not to assume that they are standing in the door like George Wallace trying to prevent me getting into the office of mayor only because I am black. Those defectors see in this campaign a new zeal, a change in this city, which would throw out these people who have been ripping and raping this city (applause). They see a man like myself, who has spent his life ensconced in politics, trying to bring people together, trying to unify. Everybody in this city must be considered. I reach out to each of them in a different way. I reach out to the Polish people. The Germans. The Scandinavians, the Irish, the Jews. I reach out to the Mexican people, the Puerto Rican people, the Cuban people. I reach out to my own people. I exclude no one. This city cannot grow. It cannot thrive, it cannot be the oasis here in the middle of this country that it should and must be, unless we get that behind us. But to accuse me, even remotely, of being exclusionary is fantastic and crazy. And it indicates a paranoia so unhealthy that no citizen has a right to repeat it. I propose to be mayor of all the people in this city. I propose to go through this city and put together the finest transition team you have ever had, that consists of a cross section of the tremendous talent this city has to offer (applause and cheers). Our plan is to bring under the umbrella of this city people from planning and policy and administration, corporate and financial and small business of Chicago, academicians, the neighborhoods, organized labor, all, all, all. Every group, as I move through this city. The outstanding thing which hits you . . . they don't change. When you go across the street, it is the same on each side. It doesn't change. People want their communities serviced by government, timely, efficiently and without begging for it, or without paying an extra bit of money to get your garbage removed. They want those things done. They want their schools to turn out more than flotsam and jetsam and they are crying for new ways to do it. They want a mass transportation system which is efficient, fair and safe. They want money passed into their neighborhoods for rehabilitation of their homes and for seed money and grants and joint ventures and low interest loans so their businesses can increase the inventories and improve their plants and do something about their capital structures so that money can be leveraged. They want to buy Chicago. They want those dollars to turn over and in order to do that you have to move aside all of these prejudices and . . . and you have to move aside that monolith that stands in the way. I propose to do that. Only that, and nothing more.

So I say to you in the dwindling hours of this campaign, political discussion in this city is hard. Some of the press do not understand, not many, they are barracudas, they don't want to talk about it (cheers) but we will get over that. We will get over that. You are the real message bearers. You are the people who understand what I am talking about. You are the people who have been fighting for the very things I am talking about. You don't have much time. It's dwindling. The votes are there. The people's ears are open. They want to hear the good sound. They want to see the open hand. They want to know that there is hope in this city. And it can be made a beautiful city. And you have got to do it. You have got to do it. The burden falls not upon me. It falls upon you. And the fate of Chicago is in your hands and in these last hours I say don't leave any stone unturned. No person who thinks as we think, has the right to the luxury, to sit at home dealing with the issues. You have the time to do it. I have a feeling that the people are open and waiting, ready for you to go and talk to them. But the battlecry of this campaign never was and never will be directly, or indirectly, remotely, race, the battlecry of this campaign is reform (applause).

This is our city, this is our city (applause).

A crowd of 350 Hispanics, poor whites, and blacks in a Westtown church meeting sponsored by the Puerto Rican Diaspora Coalition ignore the pickets outside the building who are chanting, "We want Epton," in the pouring rain, and listen attentitively as Washington answers questions from the audience:

Question: Many urban areas in recent years have suffered from two related and unfortunate developments, a dwindling tax base and an increasing demand for city services. These developments are important due to thousands of people leaving the city to reside in the suburbs, and yet who still maintain jobs and service relationships within the city. What is your plan or strategy to recover these lost revenues?

(Spanish translation)

Answer: The question can't be answered simply, it has to be answered in terms of the broader picture of municipal taxes. What I propose is a commission on tax reform that will look at the whole spectrum of municipal home rule taxes. That will take not a lot of time but *some* time. But in order to make the adjustments which are necessary, you have to have the whole picture. We are concerned about certain taxes which should not exist. For example, the last one cent increase in the sales tax. And also the head tax which has caused so much of a problem within the city. But basically, and fundamentally, the question begs for a complete and thorough study of the entire municipal tax structure in the city of Chicago, and out of our transition team we will begin to start such a study with an eye toward making certain that those who draw from the city pay their fair share back into the city (applause).

(Spanish translation)

Question: We are petitioning Mr. Kelly because we believe that our park has inadequate facilities for our growing community. From January 82 to 83 the attendance at the park has increased 43 percent. We also feel that we are being discriminated because we are in a lower income area park. Could we have your support, Mr. Washington, and your signature on our petition to Edmund Kelly? (applause).

(Spanish translation)

Answer: Yes, you will have my signature on the petition (applause).

Thank you, very, very much (applause and cheers). My answer to your question, is yes you are being discriminated against. That has been known at least for the past four years. In 1979, the issue of discrimination of park facilities, payment for park salaries in various neighborhoods, was brought up very clearly by CBS here in Chicago and by the *Reporter* magazine. We tried to redress and resolve the problem at that time. I won't go through the whole picture. Suffice it to say that we did not succeed. The Justice Department has just completed its study and actually I am not certain of the progress of the case, but the Park District of the city of Chicago is about to be hauled before the Circuit Court, for discrimination against certain areas and neighborhoods relative to the facilities of park facilities. We are going to press to resolve that matter. We are going to see that that matter is resolved without taking thousands and thousands of your dollars to defend such a suit. There is discrimination. It is your community against my community against other communities. It has got to stop before your tax dollars are eroded; and no one has a right to discriminate against you (applause).

(Spanish translation)

Question: . . . what will you do to continue day care programs which are being threatened by cuts?

(Spanish translation)

Answer: Those cuts have been visited to a great extent upon the states and cities by the Reagan program. I haven't detected a turnaround on the part of Congress toward these human service programs. Far too much of our money, far too much, over $200 billion is being used by the Reagan administration for what they call the so-called defense budget. I think Congress has taken a most sane and sensible attitude toward that, and I expect that there will be significant cuts in that defense budget. That's the first step. Secondly, it is my feeling that the change in the makeup of Congress will redirect some of those funds back into the human service areas and consequently there will be increased funding for day care. This will not happen overnight. It's going to take some time. It's going to take pressure. You are going to have to mobilize your Congressman. I will do the same, I will work hard to do that. We have got to, at the same time, work on the state levels and get those funds syphoned into the city. The city of Chicago has reached an impasse. We have to find new revenue dollars to continue the level of service that we now have. I made it clear when I first announced in this campaign that I will search and find to the best of my ability those dollars. It has got to be done. We can't increase taxes on the municipal level, and I won't support any increase of taxes there. But through a combination of pressure on the state, I hope we can raise the funds there, and we must force a turnaround of the Reagan program, I am confident that in the near future we can bring those funds back into the city of Chicago (applause).

(Spanish translation)

Three hundred white senior citizens and a smattering of younger folk, and a few blacks crowd into the recreation room of a Lake

Shore Drive hi-rise. Washington's former colleague in the House of Representatives, James Houlihan, has just described his skill in building coalitions.

Thank you very much, Jim Houlihan. That is a very kind thing that you said about me. I appreciate it immensely and deeply, but I must confess to you that Jim Houlihan came to Springfield with more than most people have when they leave. I am sure he was a well organized, very perceptive, very conscientious young man and if I had any role even minor or remotely to play in the development of such a fine person I am extremely proud. He has been unduly nice to me. I think he even lies charmingly, so (laughter) thank you, Jim, for a friendship of many years and thank you for your tremendous contribution to this campaign, which is not really a contribution to me, although I suppose people classify it that way, it is a contribution to the development of the future of the city of Chicago, because I equate this campaign not with my own narrow ambitions—they are great, but they are narrow—but I equate this campaign with the future, in a sense, of the city of Chicago which is moving through a pivotal stage and in which some strong hard decisions must be made as to whether or not the city will improve, or shall it continue in the same hidebound fashion.

There are so many things I would like to discuss with you tonight. It is just impossible, so I will just have to be satisfied to touch on several issues and hope that I can at least whet your appetites.

I see so many people here that I know, it is just amazing, and I must confess to you as I look through the audience to see those blue buttons spotted all over the place, I feel almost at home. You look so well dressed when you have those buttons on (laughter). They add something to you. Have you ever noticed that when people are wearing a Washington button they always smile, they always seem to be on the upbeat. You never see a Washington button wearer looking glum. They are looking forward. They have city building on their minds. They have coalition building on their minds. They are people who have been attracted to this campaign because they see the benefits of it. It was said the other day by Bill Berry, who heads up my transition team, who has done a marvelous job, a person who has dedicated his life to unity and coalition building and bringing people together and trying to smooth the frictions which, of course, exist between various groups. Bill is an administrator, that is one of the reasons I asked him to head up my transition team, and he has done a marvelous, marvelous job. Yesterday when we unveiled our transition team, Bill said something which will indicate to you the kind of work that he has been doing and the level of expertise we have obtained, notwithstanding the fact that our campaign is only five months old. Bill said that when I enter office shortly after April 12, which proves beyond doubt that he is an extremely intelligent person, that when I arrive at City Hall I would know more about city government, the city of Chicago, about the various aspects of city government, and know more about the budget, more about its fiscal condition, more about the potential for additional revenue, more about the necessities for budget balance than any mayor who has entered office in this city in the last sixty or seventy years. And you know something, Bill was right. We have put together a marvelous transition team which I assure you is not just filled with prestigious people who have gained eminence in the corporations, finance, small business, labor and neighborhoods, but who have also in the process of that come together and given me their awesome experiences, their tremendous talent to help run this city. And I submit to you that we have elevated the level of political discussion in this city, we have focused upon some of the more serious problems of the city. I think we have hopefully done something about the credibility of the politicians in this city and I think this transition team is a showcase piece and as you see it unveiled in various phases over the next two or three more weeks, I think you will have to agree that we have done a tremendous job in bringing this city together. I promised that I would do that. There are some saying that it is not being done because there are some strident voices that are raising their voices. Well, I don't think that is an indication of what is happening out there. If you could travel through this city with me and see in every neighborhood people who have signed aboard, people who have come forward with their agendas and their concerns, who have brought me those agendas and concerns because they know, based upon the kind of record I have been able to amass, that I will not just read it and think about it, but I will act on it. And so we have had a good campaign. But there are certain issues which obviously and clearly must be addressed.

My concern for senior citizens didn't just start with this campaign. It goes back into the early 70s, when my former school teacher at DuSable High School, Miss Mary . . . who now I think is almost 97 years old and who, incidentally, is one of my major supporters, Miss Mary Herrick came to Springfield and testified before the Executive Committee on which I was serving and when she saw me there she called me out in the usual fashion, she said, "Come here, Harold," (laughter) and naturally no one disobeys Mary Herrick, if you know her, when she raises her voice that is a roar, and you just . . . well she took me down the hall and said, "I would like to see this Department for Senior Citizens Bill without a negative vote, and I have a feeling and impression that people throughout the state are supporting senior citizens." I said, right on. I went back there and told all of those men on the Executive Committee 'I must tell you something, I don't know if you know my ire, but if you want to see my ire raised, you vote no, because my former schoolteacher is out there and she wants this bill to slide through here on a great scale.' It did. But in a sense I must confess that was a sort of opening up of my eyes to the plight of senior citizens and since that time I have spent a lot of time with it.

My concern about Social Security, I think you know that. I have perhaps one of the strongest, if not *the* strongest anti-Reagan voting record in the Congress (applause) and that record is strong for several reasons and one of the major reasons is that Mr. Reagan saw fit to put his hands upon the Social Security and Medicare programs. I will repeat it, I don't like Mr. Reagan (applause).

To make it short, it has been my responsibility, self-imposed, to do everything I could to make certain that my record reflected and my advocacy reflected the deep-seated understanding I had and appreciation I have for the senior citizens in this country. I am about to leave the Congress, and I leave with some regrets because it has given me an opportunity . . . I must interrupt at this point and say that a good friend of mine has come in, County Commissioner, George Dunne, let's give him a big hand (applause).

My concern for the senior citizens must be expressed in special government positions. I have signed on to and made it very clear that we will have a department for the aged so we can coalesce and bring together in one spot all of the varied problems of the senior citizens which should be brought together for efficiency and to make certain that the senior citizens of this city have a place in city government where they can go or send or write or call and have their problems and concerns responded to and have an agency of government which would have as its own going responsibility ferreting out and planning and making certain that the problems of the aged are attended to. It's alright to have banquets and picnics and those sorts of things, fun and games are important, but it is more important that the concerns of senior citizens be directed and dealt with on a day-by-day basis by people who have skill and concern in those fields.

It is my understanding that one of the major problems confronting this entire city, and certainly this area, is inadequate police patrols. That has got to be dealt with. I stand before you as one of the major supporters, let me stress that, major supporters of the Chicago Police Department. I was born and raised in this city and I knew when the Police Department was not so good, and I saw it developed over a period of years, come to its zenith under O.W. Wilson, and I think that we now have a good, good Police Department. I always lead with that, so that there is no confusion about where I stand and then I follow by saying it is not good enough. It has got to be improved, and under my administration it will be improved along certain specific lines. One, we are going, and I set this as a goal in the immediate future, and it can be done, without any significant attendant cost, the hiring of an additional, or placing of an additional 1,000 policemen. Believe me, it can be done. Why do I say 1,000? Well, 1,000 is not a golden figure, but it seems to be a figure with which we can work. I am not an authority on police science, I don't want to hold myself out as such. I do believe, however, that people and their perceptions know as much about police science as those who purport to do so, and it is clear that people throughout this city want foot patrols to supplement the squad patrols that move through the city. They want foot patrols. Their perception is, their feeling is that they are safer if they have them, and even if they are wrong in the sum total of what the most effective way of dispersing patrolman, since you pay the bill, you should be catered to to a certain extent. But I think we should supplement our squad patrols with foot patrols around senior citizens' homes, around nursing homes, around schools, around hospitals, to the point where people feel safer as they move in and around these great streets.

We have some more serious problems, the gang problem has gotten out of control in many sectors of this city. It cannot be tolerated any longer, and it seems to me that with adequate attention on the part of the police, working in private garb, they can ferret out some of these things. The dope problem has just gone insane. It always amazes me that young people can find the dope, but the police can't find it (laughter). It seems to me that there is something wrong with police science, or else (applause) not enough serious attention paid to that. I will find for this city, I guarantee you, from the ranks of the existing command structure in this city, the finest police superintendent that this city has to offer. I know the talent is there. The reservoir is deep, broad and of quality. We will also investigate and look at, not in an incriminatory manner, but just toward the idea of making certain that you get your maximum dollars worth in terms of efficiency, we will look to the entire police command of this city and we will suggest to the superintendent, and we will suggest tenderly, but firmly, that people be slotted on the basis of their ability and their concern and knowledge. We will have, I guarantee you, before my first four years are over (laughter) the finest police department that this city has ever had (applause).

As I said before, there are just so many issues that we want to cover and I can just touch on a few of them. Your parks, there have been many criticisms of your parks, the status of the parks, the upkeep of the parks. We will work on that. I have taken a position on the parks and it has caused me some opposition within the ranks of the Democratic Party, but I must confess to you that we have to look hard, not just to having an efficient park district, but also in saving dollars, and so we will take a hard look at the Park District, and if we don't see what you say *you* don't see, or we see what you do see, we are going to have some changes. As mayor of this city I am not about to sit down on the fifth floor of City Hall and send out edicts like thunderbolts as to what should go here and what should go there and what should go other places. I am going to get input from those people who know best and that is the communities, and if we convert use of land from one use to another, or we use land for one purpose, the neighborhoods in this city, every neighborhood, every ethnic group will have input into how that city will be developed, how that land will be utilized.

So I offer to you for the first time in the history of this city, an open government, one which will be fair with justice and firmness. I offer you a government that will have freedom of information so you will know exactly what is being done. I offer you a government in which there will be a budgetary process that you can have input to, criticize it. I offer you those kinds of things, but above all, I offer you a steady day-to-day struggle to bring this city together. One of the kindest things said about me and one of the most cogent and accurate things said about me by Jim Houlihan is that I spent a lifetime in public service trying to bring people together to focus on our common problems. I will do that. I won't cease until I do that, and I assure you that at the expiration of four years, I just honestly think deep in my heart that with the cooperation of all you fine citizens, that we can clean up our city even more. But I need your help. I need the help of every individual here. No one shall be sacred and protected from my constant loquacious, golden-throated appeal for your help. I will give you no rest. I will give you no peace until you sign on, not to the campaign, but to be a partner in the government of the city of Chicago. So don't dodge, you can't hide, I will find you and when I find you I am going to ask you what can you do for your government because I know deep down in your hearts you want to do it. I want to be your mayor. I think I will be a good mayor, I need your help to be a mayor, I need your help to be a successful mayor and I appeal as I close, because I must go, and unfortunately the time is never long enough, but there are places to go, speeches to make, votes to get, people to love, people to bring together, so if you permit me I will take my leave. Thank you very much.

The Winner

On April 12, 1983, on the 122nd anniversary of the start of the Civil War, with slightly more than 52 percent of the vote, Harold Washington broke the already wounded back of the Democratic Machine in Chicago to become the first black mayor of the city. Since the mid-seventies, the Machine had received a series of potentially mortal wounds, though there were few in the city who would bet on its early demise. An independent alderman elected here, a reform Republican state's attorney elected there, Ralph Metcalfe's revolt against Daley and his defection in 1974, a sizeable vote for Mayor Daley's independent opponent the next year, Byrne's win in 1979, and Washington's victory as an independent Congressman in 1980 all pointed to the end of the Machine and, in fact, it was not at all the healthy robust animal it had been since Anton Cermak put it together in the thirties, but that it would so soon be destroyed in one fatal blow by the same coalition that had been so roundly defeated so many times and so betrayed by its most recent banner holder was hardly dreamed of by most of those who claim to understand Chicago politics.

To give all the credit to Washington for that victory would be a grievous insult to all those who created the movement—the crusade—that Washington rode to that victory. But that movement would have remained a movement without the charisma and intelligence of Washington. There was not another contender for the role who could have pulled it off. As Judge Pincham said, the tragedy of segregation and discrimination is not that it prevents access so much as that it prevents dreams. There certainly were several able contenders for the race but none of them had that intense personal vision—that charisma and political stature that is the result of such dreams. Washington was not only a respected Congressman, he had a 20-year illustrious legislative history and even more years in the Democratic Party. No fly-by-night, no upstart, no gadfly, a seasoned politician who knew his craft and had paid his dues. Blacks understand what thirty years in the Machine means: devotion to politics, the will to win. They also understand what breaking with the Machine means: courage, devotion to ideals, vision, determination. That he had won against the Machine was a crucial factor in his favor. If he had already done it three times, he could do it again, perhaps even bigger.

Even that history of his, however, could not initially win the black vote. It took the televised debates, in which he shone beside his opponents, to begin to win the support of all those people who were furious at Jane Byrne—blacks and liberal whites, blacks who had registered to vote to defeat Byrne but who had waited to see, and whites who had never heard of this new Washington.

The question arises, considering their general wariness, why did not more blacks than the tiny 3 percent who voted for Epton turn on Washington when his infractions became the central issue of the media coverage? Why did they stick by his side—indeed vote in huge numbers, even register to vote for the first time after the primary in order to vote for him—when so much of what they watched of the television coverage was about his blemished record? They were reading and hearing the same thing whites were and Washington's support among whites slipped badly as all those attacks were released. Vernon Jarrett, a *Tribune* columnist, the only black columnist in Chicago, points out that blacks are more forgiving than whites. Since their days of enslavement, blacks have forgiven whites, Jarrett says, not so much out of kindness but out of the recognition that their survival depended on forgiveness. One cannot live without forgiveness when one is so gravely mistreated for so long. The alternative is unrelenting rage, illness. We have seen over and over again the consequences of black rage—violence, depression, illness. Rage, unmitigated by forgiveness, is intolerable. So it is that blacks have learned forgiveness that whites cannot—need not— conceive, that has no meaning in their lives, the forgiveness that Christ taught—"Father, forgive them; for they know not what they do," that white Christians have had such difficulty with.

Martin Luther King built a huge movement on Christ's message, "Love your enemies, bless them that curse you, do good to them that hate you, and pray for them which despitefully use you, and persecute you."

Having forgiven whites for so long and having forgiven so many of their own people who have wronged them, should blacks now have refused to forgive this man of such sterling qualities who, years ago, made some mistakes but who, today, seems to hold such promise for them? To the charge by some whites that he was not "the best candidate the black community could produce," they sent a thundering message: 97 percent of their votes. Washington was, indeed, their best candidate—smart, well-educated, an experienced politician, charming, witty, idealistic, practical, too, and cautious. He was their best candidate and, as Mike Royko said on the day after he won the primary, he was not only the *black's* best candidate, he was also the *white's* best candidate: "The fact is, Washington's credentials for this office exceed those of Byrne, Bilandic, Richard J. Daley, Martin Kennelly, Ed Kelly, Anton Cermak and most of the men who held the office of mayor of Chicago."

There are those who say that so many blacks voted for Washington merely because he is black, that they would have overlooked any crime committed by a black—reverse racism, they call it. The record emphatically denies that charge; blacks have for most of their history voted for whites, often against their own people, most recently in the 1983 aldermanic election in which they elected Lawrence Bloom to a second term as alderman in a ward that is more than 65 percent black and in a contest in which Bloom was opposed by six blacks, among them some creditable candidates. He won a clear majority in both the white and black sections of the ward.

One of the most dramatic instances of the record of black voting occurred in 1977, when blacks overwhelmingly voted for the incumbent mayor, almost ignoring the black who ran against him because he was an unknown, an upstart, with no reputation in the community. That candidate, as we know, was Harold Washington. He was running as an independent; he took 11 percent of the total vote. Again in 1982 when he declared his candidacy after widening his reputation by winning a race for Congress, only 20 percent said they would vote for him. Only when his qualifications emerged in the television debates and on the campaign trail was there a groundswell of support. Had Robert Shaw or Wilson Frost, two regular Machine aldermen with little to recommend them, been the candidate besmirched by his opponent as Washington was, they would have gone down to an ignoble defeat.

James Joyce once said, "I am a man of simple tastes," a remark thought hugely funny by some of the readers of his complex, original, inventive work. There is, though, in that remark a subtle and profound truth. Joyce sought to tell the truth about the human condition, the simple truth in the sense that truth is always simple as Shakespeare understood when he described "simple truth miscall'd simplicity." It could be said of Washington, too, that he is a man of simple tastes. His chili recipe is famous. A favorite dish is macaroni and cheese. How simple can you get? But he is also famous for the big words and lofty phrases that reflect his vision of a complex world that cannot always be described in simple terms. It is not true, as some maintain, that complex ideas can always be expressed simply. A highly complex man, not always easily understood, his life history nevertheless reveals a continuous effort, often constrained but always straining to tell the simple truth—about the conditions under which his people have lived too long, the simple truth of what is needed to attain justice, and the simple truth that he is, above all, a man like other men. It is to the mission of making that understood by all that he has devoted himself.

Certainly Washington has his defects—who among us does not? It is said by many close to him that he does not suffer fools, not the best quality in the mayor of a big, complex city. It is also said that he *surrounds* himself with fools, preferring to shine in a heap of rubble and preferring to maintain control. That, too, is not the most admirable quality in a man seeking to govern. Both statements are true of Washington—and false. He does not easily abide fools. He prefers to make his own decisions, trust his own judgments. Yet he was initially heavily influenced by several people in the campaign who are seen as fools by others, the more radical elements of the movement, indeed those who had been highly instrumental in the voter registration drive and the preliminary planning for a mayoral campaign.

The pressure on him, for instance, during the primary to announce that he would fire the police superintendent may have been the most foolish advice he received. He spent two days agonizing over it and finally gave in. He then spent too much time during the six weeks of the general election overcoming that foolish move based on the short-sighted, paranoid strategy that he could not, anyhow, win many white votes so that he should go ahead and make that highly emotional play to blacks who held the police chief responsible for a great variety of crimes against blacks, a charge that was only partly true. An administrator can issue orders but he cannot control all the behavior that goes on in the streets. This is not to say that the police department did not need massive reform, but that reform could—should—have been couched in the terms Washington used after the primary, not the ones he used before, words of constructive reform rather than hostile rejection.

The day after the primary, a black policeman answered a distress call I put in. When my business was finished, I offered him coffee. It was midmorning. He told me of the events in the station house when he reported for duty. "In all my years on the force, I have never seen such rabid racism, such vicious hatred. Washington sure didn't help by those blasts at Brzeczek."

That assumption that he could only win a tiny proportion of white votes plagued and befuddled the campaign all the way to the end. The "numbers" man of the campaign and Washington's close advisor, David Canter, says that the numbers of white votes came as "a complete surprise. We expected a lot less," he says, as he reviews the percentages of votes from the all-white wards (actually, they need be only 80 percent white to be so characterized). Those wards are generally considered the most anti-black and indeed, the figures show that some of them are. Four of those traditionally Democratic ethnic wards gave Washington only 4.9, 5.7, 6.8, 6.9 percent. But in the other eleven all-white wards the figures are 39, 36, 20, 18, and on down to 12 percent. Furthermore, in 55 precincts Epton received no votes, presumably all-black precincts, but in no precinct in the city did Washington receive no votes. In 880 precincts, Epton received less than ten votes, again presumably all-black precincts. Only in twenty-three precincts, however, were there less than ten votes for Washington. That the total white vote adds up to only 16-18 percent remains an indictment of racism in Chicago but the spread of votes all over the white sections of the city shows that even in the most racist communities there were some who preferred a black Democrat to a white Republican or a black to a Jew or to whom Washington appeared to be, despite his race, the better candidate. Which leads us to wonder how many more such votes he might have won had Washington given more of his time to campaigning among whites.

It should be noted, however, that "white" includes Latino and that some of those "all-white" wards have sizeable Latino populations that gave Washington an estimated 65 percent of their votes.

It could also be that some of those "white" votes were actually black votes, since there are a few blacks scattered among all but a few of the mostly white communities, even in Bridgeport. In a couple of wards, there are sizeable black contingents. So some of those "white" votes were most likely black, a fact completely overlooked by the other analysts. It is also likely that some of the "white" votes were Asiatics, many of whom share the racial prejudice of whites against blacks but who are less fervent in their hate, partly because they, too, have been excluded from political power. Interestingly, it is speculated that Latinos are split in their attitudes, with Puerto Ricans more friendly and open to blacks while Mexicans are more strongly anti-black. Puerto Ricans have a strong history of political activism in the U.S., while Mexicans tend to avoid politics. So there is a strong possibility that it was Asiatics, Hispanics, and blacks living in the "all-white" wards who gave Washington much of that 16-18 percent of the "white" vote.

On the other hand, there are only 95,000 registered Latino voters, even fewer Asiatics, and the Lakefront is a high-rent area, not likely to be the home of many Hispanics and Asiatics. The Lakefront gave Washington 45 percent. As was said in the previous chapter, the director of the Lakefront campaign expected to carry his district and might have, had Washington and his staff agreed with Stevens and campaigned there, taking advantage of help offered by white politicians such as Lawrence Bloom, whose offers of help were never used. A charge that this distorted view of white voters was limited to the blacks in the campaign, however, is not true. The whites on the staff shared the same view. Bloom remarks, "Not enough people in that campaign understood enough about city politics." Perhaps Bloom is right. Or perhaps Washington and his staff—white and black—were simply too cynical about whites. Washington's sophistication may have failed him.

Washington did, indeed, surround himself with a great array of people clearly not competent for the jobs to which they were assigned—"nincompoops," in the words of one veteran in Washington's entourage, energetic, hard-working, incompetent nincompoops. On the other hand, there are also close to him some of the most competent, least foolish people in the community. Edwin C. "Bill" Berry, the chairman of the campaign and then the head of the transition team, remained close to Washington throughout the campaign and, as the former head of the Chicago Urban League for twenty years, is one of the most highly regarded men in the black community. He was not the only one who consistently had the ear of Washington.

It is said by many apologists that those nincompoops were in those jobs only because there are so few blacks with experience in politics that Washington had no choice. They are not stupid, merely inexperienced. They were the people who had worked as volunteers in the voter registration drive and they were the ones who had worked on Washington's earlier campaigns when there had been no money to pay professionals and so there, too, there had been too many inexperienced volunteer types. This was not, it was said, your ordinary political campaign staffed by pros; this was a crusade—a movement—staffed by amateurs—black and white alike. For the most part, this is an acceptable, reasonable argument. Some reply: "Well, that's ok for the troops but the top jobs? Couldn't a few pros be found for them? Even if they had to be white?"

"Are you kidding? Bring in whites for the top jobs in this black crusade? Sure, there were a few whites, but this was a black campaign, a black *grassroots* campaign. If all the top jobs had been staffed by whites, we would have had revolt instead of the euphoria that prevailed in that office. Raby tried to do it and all hell broke loose."

"Well, ok, but how about some of the worst characters who, after a few weeks, became a serious obstacle, alienating all those on the outside who were trying to do business with the campaign?"

"Yeh, well, Harold does have a problem. He can't seem to fire people, even when they make trouble for him, until disaster sets in. I hope he has learned his lesson in the campaign and doesn't do the same thing in the Mayor's office."

"It's not that he can't fire them. He won't. He wants them around because he can control them. Harold runs his own show. If he had been willing to give up control, he would have hired a professional campaign manager instead of Raby."

Don Rose enters the scene. He has known Raby for more than twenty years and he defends him as a pro. Washington was right to hire him and wrong to fire him. Raby lost his own race for alderman by only 275 votes. But he did lose. Washington lost only one race in twenty years and that was the improbable mayoral race of 1977. But Washington won most of his races with the aid of the Machine. Raby ran against the Machine. So did Washington in his last four races.

There are many who disagree with Rose, who call Raby Washington's first nincompoop of the campaign. They insist, in fact, that many of those incompetent staffers were hired not by Washington but by Raby. In the last few weeks of the campaign, Raby was "eased out" and replaced by Bill Ware, who ran Washington's Congressional office, widely considered highly competent, a University of Chicago Law School graduate, who became Washington's chief deputy mayor.

Now enters Chris Chandler, white, an experienced journalist who also worked in an earlier campaign to unseat Mayor Daley. Chandler was the first press secretary in the Washington campaign, was on board even before Washington, and in the jockeying for position held fast to a leading role though he was never again actual top banana. He moved with Washington to City Hall to be second in command of the press office.

"There was a racist assumption in the media from the start that a black campaign had to be disorganized," Chandler says, "and they overplayed every snafu." Those snafus are excused by Chandler as a consequence of the "heat of the campaign." "This was no ordinary campaign," he explains, "it had international attention and the number of calls from all over the world was incredible. On the day of the mixup over Wally Phillips' show [a local radio talk show at which Washington failed to appear], we had television crews from six countries. We had a hundred media requests a day.

"This campaign was a remarkable achievement," Chandler adds. "The paid staff went from a half dozen people at the beginning to 137 with 10,000 volunteers at the end. On Election Day, every precinct in the city was covered. It was Harold's genius that kept the whole ship floating. He has an extraordinary ability to relate to all kinds of people."

But what about that charge that he surrounds himself with nincompoops? Utterly untrue, says Chandler. "Sure, there were lots of amateurs and when you have that many people working in a campaign, especially with a lot of people with no experience in politics, there are bound to be lots of kinks. When I worked for Friedman, we didn't have any kinks. We had forty people in one office. Washington had 137 people in twenty-eight offices."

What about Raby? Was he the first nincompoop? Chandler says that Raby was not a nincompoop but he did become the central problem. He had been viewed by many as the best choice for campaign manager. But it soon became apparent that he was not the best man for the job. Not only did he hire incompetent people, Chandler says, but he established his own policy-making group and chain of command whose ideas were contrary to Washington's and other key members of the staff. A group of corporate lawyers and business people, along with pollster Pat Caddell and media specialist Bill Zimmerman, and others, "met regularly in Wayne Whalen's living room, where Raby was living, to make policy that was in opposition to Washington's and that Raby imposed upon the campaign," Chandler says. What were the issues? Well, Chandler says, it was mostly a matter of elitism as opposed to a more democratic way of doing business. It was mostly white, mostly middle class, mostly elitist. For instance, on the day after the primary election, Raby called a press conference with Caddell and Zimmerman to explain how the election had been won. Caddell from the East Coast and Zimmerman from the West Coast, both of whom came in on an indigenous movement that had built and won the campaign, and Raby, who had come into the campaign late, on their own, with no discussion with the candidate, arranged to tell the media about this campaign about which they knew practically nothing, Chandler says. But it was too late for Raby to exercise much control. Washington had taken over and brought in his own people. The question is: was Raby doing anything so unusual by calling that press conference and meeting with those people, in his role as campaign manager? Isn't that what campaign managers do? Well, yes, Chandler admits, but this was no ordinary campaign, no ordinary candidate. Washington runs his own show. And, according to Chandler, that is how it should have been. Washington was far and away the most accomplished and experienced politician associated with this show; he should have been calling the shots.

Raby was not fired, Chandler says, only because Washington did not want another charge of disorganization against him. His actual diminished role in the campaign, despite the efforts to keep it quiet, did leak to the media, however. By the time a glowing profile of Raby appeared in the *Magazine* of the *Chicago Tribune*, he was on the outside of any serious campaign activity.

Interestingly, Raby had acquired, in the sixties, the same reputation in the civil rights movement. He acquired a name used for some blacks for many years: Uncle Tom. In the sixties, however, the term was not so polite. He was called by certain groups a "white man's nigger." In fact, he operated then much as he did in the Washington campaign. The cast was different but the plot was the same: a spacious living room, a group of white professionals and businesspeople, policy-making, Raby the emissary to the movement. His loyalty, like that of all Uncle Tom's, it was said, was to those rich whites.

But wait. There is another view. "Raby represented the most progressive forces in the campaign," says a long-time political activist on the Washington staff and a long-time associate of Raby's. And Rose says, "He saved it [the campaign] from total catastrophe and won the election."

But Lawrence Bloom, independent alderman and another long-time friend of Raby's, says, "He's never struck me as a take-charge guy who could get things done." Bloom adds, "Raby is a guy who is always worried about racial polarization, working to change it."

Raby, of course, has a different view of the events. He was, on the one hand, never exiled to Siberia. It was simply that "the Democratic nominee brought in some additional people and distributed some of the responsibilities of the campaign to these people." On the other hand, he says he has no explanation for his exile, that he has some theories but "is not interested in reading them in print."

Did he actually set up a policy-making body at odds with the candidate's ideas? It wasn't a policy-making body, it was a strategy committee. The campaign had none when he took over and so he created one. "That might have caused some tension," he admits. But the steering committee that existed when he took over, he says, "was merely a place to put people who deserve a role or who had influence but the committee had no real responsibilities." More important, there were people on the steering committee "who were more interested in their own relations with the press and so leaked everything, making it impossible to create the drama that is the heart of the campaign." He tried to get input from Washington, suggestions for people who should be on the committee, but they were not forthcoming. "The candidate made his own decisions." On the other hand, Raby insists, Washington either "participated or signed off" on all the decisions made by the strategy committee. Well, apparently not the crucial decision to schedule a press conference with Caddell and Zimmerman the day after the election. Of the accusation that the strategy committee was elitist and didn't reflect Washington's view that the campaign should be democratically organized, Raby says, "strategy comittees are not democracies. I told people that I was not willing to share the decisions of the strategy committee because to do so would be as if I was telling Richard Daley what we were doing."

What was Raby's view of the decision not to campaign in the white communities until close to the end of the campaign? He didn't agree. He voiced his disagreement. It seems that his disagreement had not much impact. Washington followed his own instincts.

Raby defends himself by saying that when he came into the campaign on Dec. 15, "Harold was 13 percent in the polls, there was no office, no staff, no budget, no one raising money, and an enormous number of people demanding resources to do their job in the streets. I didn't sit down and philosophize about Harold's positions. I tried to respond to the environment I was in. I didn't create the environment." To the accusation that he hired incompetents, he says, "Byrne and Daley would probably have liked to have such incompetents."

On the last, Raby may be right. After all, Washington did win. But he was in a three-way race in which the other two candidates were splitting most of the white vote, leaving a clear channel for a black candidate to walk through with relative ease. Ease, if most of the blacks voted for Washington. But there is a question in the minds of many about whether he might not have won with a bigger margin if the campaign had been better organized, if Raby had made more effort to harmonize the various elements demanding attention, if he had been able to gain Washington's confidence. It must have been abundantly clear almost from the start that Raby's idea of a strategy committee was not the candidate's. Perhaps Raby did try his damndest to get Washington to cooperate and found himself bucking against a candidate who insisted on running his own show. Or perhaps he presented the strategy committee as a fait accompli and offended the candidate's sense of what a campaign manager should be doing.

The storm over Raby highlights the larger storm that surrounds Washington's image as a man who needs to control, who often makes poor personnel judgments, as a man who is, in the words of one of many critics, "a lousy administrator," and alternatively, who is seen as a brilliant administrator, a good listener, but a man who runs his own show. How was Raby hired? What did Washington know about him? Why did he hire him? Well, he knew that he was a black who had many ties into the white community and the middle-class black community, a real asset to a campaign that had been built entirely on the South Side among blacks, most of whom could not be described as middle-class. Berry told him that. He knew that Raby had run and only barely lost an aldermanic campaign in an integrated community. He also knew that Raby had worked for Governor Walker and for the Peace Corps, and had appeared to be a civil rights leader in the sixties, an associate of Martin Luther King's. Pretty good credentials. His organizational skills? Well, he had organized quite a lot, it seemed. His loyalty? Well, he'd been loyal to Berry. Chandler says Raby looked like the best choice.

Others say he looked like the worst choice, that he was never recommended by anyone involved in the voter registration drive, and that his appointment came as a shock and not necessarily a pleasant one. Others were recommended: the campaign managers of Coleman in Detroit, Berry in Washington, and Young in Atlanta, all seasoned political organizers. Only one of them knew Chicago, however. Did Washington hire the director of this show, the most crucial person beside himself in the campaign, because he sensed in Raby a yes-man whom he could control, a nincompoop who would not dim his light, who would take orders? Or did he hire him under pressure to name someone who was connected to some big bucks and big prestige in the city? Or did he hire him because his credentials indicated he was the best man for the job? Berry insists that Washington makes all his own decisions. "He is very much his own man," he says. Whatever pressure was brought to bear, the decision was his alone. Nobody knows why Raby was hired. Maybe Washington just didn't know him well enough. Maybe it was true that he chose him because he sensed in him the yes-man, only to discover that Raby was yessing the wrong people.

Tim Black, another long-time political activist and friend of Washington's, says, "He is normally careful to select people who can do the job. He is the boss, but they can carry out the orders. The reason he's always been able to get so much done is because he's had people on his staff who could do it well and who were loyal." Black says that Washington made the mistake with Raby because he was under a great deal of pressure to find someone in a hurry and because there was pressure to hire him.

To say that Washington had a mess on his hands which he somehow managed to handle and win an election leads us to accept Chandler's estimate that it was his "genius that kept the whole ship afloat." That he rejected Raby because he marched to the wrong drummers indicates that Washington is, indeed, his own man, that he cannot be manipulated and outmaneuvered in the end; in Chicago, after its recent experience with a mayor, a singular quality for the mayor to have.

Washington is a proud man, some say too proud. There were some who feared he would lose the election because his pride prevented him from attacking his opponent, requiring him to cling to some higher standard: "I will not lower my own dignity to match his." But his pride was not so great that he could not admit his error. He admitted that he should have gone on the offensive against Epton. Still, there is something to admire in a man who, out of pride, would choose to risk his career rather than join his enemies.

Washington's pride is not that of a person who has acquired values and standards that he refuses to compromise. In fact, he has learned the art of compromise very well and his long legislative history shows that he has finely honed that skill. Politics, they say, is the art of compromise. He has learned well how to, occasionally, sacrifice one valued position in order to get something else done. Nor is it vanity—the vanity of thinking too highly of oneself. Washington's pride is both tempered and enlarged by his racial heredity. It is not merely the pride of person but the pride of the black person. He will not be scorned by those who believe it is their right to scorn him or, worse, those who scorn blacks out of the deep roots of racism of which they are hardly aware. He refuses to produce more to stand in the same place. At the same time, he has dreamed of standing at the top. *Whitey, not only will you not scorn me but you will admire me. Not only will you not shut me out but you will seek me out. Not only will you not ask me to wait another hundred years but you will wait for me. Not only will you not deny me the vote but you will vote for me.* It is a powerful source of pride, born of years of discrimination and segregation. Washington learned it at his parents' knees. He also learned it from Edgar G. Brown, the soapbox orator at 47th and South Park, from the librarians at Hall Branch library, and from Martin Luther King, Jr. It is a thread that has woven its way through the black community, touching some, touching some mightily. There are some blacks who have achieved highly for purely personal reasons—but not many. For most, their accomplishments are motivated not only by personal ambition but by racial pride. *We will show them that blacks are as good as, even better than, whites.*

To understand the depth of this feeling it is necessary also to understand there is in every black, as in every Jew, some trace, however slight, of self-hate that results from having been told so long that they are inferior. It is by now commonplace that the oppressed tend, to some extent, to come to believe about themselves what is said of them, to identify with their oppressors. The most obvious example of that self-hate is the almost universal use of the word "nigger" among blacks to refer to each other. There is, of course, an opposing view of the use of this pejorative, made famous by Lenny Bruce in the fifties, that, if you use an epithet enough, it removes the sting from it. Perhaps. But repetition doesn't seem to have removed the sting from son of a bitch or schmuck. In fact, nigger is now used even as an affectionate term, "He's my favorite nigger," but at its heart, the term remains an epithet and reflects, in its use, what may be deeply hidden but remains: a sign of identification with the oppressor. That it is still an epithet is made obvious by the fact that a white who calls a black a nigger is asking for trouble. It is a red cloak to most. *We can smear ourselves but you may not.* The word "kike" seems to have disappeared from use among Jews but remains an epithet among antisemites. However, I clearly recall in my youth the practice of Jews calling other Jews kikes.

It is in reaction to that identification with the oppressor that racial pride is born; that identification is an intolerable condition, especially for the talented, the insightful. To shed that identification, to prove the proposition untrue, becomes a matter not only of personal ambition but racial ambition: *I will prove to them that being black is no more an obstacle to success, given the opportunity, than being white. Blacks are as capable as anyone else.*

For most, this mission is translated into some kind of service to the community: in politics, the law, medicine, communications. In fact, it is difficult to find a successful black professional who does not see his or her success as an achievement both personal and racial and who does not somehow perform some service to the community, even if that service is merely in the contribution of money to a service organization. (This is, incidentally, quite a different stance than that of many women who achieved success when it was difficult for women to find a place in the male world.)

Washington has become a symbol of that racial success. It was that racial pride that was a large spur to his dreams, his ambitions. It was that racial pride, as much as his personal pride, that prevented him from levelling attacks at Epton that were, in fact, quite clearly justified by the record and recommended by his advisors. *That kind of a political campaign is the white man's game. It is as common as corn in Iowa. We will not play it. This campaign—this black man's campaign—will be honorable, will stick to the issues. If, as it appears will happen, I am elected—or rejected—because I am black, it will be truthfully said that I was elected on a campaign of the highest aspiration.*

Washington is also a secretive man, another trait not necessarily desirable in a big city mayor. George Bernard Shaw said, in 1933, "An American has no sense of privacy. He does not know what it means. There is no such thing in the country." A typically exaggerated Shawism, of course, but like all his bombastic blasts, it has a certain truth. Washington seems to be one American who violates Shaw's dictum. Yet one of the planks in his campaign that he repeated over and over again, apparently a deeply important one for him, was for an open government, a government to which everyone has access. His secretiveness, it seems, concerns his private life.

There is hardly anyone who knows Washington, personally or professionally, who does not comment at some point, "Harold is a most private man." His campaign press secretary, Dave Potter, complained bitterly that he would share none of his private life—even the chili recipe for which he was famous—with the press. "Keep to the issues," Washington insisted. Rumors about his sexuality float freely about the black community because, not only has he been unmarried all of his adult life, but he has kept his relations with women completely private. Those who know him well laugh at the rumors but understand them. It must have caused him no little pain to bring into public view as his fiancee a woman to whom he had been close for twenty years, very privately. His advisors insisted: in Chicago a mayoral candidate must have a spouse, if not a spouse, at least a fiancee. The press badgered him about when he and Mary Ella Smith would marry. She was badgered, too. And profiled as his future wife. The notion that a man of sixty who had been married only once, as a teenager, is not likely to marry again did not prevent the reporters from regularly asking about his marriage plans. In one such exchange, he replied, "Buried? I've lived in Chicago all my life and intend to be buried here. Oh, you said married," and laughed it off. He had given in to the political requirement to have a fiancee but he would not be intruded upon. (Had he succumbed to pressure, as Jane Byrne did, and gotten married shortly after the primary, no one would have been more surprised than Ms. Smith. As for Byrne's political marriage, rumors were wildly flying at the end of Byrne's regime that she and the man she had married under the pressure of Chicago politics were now about to split up.)

I have no small amount of conflict about violating Washington's privacy, having been a long-time admirer and always respecting his privacy. I have, therefore, avoided assiduously any details about his personal life, dealing only with his public life, assuming that his call for open government included an open book about his own public life, including my analysis of the causes of his legal mistakes in the sixties. Unfortunately for him, those mistakes became part of his public life, a part that, in his need for secrecy, he refused to discuss beyond his public apologies, but a part that begged for explanation. But I leave Washington's private life to some more American snoop than I.

The issue of Washington's failure to vigorously pursue white votes has been raised in the previous chapter and again in this one; it was a tactical error. It was, also, the consequence of a paranoid assumption that few whites would vote for a black. But it is just not enough to make those assertions and go on. Especially in view of the charge that whites were systematically excluded from the campaign—yes, there was that charge, too—it is vitally necessary to examine those propositions:

• There was an expectation at the start of the primary that some whites would immediately come on board, with their support and their money. Especially Bill Berry, chairman of the campaign and long-time associate of a group of white business and professional people who had supported for years his efforts to upgrade black opportunity, expected those people to join the campaign. Berry said, toward the close of the primary, that he felt that his whole life was wasted; when it came to upgrading opportunity for a few blacks, his friends in the white power structure were right there. A black mayor was another story. There was no support forthcoming from those people for Washington's campaign. It was, perhaps, the bitterest disappointment of Berry's life.

• There was an expectation that the white independent elected officials would support Washington. One did. The one viewed as most progressive endorsed no one; he was running for re-election in an all-white ward. The rest endorsed Daley.

• There was an expectation that the Democratic Party would, after the primary, support the winner of the Party as it had for many years. It didn't. Even after it gave Washington its official endorsement, it did nothing to assist in the election and a goodly number of the party leaders worked quietly for his opponent.

• There was an expectation that a substantial section of the Lakefront would automatically vote for Washington as they had always voted for anti-Machine candidates. But the polls early in the primary indicated that they wouldn't and, in fact, only 22 percent did vote for him in the primary.

• There was an expectation that Epton would conduct a campaign on the issues after he made a post-election speech saying, "I don't want any votes based on color," and after he proposed that he and Washington issue a joint statement disavowing racism. Washington refused. He was black, a victim of racism. It was not up to him to disavow it. A few days later, "Bernard Epton, Before It's Too Late," appeared on the television screens. Epton said it wasn't a racist slogan; it referred, he said, to Washington's "criminality."

• There was an expectation that, having endorsed him because the world can no longer tolerate racism and because he was clearly the superior candidate, the newspapers would support him. Instead, they conducted a relentless campaign against Washington, if unwittingly, that even the most sensitive whites in the city did not fully comprehend because, like everyone else, they did not trouble to closely analyze what was being reported in the press. Finally, at the end of the campaign, the newspapers reiterated their endorsement, this time damning him with faint praise. He was a badly flawed candidate, they said, but the best of a bad lot.

None of those expectations were unrealistic. They emerged from a sober analysis of past Chicago politics. Unfortunately, they did not correctly estimate the depth of racism in Chicago, among the ethnics, among the white liberals, among the politicians, and among the media. Only the most cynical of blacks could have anticipated the depth of that racism. Washington is not a cynic. Sophisticated, knowledgeable, wise to the ways of Chicago politics and to the ways of the world, yes, but not cynical. Pragmatic, yes, but not cynical. Idealists, even when they weigh their idealism against their pragmatism, are not cynical; the two are irreconcilable.

Those failed expectations were mighty blows. Washington said, on the night of the primary, "I reach out my arms to all the people in this city." The whites said, the next day, "We don't want your embrace." He said, "I will govern this whole city," and they said, "We don't want you to govern because you are black." He said, "We will heal the wounds of this city," and the whites said, "We don't want your doctoring because you are black." They then put up a smokescreen; they called him a criminal for minor infractions against the law committed many years earlier. No one said that he was one of the few people ever to go to jail for failing to file his tax returns. No one said that those clients he bilked, between the five of them lost $205. No one said that his campaign debts were tiny beside those of many other candidates. No, they said he was a criminal and should be punished for those crimes, and besides, his campaign was disorganized and he was running a reverse racist campaign, playing only to blacks.

Washington is a proud man, a proud black man. He walked into St. Pascal's Church on Palm Sunday. He went into Bridgeport, into the ethnic enclaves of the city with his head high, wearing his puckish grin, and extending his hand. He reminded me of the little girl who alone entered the school in Little Rock in 1954 and Autherine Lucy who alone entered the University of Alabama in 1956—scared, courageous, proud. He may have been saying, "They will never know the intensity of my anguish. They will never know what pain they give me. They will never have the satisfaction of knowing that, after all these years, they can still wound me. Am I not a man?" And another set of thoughts: "How can it be that, merely because my outer skin is another color, they despise me so? How can it be that they can be so willfully ignorant of my humanity, our humanity? How can a man or a woman be so cruel to another human?"

And with these thoughts perhaps came others: "I will not go to them. I will not seek their help. I will not degrade myself so." Not politics? Not the way to win a citywide election when the blacks represent only 40 percent of the population? Not the way to establish a base from which to govern? Of course. And so he finally had to say, "All right. I'll go." He should have gone earlier? There were more whites of good will out there than he knew about? Certainly. There was a certain amount of paranoia in the decision not to go? Probably. Knowing the correct thing to do, he still avoided going until it was almost too late? Politicians must have thick skins but must they be automatons? But he did finally go. He was determined to win. Had he been white, there would have been no question about his being mayor. It would have been automatic the night he won the primary. Only because he was black was he engaged in this bitter fight to the finish. He would claim the title, against all odds, not only for himself but for all those who had made this victory possible, all those who had worked to prepare the way.

Did he exclude whites from his staff? Some. Not all. Some proved too valuable and too loyal. But some of the whites on the staff and some would-be advisors were less valuable, less loyal. They reaped the rotten harvest sown by those in the city who turned their backs on Washington. It was inevitable that they would bear the brunt of the anger of the blacks on the staff. How could it be otherwise? In the sixties, many blacks dissociated themselves from the whites with whom they had worked for years. Not because they loved them less but because those whites came to symbolize Whitey. Unjust? Of course. Irrational? Perhaps. Oh, what a tangled web whites wove when first they moved into that grove.

Washington's visit with Walter Mondale to St. Pascal's Church reminds me of a story, with minor variations, told me at various times over the years by three different women. The first grew up in Detroit, the second in Cleveland, the third in a small mill town in southern Pennsylvania. They all lived in integrated sections of town—poor sections of town—and attended integrated schools.

Each one, while in kindergarten, took home after school a little black classmate who had become their fast friend. When they reached their front doors, their mothers said, with variations, "Who is your black friend?" The tone in their mother's voices told the children they had committed a sin. Each one recalls looking into the faces of their playmates and seeing pained humiliation. Each of the black children went home. The white girls never forgot. Did those black children soon go again into a white home?

More than at any time in his career, Washington as mayor must continually struggle with those conflicts in his personality: to control his contempt for those less capable than he, his temptation to surround himself with just such people so that he may feel his own aura more deliciously and exercise control, to restrain his pride when compromise is required. He needs to learn to open himself to those who need to know.

He has said he would like to be mayor for twenty years. At 61, he is looking forward to a long, vigorous life, not even contemplating the solitude and leisure or the decrepitude of old age. Before he can realistically anticipate those twenty years in Chicago's City Hall, however, he must get through the first four. They will be difficult, because he will be watched as few elected officials have ever been watched.

Blacks will watch him: is he living up to their expectations? Will they continue to forgive him if he errs too often in their eyes? Has he promised more than he can deliver? Will they understand that his resources are limited, that he is but one cog in a long chain of command? If he is honest with them, if he tells them the simple truth, they will be, as they have always been for white mayors, forgiving, willing to wait. Whites who say that he has unrealistically raised black expectations do not understand the patience and understanding of black people. It is part of that hidden racism: "They are too dumb to distinguish between campaign rhetoric and realistic promises." Blacks get angry not when all that is promised is not forthcoming; they understand politics. They get angry when they are betrayed, not when promises are slow in being fulfilled, but when promises are crudely broken. There is nothing in Washington's long career to lead anyone to believe that he will crudely break his promises.

No, the watching that blacks will do will not be with a cold eye. They will take an empathetic view—wary but generous.

It will be the whites who will cast a cold eye on Washington, waiting for him to slip up, to blunder, to steal, to plunder. They will not forget his past mistakes, they will not forgive his errors. Those who voted against him will shout, "I told you so," at every little misstep. Those who voted for him will count the missteps carefully, evaluating them, judging them, hoping they cast the correct vote but always wary.

It is said that, as has happened in other cities where black mayors have been elected, soon after the election, business will go on as usual. If the mayor is a good one and if he has the right circumstances, the city will prosper, as Atlanta did under Maynard Jackson. If the mayor is not so good and the circumstances bad, the city will decline, as Cleveland did under Carl Stokes. But those who predict business as usual in Chicago do not understand this city, do not understand that politics in Chicago is not just the means to govern the city; it is, as with baseball, a local obsession. That the rules have changed, that the power has shifted is not taken lightly in this Machiavellian city, this city of political chicanery and cunning, of political intrigue and maneuver.

Washington promised to cleanse the city of its political chicanery. That is tantamount to threatening to take away the balls and bats at Cubs and Sox Park. He may be able to create a fairer government, a more open government, but he cannot rid the city government of its intrigue. Nor am I sure he wants to; he is a product of this city and its Machine. Much of that experience was painful but it also had its good moments, its moments of glee. Chicago's City Hall and its precincts are hardly imaginable without political intrigue.

The whites who so bitterly opposed Washington did so out of hatred for blacks—they feared, they said, and perhaps they genuinely did, that he would move his people into their neighborhoods and expose their women to rape. But even more, they resented the black takeover of their beloved *amour*, their favorite plaything, the source of their wealth: the political structure of the city. Washington said, during the campaign, that they feared reform. I'm not so sure. I'm not so sure that many of them would not have welcomed some reform, for many were cut out of the pie. Reform accomplished by whites might have been welcome by many. Jane Byrne promised reform and won big. But, real or only imagined, whites held the power in their sweaty palms throughout the history of this city. They let a few blacks in to share the spoils. But a genuine transfer of power? A black mayor? *Great God in Heaven, deliver us from that. We will watch that son of a bitch and every time he steps out of line, we will create one rung up the ladder to our own return to power.*

History was made in the winter and spring of 1982-83 in Chicago. The Democratic Machine was ripped to shreds and a black mayor was elected despite a scurrilous racist campaign against him. It was an uncharacteristically, unseasonably warm winter. There are those who believe that God was looking down from his heaven at the events in Chicago and offering his cooperation, his blessing. Others, with another view of the universe, believe that nature, recognizing the gigantic effort being made to bring balance and order to a disordered city, to bring the city in closer touch with nature's own order, bestowed its benevolence. It was predicted that a high turnout would help Epton. It rained all day on Election Day. It turned cold and nasty. Nature—or God, if you prefer—was doing its job. Nevertheless, the turnout was the biggest in history, beyond all predictions, breaking all records. It got so high towards the close of the day that the pundits began to reconsider: such a large turnout could only help Washington. It indicated that blacks were voting as they had never voted in Chicago. They were defying even nature's benevolence—"Don't do us any favors. This is ours. We'll do it ourselves."

Of course, true order and balance will not be restored even in the four-year term to which Washington was elected. Even after another four-year term. Too much is out of joint. Too many babies—mainly black babies—will continue to die. Too many youth—mainly black youth—will continue to be unemployed. Too many old people will eat dog food. Too many will sleep in train stations and apartment lobbies. Too many children will not learn to read. Too many poor sick people will die enroute to County Hospital, turned away from the private ones that treat only those who can pay. Too many will be malnourished and undernourished. Too many will continue to be hungry. Too many will continue to live in hovels. Too many will remain segregated. Too many will be victims of violence, criminal violence and police violence. Too many will continue to hate. For these are the problems of our urban society that cannot be solved by local government but must be attacked by the larger powers that influence and govern American society. As mayor of the second largest city in the nation, however, Washington can be a leading force for change. He has pledged to play that role—it was one of the major pledges he made in his campaign. The nation may never be the same; Chicago surely will not.

Nor will Washington be the same man who dared to run for mayor in 1977 and then again in 1982. His life-long dream was realized at the close of that election, in 1983. No one can ever be the same who has made a lifelong dream come true, especially if that dream was made a reality by the generosity and back-breaking work of thousands of others. He is now mayor of Chicago, a hero to blacks everywhere, even in Zaire, and a hero to many whites who also cherish a dream of peace and personal fulfillment for all. Quite a mantle, Harold.

A glass brimming, not spilling,
the green trees
practicing their art.
'A wonder
from the true world,'

he who accomplished it
'overwhelmed with the wonder
which rises out of his doing.'
(From "Notes of A Scale," in *With Eyes at the Back of Our Heads,* by Denise Levertov)

Epilogue

The hall is overflowing with a standing-room-only crowd, mostly black but with a substantial number of white faces, over 4,000 of the people who worked in the campaign. Sneakers and snaky sandals, the black oxfords of the old, blue jeans, a cowboy hat, elegant high fashion dresses and suits, some not so elegant but obviously brand-new clothes, new outfits bought to wear to this historic event, white suits, red hose, red dresses, white hose, silver foxes, minks, fake furs, gold jewelry, hats with nose veils, broad-brimmed straw hats, corn-ribbed hair with bright tassels and white-haired old folks—businessmen and busboys, lawyers and welfare mothers, bankers and bellboys, doctors and orderlies, ward heelers and community organizers, children, people in wheelchairs, Asiatics, Hispanics, Poles, Jews, WASPs, and blacks. Through the crowd, reporters from all over the country, wearing their plastic badges around their necks, wend their way, interviewing people, observing reactions, to report back to their communities this historic inauguration of Harold Washington at Navy Pier, one of Chicago's unique landmarks, stretching 3,000 feet into Lake Michigan, built at the cost of $4.5 million in 1913-16 as part of the Chicago Plan as a shipping and recreation center but never much realized as either. In the mid-seventies, the great dance hall at the end of the pier was renovated and is today surely one of the city's most graceful architectural assets. Across its high domed ceiling rows of lights glimmer to enhance the already splendid circular room. Plush red carpeting muffles the sounds of scraping chairs and high-heeled shoes. The glass doors that serve as walls of the great hall and open onto a balcony overlooking the lake, on the main floor, and the huge windows that line the balcony are a particularly lovely symbol for this remarkable departure from tradition: a new mayor who promises an open government is inaugurated in this wonderfully open hall, with the sky and water in clear view of all who turn to look. For this occasion, 4,000 white roses—the symbol of fragrance and beauty for most of the world—grace the hall and the corridors.

Chicago mayors have traditionally been sworn into office in the somber chambers of the City Council, a brief ceremony marked with no pomp. Today, Morris Ellis's fine band plays "Colonel Bogey's March," to accompany the mayor-elect as he walks down the long aisle to the stage, after having opened the ceremonies with a medley of international songs and in the middle, playing Aaron Copland's, "Fanfare for the Common Man." (Washington selected the music.) Gwendolyn Brooks, poet laureate of Illinois and preeminent black poet, reads from her work and Studs Terkel, now a well-known author, for many more years a staunch supporter of liberal causes and a talk show host, reads from the work of Carl Sandburg. Cardinal Bernardin, head of the Chicago Archdiocese, opens the ceremony. The head of the Jewish rabbinical association says the morning prayer of the Orthodox ritual, a prayer for fair and just government. The audience applauds. The Greek Orthodox bishop and a black Protestant minister offer prayers for unity and good will in the city. It is a short ceremony—less than two hours—but it is the first such ceremony in Chicago's history. It is not a three-day party in a hotel; it is an elegant inaugural. There are not 200 people; there are 4,000. But those original 200 are here.

On the stage, in three tiers, sit 179 people: the aldermen and women, their spouses, the governor and his wife, the elected Democratic officials, county, state, and federal, and honored guests: Washington's family and some friends, and traditional community leaders from labor, business, and the ministry.

Dick Gregory, uninvited by the committee, sits next to the aged Nick Melas, county treasurer. Al Raby sits in the audience with the rest of the people invited because they helped to win.

The crowd boos when Governor Thompson is introduced. Jesse Jackson is not introduced.

The crowd cheers wildly as Washington says, "My election was the result of the greatest grassroots movement in the history of Chicago." The old guard aldermen sit on their hands. The crowd cheers most when the new mayor announces that he will fire the people hired by Byrne in the closing weeks of the campaign, when she padded the payroll with her friends—80 percent more people were hired in April than in any previous month before. The old guard sit grim-lipped when Washington says, "We will not tolerate business as usual." He ends his speech by quoting John F. Kennedy's famous lines, "Ask not what your country can do for you; ask what you can do for your country."

The speech is described by some as "presidential," by others as "negative," "too strong." It was strong. "With malice toward none," he said, he revealed the condition of the city's finances, grim indeed. "The situation," he said, "is serious but not desperate." He is proclaiming to the city that he will be tough, truthful, tenacious about restructuring the operations of the city. In a rare mood of concern for the impact of this speech, he reads from a prepared text, prepared by his speechwriters, edited by him.

The crowd sways with a blissful joy of accomplishment and fulfillment. Washington's religious coordinator since 1979 says, "I'm so proud I feel like a fox."

Father Mitchell, a young priest from St. Pascal's Church, the scene of a vicious attack on Washington during the campaign, is one of the many priests present. He is a product of the sixties, was at Kent State University when "we shut it down," worked for Senator George McGovern in his race for president in 1972. His invitation came as a special favor through Father George Clements, the black priest who is a leader of religious activists in the city. Mitchell and his fellow priests at St. Pascal's are working to overcome the racism in their parish that took them by such surprise, he says.

Even the old guard smiles over their champagne. The mood is temporarily contagious.

Across the street from the pier, in a little park, about 60 people from the Southwest Parish and Neighborhood Federation and the Northwest Neighborhood Federation light "candles of understanding" hoping that the Mayor-elect will stop on his way to the ceremony and talk with them. He doesn't. They understand, they say. "He has a tight schedule." The people came to ask, "Are we part of this city, too?" Later, Mike Smith, co-director of the Northwest Side group, complains bitterly that his community—the site of St. Pascal's—has been grievously ignored by the mayor. During the general election, a meeting was arranged at which the two candidates would address themselves to several pressing community issues. The day before, Washington cancelled. More efforts were made to meet with the candidate, to no avail. "I can understand, from a human position, why a person wouldn't want to expose himself to another shameful situation like St. Pascal's," Smith says, "but a politician has an obligation to go to all the neighborhoods." Smith admits that he was told that the decision not to visit his community may have been made because another incident would be too damaging to the campaign, would arouse too much fear that a black mayor would not be able to govern. However, Smith insists, he should at least have sent a representative to the candle-lighting. Instead, he says, the mayor's spokesman denied any knowledge of it after a concerted effort made by the organizations to insure that Washington did know of it. For the future, Smith says, "We are very determined to have the mayor come out and listen to our community. We think that perhaps he has no understanding of us."

The crowd continues to enjoy itself though the champagne is gone. They are waiting for the Mayor to make a quick appearance on his way out. Meanwhile, the staff goes off to its own, private party at a Lake Shore Drive hotel. The press is barred. "How can we relax with you guys snooping around?" I am acceptable, along with a few friends who are well-known to the staff. As a biographer and not a working journalist, my snooping is ok.

I check my high-heeled shoes under a sofa and wander about to talk to these people who have been so helpful in the writing of this book and other friends who have been invited to this most joyful party, the first occasion in six weeks on which these people can relax. It's a time for drunken reflection, for jokes, for "profound" inanities.

Some of us move with some of Washington's press crew to the "Inaugural Ball" at the Hyatt-Regency, given by a group of supporters, $10 per person, a gala party but stiff and impersonal. It doesn't suit our mood. We want a familiar setting, Riccardo's, where it's a typical Friday night, noisy, crowded, drunk, a second home to many of Chicago's writers. Some of us stay out until dawn.

April 30, 10 A.M.: The mayor's first press conference. The room is jammed. Harry Golden, Jr., veteran City Hall reporter for the *Chicago Sun-Times,* suggests that we explain to the new mayor that his predecessor cut off much of the space in this room by having a pedestal built out into the room to raise her up because she was embarrassed by her diminutiveness. "It will cost too much," Golden imagines the mayor saying, prophetically anticipating Washington's announcement that he will return to the city

20 percent of his salary "until the crisis in this city abates," as a start to cutting executive salaries in the austerity program that has become so necessary since the disclosure of the full facts of the city's finances. Of his $60,000 salary, he will return $12,000, thus, he says, maintaining his title, "the poorest politician in captivity."

Golden says he will tell Washington where Mayor Daley's huge desk can be found, the desk that Byrne moved out of the mayor's office because it dwarfed her.

Mayor Washington appears, looking fresh and rested. After the inauguration ceremonies, he hosted an elegant reception for a few friends and family and went home to bed early, the first time in many weeks. He smiles, looks over the crowd, and says, "Mr. Golden, are we ready to begin?"

"Yes, Mr. Mayor, we are ready."

"Good morning, ladies and gentlemen. It says here [pointing to his prepared text] that I'm supposed to say, 'I'm so glad that so many of you turned out to wish me well' [laughter] and if it didn't say that, I'd still feel the same. Thank you so much." He cannot resist his own quiet wit. Then, on to business. He is serious, unsmiling, wearing that bearish look that is such a contrast with his bright impish grin, that look that so many Chicagoans have already come to know.

The first appointments are disclosed: some holdovers from the Byrne administration, especially those who hold the secrets to the Byrne budget that allegedly holds all kinds of hidden funds accumulated by dipping into regular budget items to finance such things as $800,000 worth of luncheons and dinners charged to the Office of Special Affairs but not budgetted for. A black chief of the corporation counsel's office, the first in history, a crucial job in the city government, a job traditionally held by a political appointee with no serious credentials for the job. The new appointee, James Montgomery, a highly-regarded attorney whose reputation in the civil rights movement is widely known, strongly reflects Washington's reform effort. Angelo Geocaris, a liberal millionaire businessman-lawyer, will work for $1 a year as special liaison to the business community.

Unsmiling, straighforwardly, he announces that he has asked

certain members of Byrne's staff to stay in place temporarily to "insure a smooth, orderly transition." He does not say that these requests were made necessary by Byrne's refusal to assist that transition before she left office.

The appointments are about equally divided between black and white, between new appointments and holdovers. Washington is making it clear that there will be equal opportunity but there will not be the black takeover that so many ethnics feared. Only one woman out of eight appointments, the woman who was fired by Byrne from the job she had been appointed to by Byrne's predecessor after he fired Byrne from that job. Byrne had fired highly qualified black Sharon Gilliam to replace her with a white friend, the first of many such changes in City Hall under the previous mayor.

Radicals? None. Reformers? Some. But who knows what these holdovers from the Byrne administration may have preferred all these years? In a reform administration, they may perform differently than they did under previous orders. George Spink, assistant director of the Mayor's Office of Special Events under Byrne, who incurred the wrath of the administration by publishing some of the department's dirty linen, says that he always had the feeling that new Acting Comptroller Walter Knorr was never happy having to do what he was asked by the former mayor. Perhaps he will enjoy helping Washington run the open budgetary process the mayor promised in his campaign.

Asked by a reporter about the power struggle between the mayor's supporters and the old guard that is about to occur in the city council, Washington says, with a straight face, "I don't know why I am involved in that struggle . . . . I have a deep-seated and vested interest in the outcome but to embroil me in that controversy is somewhat presumptuous, I would say." Pushed further by another reporter, he says, "I would hope that my . . . reform propensity would permeate the discussions there." It is no small issue, that power struggle, and may mean the difference between reform and no reform for the city. He cancelled an appearance he was to make at the New Orleans meeting of black mayors to stay at home and work behind the scenes to influence that struggle.

There is little he can say, however, on this Saturday before the city council convenes officially. Humor is the best way to handle touchy questions like this. The reporters appreciate his position, laugh heartily, are friendly. He is embarked on that honeymoon that all new chief executives get for the first few months. We wonder whether he will be equally humorous with the first visitor of the day, Alderman Vito Marzullo, the eldest and among the most venal of the "barracudas."

It is the end and the beginning, the end of the campaign, the beginning of a new administration, an administration born of great hope and great despair, of love and hate. Is it the end of an era, an era of white-dominated politics, of Machine-controlled politics? Is it the beginning of true equal opportunity in this city? Is it the beginning of a great era of reform? Is it the beginning of the transformation of a city? Will Harold Washington earn the title he covets: greatest mayor of Chicago?

INDEX